D1601222

Race Relations
Within
Western Expansion

RACE RELATIONS
———— Within ————
WESTERN EXPANSION

Alan J. Levine

PRAEGER

Westport, Connecticut
London

Library of Congress Cataloging-in-Publication Data

Levine, Alan J.
    Race relations within western expansion / Alan J. Levine.
      p. cm.
    Includes bibliographical references and index.
    ISBN 0–275–95037–9 (alk. paper)
    1. Race relations—History. 2. Culture conflict—History.
  I. Title.
  HT1507.L49 1996
  305.8—dc20   95–43772

British Library Cataloguing in Publication Data is available.

Library of Congress Catalog Card Number: 95–43772
ISBN: 0–275–95037–9

First published in 1996

Praeger Publishers, 88 Post Road West, Westport, CT 06881
An imprint of Greenwood Publishing Group, Inc.

Printed in the United States of America

The paper used in this book complies with the
Permanent Paper Standard issued by the National
Information Standards Organization (Z39.48–1984).

10 9 8 7 6 5 4 3 2 1

Contents

Introduction

This book is a work of synthesis in a field in which the writer is not a specialist, and in fact, treats a subject that he finds rather repugnant; a fact which may call for an explanation.

I first became interested in racial matters in the late 1970s as a result of a growing dissatisfaction with the bizarre tone of public discussions of that subject. I was already familiar with the development of the European colonial empires, and the pseudoscientific racial theories that grew into the ideology of Nazism, and knew a bit about black slavery in the United States. But what I heard often could not be squared even with what I already knew, and this worried me. Although I did not enjoy reading about slavery and the slave trade, and white mistreatment of Amerinds, I was determined to learn more. Rather to my surprise, the general level of scholarly literature on such emotional issues as the overall theory of race relations, slavery, and white-Amerind relations proved very high; possibly a good deal higher than the level of work on the history of the Cold War, my own field. I found that some of what I had believed was wrong, but also that much of what I had suspected to be nonsensical or exaggerated was indeed such, or worse. Unfortunately the work of such outstanding scholars as Winthrop Jordan, Kenneth Stampp, Michael Banton, Philip Mason, Wilcomb Washburn, and Alden Vaughan (to name just a few) seemed to have little to do with what was usually said in a public arena (including our educational institutions) that seemed to be, and still is, dominated by charlatans. There seemed to be no bridge between them and the public. This book is an effort to build such a bridge, one situated within a broad understanding of world history.

Although I have not, basically, sought to present anything original, I have tried to place a proper stress on some matters that are generally ignored, even by many specialists, and have tried to show how phenomena such as medieval expansion and slavery flowed quite neatly into the modern world. It is my belief that race relations cannot be intelligently discussed without relating them to the general development of the world. Race relations are connected with many other issues. Understanding of them has also suffered, to an unusual extent, from errors that have infested the study of history in general—notably presentism and the telescoping of developments that took place over many centuries into purely "modern" or even more recent phenomena. For example, the critical fact that the meaning of important terms, and the outlook connected with them, have changed over the centuries—notable examples are "race," "Indian," "savage," "white"— is often neglected. There is, perhaps, no field in which it is more dangerous to assume that people in the past thought the way they do today—although it is also misleading to assume the opposite.

It is, perhaps, necessary—since some early readers of the manuscript of this book have already accused the author of being a "racist"—for me to state my beliefs. I am unimpressed, to put it mildly, by arguments stressing racial differences, and agree with the views of the anthropologist Ralph Linton: "For the purposes of the study of cultural history and development, all human groups may be taken as equivalent. This does not mean that all have made an equal contribution to the growth of culture, but everything indicates that the differences which exist are due to historic accident rather than to any innate qualities of the groups in question."[1] That may be old-fashioned in an age in which many pretend that all cultures are equal— except perhaps Western culture, which is inferior—and often suggest that any criticism of (non-Western) cultures amounts to racism, but so be it. Culture is not the same as race. People are not their ancestors. They are not responsible for the crimes their ancestors committed. (Nor can they claim personal credit for their achievements.) The cultures, ethnic groups, and classes to which they belong are not eternal and unchanging; they blend, mix, and alter.

Disingenuousness has so infected the discussion of certain subjects—notably slavery, the history of Africa, and the European empires—that I am almost certain to be accused of "insensitivity" at least. I plead guilty to that; but I have tried to be equally insensitive to everyone.

Race Relations
Within
Western Expansion

1

"Colorthink"

One of the few aspects of the history of the twentieth century that might seem to offer a good reason for self-congratulation is the rapid death of racist notions, at least in the Western world. Even the South African government finally retreated from the notion that the white race is inherently superior to all others, a supposition that, if not universal, was generally accepted in the Western world in 1900. Racism would seem to be dead, or at least on its last legs, if not as an opinion, at least as an openly avowed explanation or justification. At least, at first sight, that would seem to be the case, and the disappearance of this evil would certainly represent progress.

Many would agree with John Stuart Mill's comment that "Of all the vulgar modes of escaping from the consideration of the effect of social and moral influence on the human mind, the most vulgar is that of attributing the diversities of conduct and character to inherent natural differences." It is, thus far, impossible to scientifically *prove* that there are no differences in the intellectual and moral capacity of different racial groups. For no certain way has yet been devised to measure "pure" intelligence and completely eliminate the factors introduced by such environmental influences such as early education, class, and general cultural background.

Intelligence quotients are not unimportant—they do measure operationally effective intelligence and correlate fairly well with success in life—but they are unreliable as an index of innate or inherited capabilities. Far from measuring fixed hereditary characteristics, individual IQs change consid-

erably with age. White people who are included to exaggerate the importance of the fact that black Americans, on the average, have lower IQs than
whites, should note the interesting fact that the average IQ of the Japanese
people is ten points higher than that of Western Europeans and Americans,
and is now seven points higher than it was before World War II. A clue to
the difference between Westerners and Japanese may perhaps be found in
the fact that those Japanese children so unfortunate as to be exposed to the
United States' glorious system of public education normally fall over a year
behind their compatriots who attend Japanese schools. It is also noteworthy
that black American children who are brought up in white families have
average IQs like whites.[1]

There seems to be good reason to think that any innate differences
between racial groups are not very large, and it is certain that the variations
among members of each group are far greater than any differences between
the groups. And it is an observable fact that whatever the exact statistical
distributions of such qualities may be, there are good, intelligent people in
all races, just as there are bad and stupid people of all races. It would seem
to be sensible, as well as humane, to insure that individuals, whatever their
color, are treated according to their individual merits. To the extent that the
recognition of this notion has spread, we are better off than we were.

But a look at much of what passes for contemporary political and social
thought must compel second thoughts. While avowed racism of the traditional sort may be dead, we are inundated with obsessions with race.
Race-structured thinking and race-consciousness is not dead at all; in fact it
is clearly more prevalent than it was in the 1940s and 1950s, at least among
educated persons, at least in the United States. By race-structured thinking,
I refer to an obsession with race, not in the sense of a belief in the decisive
superiority or inferiority of races, but the treatment of races as actual
discrete units, and a belief that the relations of these units constitute the
primary stuff or determining factor in history, or at least the history of the
last few centuries.

There is also a dangerous confusion of culture with race—itself a component of traditional racism. And there is even a strong tendency to slip
into the stereotyping and submergence of individual identity characteristics of traditional racism, for example, the use of personifying expressions like "*the* white man," "*the* black man," or "*the* Indian" in discussing,
and generalizing about, relationships between *groups*.[2] This race-structured
thinking—it is tempting but perhaps premature to designate it "neora-
cism"—tends to be strongly associated with the left of the political spec-
trum, while traditional forms of racism tend to be associated with the right.
(Although it was hardly the exclusive property of the right; Karl Marx and
Woodrow Wilson were utterly contemptuous of blacks.) Perhaps it is simpler and less emotional to describe it as "colorthink," for like old-fashioned
racism it tends to stereotyped thinking of human relations in terms of skin

color, even if it does not draw quite the same invidious distinctions racism did. (However, such distinctions may indeed return through the back door.)

This sort of thinking is closely related to a certain type of political ideology, the "Third World ideology," which revolves around the perception that the primary problem of the modern world is the exploitation of Asia, Africa, and Latin America by the advanced Western countries. "Colorthink" often transforms this notion into one of racial conflict, the white West (or North) versus the colored or nonwhite South, European whites and their descendants being seen as evil aggressors.[3] An extreme example of this notion was exemplified by Susan Sontag's famous remark that "the white race is the cancer of human history."[4]

"Colorthink" can be resolved into a number of component ideas:

1. That racism and racial conflict is not just bad or evil, as it certainly is, but is a uniquely evil and destructive occasion for man's inhumanity to man.

2. That racism only, or at least significantly, appears in the relations between whites and nonwhites. (Indeed, there have been attempts to redefine the term "racism" so that it applies only to the attitudes of whites toward nonwhites, and never vice versa.)

3. That racism is purely, or largely, a phenomenon of the modern world, and begins with the global expansion of the West from the fifteenth century onward. This has been called the "UNESCO thesis" or the "1492 school" of race relations, and is often accepted or repeated uncritically by otherwise sound authors. (For example, Thomas Gossett in his influential book *Race*.)[5] It is worthy noting that further subtexts often accompany this notion, although perhaps they are not necessary to it. One is that Europe's global expansion began more or less ex nihilo and was little connected or unconnected to earlier events. Another is that Europe's relations with the rest of the world were *purely* offensive or aggressive, and, during this era, there were no external menaces to Europeans.

4. And, conversely, that practically all the events of Europe's expansion can be described as racial conflicts, with (white) racism an inseparable and often determining factor in *all* that happened.

That Western expansion is often seen as a phenomenon unique, not merely in size and scope but in kind, is held to have resulted in uniquely evil forms of oppression. Among them were deliberate genocide against aborigines in areas settled by whites, a uniquely harsh system of slavery directed against black Africans, and a ruthless colonial domination of the peoples of Asia and Africa. There is a sometimes hidden, but quite often explicit, premise accompanying that described above; that such relations were not just unprecedently bad but were crucial to the present prosperity and progress of the advanced Western countries.[6] Moreover, only Western expansion is tied up with racism.[7] In a curious fashion, some wind up portraying South Africa, in the now past era of apartheid, as *both* the worst example of oppression in the world and a sort of paradigm of the world as a whole.[8]

But all of these widespread beliefs are either mistaken or must be so qualified as to be almost worthless.

There may be something particularly distasteful, even (or perhaps especially) from a coldly intellectual point of view, about racism. The condemnation of an entire group of people to perpetual inferiority on the grounds of their birth is contemptible. However, there is no reason to regard racism as a *unique* cause of horror and inhumanity. Other motives—notably religious and political fanaticism—have inspired equal atrocities. The hordes of victims sacrificed by the Aztecs to their gods and the atrocities of Crusaders against Jews, Moslems, Albigensians, Old Prussians, and Byzantines owed nothing to racial ideas. Neither did the slaughters of Christians by the pagan Romans and the Tokugawa Shogunate, or the fantastic massacres inspired by clashes of Moslems, Hindus, and Sikhs in the Indian subcontinent. Communists from Eastern Europe to Cambodia, and the Horn of Africa sacrificed millions of lives in the attempt to carry out their ideals and even destroyed entire social classes, in a way closely paralleling racially motivated genocide. Genghis Khan and the Zulu ruler Chaka were willing to slaughter millions in order to achieve a more purely political domination, while Idi Amin and "Emperor" Bokassa, operating in their smaller spheres, committed proportionately devastating atrocities for even less definable reasons. Nothing in the dismal record of racism is worse than these things; nothing could be. In their obsession with the evil of racism, many people show what Edmund Burke meant when he commented that

Seldom have two ages the same fashion in their precepts and the same modes of mischief. Wickedness is a little more inventive. Whilst you are discussing fashion, the fashion has gone by. The very same vice assumes a new body. The spirit transmigrates; and far from losing its principle of life by the change of its appearance, it is renovated in its new organs with the fresh vigor of a juvenile activity. It walks abroad, it continues its ravages, whilst you are gibbeting the carcass or demolishing the tomb. You are terrifying yourself with ghosts and apparitions whilst your house is the haunt of robbers. It is thus with all those, who, attending only to the husk and shell of history, think they are waging war with intolerance, pride and cruelty, whilst, under colour of abhorring the ill principles of antiquated parties, they are authorizing and feeding the same odious vices in different factions, and perhaps in worse.[9]

The atmosphere in New York, which has averaged near or over 2,000 murders (mostly drug-related) annually for several years, but is obsessed with those few crimes allegedly committed for racial reasons, shows that Burke knew what he was talking about.

Further, there is nothing unique, or especially bad, in the record of modern Western expansion. None of the oppressive relationships that developed—

and some were undoubtedly evil—were worse than things that can be found in the records of non-Western societies. And the latter, too, have manifested racism in various ways, although this usually takes on mystical or quasi-religious forms rather than invoking the pseudoscientific justifications common in the modern West. The more mystical Japanese extreme nationalists of the 1930s and 1940s justified Japanese superiority and domination by involving the allegedly divine origins of the "Yamato race." The caste system of India, although immensely complex and far removed from its origins, seems to have arisen as a system of racial discrimination and segregation. The lowest strata, the Harijan or Untouchables, were, and to a degree still are, degraded in a way more extreme than that suffered by American blacks. Their very touch, or even proximity, is polluting to the higher castes.[10] Comparable although less complex caste systems existed in Moslem North Africa, where Arabs and Berbers dominated segregated Negroid lower castes relegated to menial and "polluting" tasks.[11] Long before (and long after) the development of the Atlantic slave trade a brutal slave trade was carried on across the Sahara desert and around the shores of the Indian Ocean.[12] The dominant Moslem Arabs in the Sudan ruthlessly enslaved and oppressed the pagan and Christian blacks of the southern part of the country—a war is still going on there. The bloody conflict in Rwanda and Burundi between Tutsis and Hutus has a "racial" aspect; the Tutsi, the old ruling minority, is a group of Nilotic origin whose ancestors imposed their rule on the Hutus and remain physically distinct from them. Both groups ascribe innate personality characteristics to the other in a way eerily reminiscent of the sillier ideas Westerners used to entertain about different classes and races. Comparable conflicts, where "racial" and other motives are intermixed, exist elsewhere in Africa, and in Ceylon, where the dominant Sinhalese differ sharply from the Tamil minority in appearance as well as religion and language. A "racial" component also exists in the hostility of many Southeast Asians toward their Chinese minorities. Racial discrimination, without a caste or cultural aspect, exists on Madagascar, with its thoroughly mixed African-Indonesian population. The dominant element of the Malagasy people, the Indonesian-looking Merina, refuse to intermarry with Malagasy who are African in appearance.[13] These examples could be multiplied; but they are sufficient to make nonsense of the idea that racism is a vice peculiar to the Western world or to European whites and their descendants.

Moreover, race relations, although important, have not been the central, determining factor in modern history. Most of the great international movements, events, and conflicts of modern times have cut across racial boundaries. Modern science and technology originated in the Western world, but spread relatively quickly to Japan, while some parts of the Western world, and non-Western whites—Turks, Arabs, and Iranians—remained remarkably backward. Western imperialism itself cut across racial boundaries, for the European imperial countries ruled white North Africans and Middle Easterners, and even European Christian Boers, Cypriots, and Maltese, as well as Asians and black Africans. The great struggles of the twentieth century have cut across racial lines. At practically the height of the belief in the superiority of the white race, the British Empire contracted its first peacetime alliance with Japan, and British and American opinion cheered Japanese victories over Imperial Russia. World War II and the Cold War saw whites and nonwhites, Westerners and non-Westerners, on both sides of the struggle.

Race relations may be important, but they are not the single key to understanding modern history, anymore than inherent racial differences are.

Moreover, the belief in white superiority that reached its peak in the late nineteenth century was not a single harmonious whole, created full-blown, like a modern political ideology, like Communism or Nazism. The "1492 thesis" is wrong at both ends. Some constituents of "modern" racial prejudice long predate 1492, while other elements developed only slowly and much later—and necessarily, for some groups later perceived or classified as different races were not regarded as such for several centuries.

The racial ideas of the nineteenth century actually fused at least three elements, which originally had nothing to do with each other:

1. A very old belief, going back to the Middle Ages, whose origin has not yet been satisfactorily traced, in the inferiority of black Africans. This prejudice, it must be stressed, existed long *before* the slave trade or even serious direct contact with Africans.[14]

2. Assumptions of the natural inferiority of other groups, such as Amerinds and Asians, which developed *during* the age of European expansion as these groups were forced into subordination by European whites or became their enemies. The fact that such groups were ignorant, poor, backward, or merely dominated became the source of false generalizations or self-fulfilling prophecies to the effect that their social inferiority or subordination was somehow "natural," and was permanent and biological in origin. George Orwell, a veteran of the Indian Imperial police who lived in India and Burma, once neatly described the mental process behind this. Commenting on how Europeans contemptuously treated "natives" in India, he remarked, "it's very hard not to, seeing that in practice the majority of Indians *are* inferior to Europeans and one can't help feeling this, and after a little while, acting accordingly."[15] With the enslavement of large numbers of African blacks a similar and stronger process operated to greatly intensify the preexisting prejudice against them. In a sense, the European preponderance in the world, the enormous economic and technological gap between the West and the rest of the world, and the social interactions involved in colonization, imperial rule, and slavery caused Europeans (although not all of them) to acquire a swelled head during the eighteenth and nineteenth centuries.

3. Anthropological pseudoscience developed in a way connected with the self-flattery described above. The early ventures into physical anthropology of eight-

eenth- and nineteenth-century scholars—or quacks—were often far from accurate. Especially in the midnineteenth century reams of studies, often of an
indescribably silly nature, "proved"the inherent superiority of whites over
blacks, and to a lesser degree of whites over Amerinds and Asians, but also (and
quite independently) of some whites over other whites. This deformation of
science was not just an expression of the "swelled head" syndrome and became
of tremendous importance in itself. A certain type of racism—the worst sort, in
fact,—was largely the result of this pseudoscientific claptrap, a point we will
return to later.[16]

Moreover racism appeared in several different contexts during the era
of Western expansion. That expansion, after all, took several forms, and
while racial notions appeared in all of them, racist ideas were not of equal
importance in all contexts. Race relations can be said to have operated in
three different situations:

1. Masses of European settlers, from the fifteenth century onward, colonized lands
   inhabited by relatively primitive peoples in the Americas, Australia, New Zealand, Siberia, the Eurasian steppes, the southern tip of Africa, and the Canary
   Islands. The natives of these areas were assimilated, or destroyed, or subjugated
   to one degree or another, and European immigrants became the numerical
   majority.
2. Enslaved black Africans were brought to some of these areas as a labor supply.
3. European countries gained control of vast areas of Asia and Africa, which were
   relatively densely populated, and ruled them as colonies. Often they were
   inhabited by civilized peoples; and no large-scale settlement by whites could be
   expected. This phenomenon constituted imperialism in the strict sense of the
   word.

In distinguishing these three currents, of course, caution is advisable. In
some cases, large numbers of Europeans settled among peoples who were
not primitive and whom they could never expect to absorb or outnumber.
Much of Latin America, from Mexico to Peru, is a borderline case; the
Spanish conquest resulted in situations of mixed race and, sometimes, of
culture. French settlers in North Africa, British settlers in Kenya, British and
Afrikaaners in South Africa, and Russians in parts of Central Asia and the
Caucasus were always minorities. Nor were all slaves in Europe's overseas
extensions black, for Amerinds, Malagasy, and East Indians were enslaved
or bought by Europeans. Nevertheless, three quite different patterns can be
discerned.[17] This book will explore all of them, and the development of race
relations in each, in greater detail.

It should be noted from the outset that race relations cannot be studied
in a vacuum, or just as an interaction taking place between Europeans and
non-Europeans, or whites and "nonwhites," with both "sides" remaining
essentially unchanged through the centuries. Indeed, the very idea that
there was a non-European "side," or that "nonwhites" over the last few

centuries can be said to have shared any real feature other than some degree or other of subordination of Europeans—and often not even that—is itself a highly suspect concept, smacking of an inversion of the older forms of racism. Racial myths apart, the peoples Europeans dealt with ranged from highly civilized East Asians to utterly barbaric Pacific islanders; they differed too much to have only one form of interaction with the West.

Both Europeans and the peoples they encountered have changed greatly, as have the mental frameworks within which they operated. As Philip Mason has noted in his brilliant, although strangely little-known, work, *Patterns of Dominance*, racial conflicts, in their modern phases, have been just a special case of a worldwide reaction of the oppressed, or merely subordinate, against domination, which is entangled with still other issues. In this revolt "against inequalities and ritual taboos that have become irrelevant to modern life" both former rulers and ruled have become anomic. "It is not simply a matter of the underprivileged moving up into the places left vacant by their former superiors. *There is nothing left to move into.*"[18] (My emphasis.) The present writer is not sure that the last sentence is really true, but widespread beliefs along those lines may explain much about contemporary Western, let alone other, societies.

It should be noted, too, that the very concept of "race" has changed over the centuries. The word itself only came into use in English in the sixteenth century, and for long was barely distinct in meaning from "nation" or "people." It was sometimes even used to refer to family or social class. Its meaning was narrowed to a biological (or pseudobiological) classification over a long period. Indeed in British, as opposed to American, English, it was not fully restricted to that definition until after World War II. And, as we shall see, classifying various groups as different "races" was a development over time—East Asians and American Indians were for long perceived as "white." And the impact of racial classifications and/or racism varied enormously. In some cases, racism turns out to have been far less important than is generally imagined; in others, it may have had a longer, deeper history than is usually supposed.

For race, or rather beliefs about race, rarely appear as a clearly independent or isolated factor in the developments chronicled in this book. In initial contacts between Europeans and others, differences of skin color would often coincide quite neatly with differences of belief, language, religion, social class, and degree of civilization. But, as we shall see, that original coincidence of all categories of classification could, and often did, change with remarkable speed. Racism could be encouraged by this original coincidence of all forms of difference, or inflamed by the attempt to artificially preserve social differences, which, while once real enough, had ceased to coincide with reality.[19] South African apartheid, from 1948 to its disappearance in the 1990s, can be seen as the ultimate effort of the latter sort.

2

Origins of Western Supremacy

One of the problems in understanding later events and the relations between the Europeans and the other peoples of the world is a dangerous confusion over the origins and the earlier phases of the expansion of Europe. There is a widespread assumption that expansion was a purely modern phenomenon, directed only at Asia, Africa, and the Americas. There is also a lot of confusion, too, about how that expansion became possible. It is widely supposed that European societies became sharply differentiated from—or more advanced than—others, only at a late date, perhaps at the supposed divide, wherever that is set, between the Middle Ages and modern times, or even as late as the Industrial Revolution.

That is far from the case. The superiority of Western technology and science, and particularly in the ships and weapons that made extra-European expansion possible, was neither a sudden or purely modern development. Long before the modern era, Europe, or at least its Western parts, had become a particular kind of society, quite different from the other civilized societies of the world—except for Japan, whose development showed remarkable parallels with that of Western Europe. Nor was Europe's expansion a purely modern phenomenon.

There is still a widespread assumption that the West was only a bit further advanced on the same "road" as Asia and Africa. This notion derives from a belief in a simple, unilinear social evolution, still common among most Westerners as well as Marxists. To some extent it reflects a normal, egocentric assumption that one's own society is the natural, inevitable culmination of historical development. (Unfortunately, when questioned—nowadays such assumptions are often derided as "Eurocentric"—it is by people who themselves have no clear ideas about, or even interest in, social evolution, and merely wish, for one reason or another, to deride the Western world, or certain of its traditions.)

Most of the non-Western world was locked into other patterns, which, for one reason or another, did not lead to the development of modern science and technology, and the strength and influence they produced. Europe enjoyed significant environmental advantages, and it "alone managed the politically remarkable feat of curtailing arbitrary power, thus reducing risk and uncertainty, encouraging more productive investment, and promoting growth."[1] It is necessary to understand some crucial features of the non-Western civilized world, and why the development of the West was distinctive. And it must be remembered that the "non-Western world" came first. The West—and this is true whether the latter is defined as a distinctive post-Roman development or just as continuation of Greece and Rome—is a "secondary" civilization, a result of the spread of civilization from its original homeland in the Middle East.

THE NATURE OF THE NON-WESTERN CIVILIZED WORLD

In the precolonial era, the civilized lands from North Africa to the China Sea belonged to several quite different civilizations. But, despite cultural differences, nearly all were ruled by states of one kind—a very old, very durable sort of political formation familiarly known as "Oriental despotism." Because we live in an era hypersensitive about labels, it should be noted right off that "Oriental despotism" was not limited to Asia. The civilized Amerindian states were Oriental despotisms, so were some states in the Western world—notably the Roman and Byzantine Empires, and post-Mongol Russia. Nor did every government in Asia fit this pattern. Japan was a feudal monarchy, not an Oriental despotism. From the dawn of history, Oriental despotism was the predominant form of government for civilized mankind—of whatever skin color. It must be stressed that we are dealing here with a social and political category, not a racial, or even a cultural, one.

This type of regime has been explored by many great political commentators over the centuries; most thoroughly by Karl Wittfogel. Although some of his views remain controversial or subject to modification, Wittfogel argued convincingly that the roots of Oriental despotism lay in the environmental conditions facing the earliest civilized peoples. Although farming and towns first appeared in the highlands of Anatolia and neighboring areas, the focus of early civilization soon shifted to the river valleys, often in arid or semiarid surroundings. Elaborate engineering works were needed for irrigation and flood control. The building and control of those works, and the massive labor gangs they required, promoted the consolidation of the river valleys under governments far more powerful than the so-called "absolute monarchies" of early modern Europe. Unlike them, they completely dominated economic life. Similar environmental conditions elsewhere, and the example of the river-valley civilizations, promoted the spread of Oriental despotism. Conquest and imitation spread it even to areas where the "hydraulic" agriculture originally associated with it was not needed. Russia was the most notable example of this; the Mongols, who had picked up the techniques of Oriental despotism in China, imposed it on the conquered Russians. The Greco-Roman world adopted Oriental despotism in a different way. When the internal crisis provoked by slavery, the ruin of the free peasantry, and Rome's overextended government destroyed the Roman republic, the empire adopted the methods of rule long established in its Eastern provinces.

The societies ruled by Oriental despotism had only limited possibilities of development. They were dominated by bureaucrats or priests disinterested or hostile to progress. They were not apt to encourage the critical thinking or experimentation fundamental to science. The growth of private property was severely restricted (China was a partial exception) and merchants led insecure lives, vulnerable to rulers and officials. Legal systems were weakly developed and royal monopolies were common. Although many rulers in Europe and Japan were not admirable characters, excessive "conspicuous consumption," debauchery, and outright terror were far more common in Oriental despotisms. Technological development tended to freeze at about the level of the Iron Age. (China was again an important exception.) This type of society might not generate much progress, but it was very strong. Revolution, barbarian invasion, or religious conversion might disrupt it, but a shattered civilization was soon rebuilt on the same old basis. There was little chance to develop vigorous capitalism, scientific method, or the balance of social forces necessary for liberty and a dynamic economy.

Other forms of government and society could only arise where agriculture did not depend on large-scale irrigation. Japan never became an Oriental despotism because mountains split it into small patches, allowing only locally controlled, small-scale irrigation. The Western world, based on rain-fall agriculture, had another alternative. It, nevertheless, was partially sucked into the despotic maw.[2] It was freed to travel a new road only by a fortunate conjunction of events. The Western part of the Roman Empire was conquered by the barbarians, while the eastern half preserved part of the classical heritage and stopped the Arabs from invading Europe from the southeast. This allowed the development of a new type of society in medieval Europe.

Other environmental and social factors, perhaps loosely and indirectly correlated with those discussed above, favored Europe's development as opposed to other parts of the world, especially those in the tropics. It is a fact—that Europeans and North Americans are apt to forget—that temperate-zone countries are in many ways nicer places to live in. This is particularly true when the factor of disease, until recently neglected by historians, is considered. Communicable diseases and parasites are far more common in tropical areas, and even subtropical ones, than in countries where cold seasons exist. W. H. McNeill has suggested that its exceptionally fierce disease environment alone was the main reason why sub-Saharan Africa lagged behind even other tropical, much less temperate, areas.[3] Sleeping sickness, yellow fever, and malaria were especially bad, while the tsetse fly made the horse unusable over large areas. In the Nile valley, and in Asia in general, water sources were contaminated and worm infestation universal, along with malaria, high death rates, and constant enervation. It should be noted that malaria in children can produce convulsions and resulting brain damage and retardation.[4] (That may have been a contributing cause to the impression, among whites and Asians, that the Negroid race was not very intelligent.)

Except for the Mediterranean basin, Europe enjoyed a high degree of geological stability, and suffered fewer natural disasters—earthquakes, volcanoes, floods, and drought—than other areas of the civilized world.[5] Although river basins in other parts of the globe and the loess soil of the North China Plain were more productive, Europe generally enjoyed good soils. By contrast, tropical soils, except in alluvial flood plains or volcanic regions like Java (which also enjoys an atypical rainfall pattern), are generally not very fertile. The combination of high temperatures and high rainfall leaches nutrients out of the soil. Nor are tropical forests very valuable. As everyone now knows, the equatorial rain forest is only a seemingly rich environment based on poor soil. Clearing it does not produce good farmland. Nor are the trees of much value compared to those in temperate-zone forests; the stands of trees are heterogeneous and desirable trees are thoroughly mixed with useless ones. Tropical grasslands compared unfavorably with prairies and pampas for farming or cattle-raising. Even fishing is less productive. Tropical fish tend to swim in mixed schools containing many inedible types; even the edible fish yield less food than their cold-water counterparts.[6]

A perhaps insufficiently noted factor in the relationship between the hot or tropical areas of the Old World and other regions is that in prehistory and early historical times, most crops, and especially most of those that were the first to be domesticated, and were suited to temperate and even subtropical zones, rarely grew well in really hot regions, and vice versa. (Wet rice agriculture was an outstanding exception.) And that limited the spread of cultures based on those crops. The Near Eastern crops that spread easily into Europe and were adopted by the Egyptians and the highland Ethiopians, and the many plants the latter domesticated locally, did not flourish in most of sub-Saharan Africa. Ecological limits thus prevented the easy spread of Egyptian or Ethiopian culture over the continent. The sub-Saharan Africans had to develop their own crops, or borrow others from India and Southeast Asia. Even crops of intermediate zones, or the warmer part of the temperate area, for example, the classical Mediterranean agriculture, were often quite confined ecologically. It was no vast coincidence that the grip of the Roman empire and classical civilization, in areas of Western Europe beyond the limits of Mediterranean agriculture, was weak, and that the Moors did not stay long in those areas of Spain beyond the "line of the olive." This, along with the factor of disease, was responsible for the fact that, until modern times, agricultural peoples from the temperate zone only slowly expanded into tropical areas, while expansion by tropical farmers into temperate areas was even less common. The Polynesian settlers of New Zealand found that none of their domesticated animals, and only the sweet potato of all the crops they had known in Tahiti, did well even in the warmest areas of their new country, and then only with the greatest care.

The various Old World civilizations tended to suffer from specific environmental inferiorities compared to Europe. The Europeans' nearest neighbors, in the Near East and North Africa, were located in areas that were largely arid and not very populous. They lacked iron and timber and already depended on importing these things from Europe in the Middle Ages.[7] India and China were so situated that the overland expansion of those civilizations from the Indus and Yellow river basins took them into hotter and more disease-ridden regions. Settlers and officials in the new areas suffered high death rates. The Indians never fully assimilated the conquered peoples of the south, perhaps one element in India's lack of unity.[8] Europe was—relatively—less exposed to invasion by the nomadic horsemen of the Eurasian steppes, the most formidable enemies of civilized men, than China or India. On the whole, wars, although bad enough, seem to have been less destructive in Europe than other parts of the world, and, since farming did not depend on elaborate engineering works, agriculture could recover faster there from wars.

Other social factors may have been more favorable in Europe. There may have been less gross social inequalities. Moreover, Europe's demographic pattern always differed somewhat from that of most civilized societies. (The Southeast Asian peoples were another exception.) Europeans held their population growth well below the maximum, allowing them to preserve forests and use land for livestock raising that would otherwise have gone to growing grains. This ensured supplies of timber and a good diet. This was achieved at the cost of comparatively late ages for marriage and maintaining a high proportion of unmarried people. (Asians were, and still are, horrified by the number of unmarried people in the West.) Yet another European social advantage—or a lack of self-inflicted handicaps—is often overlooked. Many peoples treated blacksmiths and metal-workers, professions essential to technological advance, as outcastes and pariahs.[9] This was so far from being the case in Europe that "Smith" and its counterparts in other languages (Schmitt, Herrero, Kuznets, Kovacs) became common, honorable family names.

Other regions of the world were hardly in the running. Although it is unfashionable to say so, sub-Saharan Africa was one of the more backward parts of the Old World. When the colonial era began, the sub-Saharan area, especially West Africa, was not as primitive as Westerners used to think. Some West African cultures were highly complex and "deserved the name of civilization on every count save that of literacy."[10] But, save for Ethiopia and the fringe of Moslem territory along the southern edge of the Sahara, the cultures of black Africa were preliterate. Even Ethiopia, although one of the oldest Christian countries in the world, with some tantalizing social similarities to medieval Europe, and undoubtedly civilized, lagged far behind Europe and Asia. The reasons for this are not hard to understand. We have already noted the ferocious disease environment. Black Africa was remote from the original centers of civilization, largely isolated by some of the most formidable deserts in the world. The configuration of the coast as well as the prevailing winds and currents rendered West Africa almost inaccessible by sea until the fifteenth century; any European or North African ship sailing south past Cape Bojador found it hard to return, while West African ships, had any existed, could not have beaten their way north. In any case, the nature of the coast and the lack of offshore islands gave the natives no incentive to develop sea-going vessels. Even the nearby Cape Verde Islands were settled only by European colonists. On the east, sea-going cultures under Arab influence developed relatively late—nearby Madagascar was uninhabited until colonized by Indonesians, not Africans. Even Ethiopia, situated on a high plateau, which was cut up by mountains and vast canyons that made internal travel difficult, was accessible only from an exceptionally hot and unpleasant desert coast. It was relatively isolated from other civilized areas.

Nor is tropical Africa rich. Its soil, not too fertile to start with, was often exhausted by shifting agriculture. Even its river deltas seem less fertile than their Asian counterparts. There are few navigable rivers, and endemic diseases made the use of draft animals impossible over large areas. Hence most black Africans remained thinly dispersed Iron Age peasants, comparable to the Northern Europeans at the time of Caesar. It has been estimated that the whole continent, including Egypt, contained only 10 percent of the world's population by the time of the European Middle Ages. The dilemma imposed on Africa by geography may be appreciated if one tries to imagine how Europe would have evolved had its only link to civilization been through the nomads of the Russian Steppes.

Most Africans lived in small tribal communities; most of the larger states were what historians have dubbed "African" or "Sudanic despotisms." Perhaps inspired by the example of ancient Egypt, they resembled the Oriental despotisms discussed earlier, although they were based on slave labor rather than hydraulic agriculture. Other features common to African despotisms were divine kingship and human sacrifice.[11]

Although the people of Mesoamerica and Peru had created civilizations of their own, almost certainly independently of those of the Eastern Hemisphere, they remained thousands of years behind those of the Old World. This was probably largely due to the latter's larger populations and more numerous cultures. The civilizations in the New World were mostly located well inland on high plateaus, instead of river valleys and coasts, which hindered their interaction and spread. One factor in retarding the relative development of the peoples of the New World was the fact that, unlike Eurasia, the Americas were laid out on a north-south axis. New developments had to pass through more varying climactic zones than in the other hemisphere. The Americas also lacked large animals capable of domestication—and their main crop, maize, took longer to develop than such Old World staples as wheat.[12]

THE EUROPEAN DEPARTURE

We have already noted that the West did not just arise in more favorable circumstances, but developed a new type of society. The words "medieval" and "feudal" are too often applied as terms of abuse, and as descriptions of a wide variety of backward countries or eras, including pre-colonial Asia. But medieval Europe was an unusual society, and feudalism, one of its most prominent characteristics, was a fairly rare phenomenon in history. Only Japan had a culture and social structure closely resembling that of medieval Europe, and it was no accident that Japan was the only non-Western nation able to modernize quickly. As E. L. Jones has remarked, "in certain respects Japan was as 'European' as if it had been towed away and anchored off the island of Wight."[13] Many of the distinctive and "modern" aspects of our civilization, from parliaments to the scientific method, originated in the Middle Ages.

Even during the so-called "Dark Age" before the eleventh century a framework was formed that led to the modern world, despite the prevalence of some unbelievably idiotic superstitions. The pluralist, multicentered character of Western Society was established at an early date by the geographical dispersal, without total disintegration, of political power through feudalism, and by the division of power between the secular authorities and the Church. These things operated both within the various countries and internationally in the struggle between the Holy Roman Empire and the Papacy. Feudal society was more open to the growth of business than Oriental despotisms; the nobility might despise merchants, but it needed them, and the merchants—and ex-serfs—gained a degree of freedom and security behind city walls. In the later Middle Ages, the aristocracy and the bourgeoisie established corporate representation as "estates" to defend their rights, and parliamentary institutions and constitutionalism developed. A long and complex process began that led to the development of democracy in the more fortunate Western countries as the rights first secured by the upper classes were acquired by the lower social strata. (Much modern commentary has tended to stress those later stages, where the middle and lower classes aligned with royalty against the aristocracy, or the following period, when kings and nobles were allied against the lower groups. But it was the early curbing of central authority that was the critical departure.)

In parallel with these crucial social and political developments, there was another critical departure. As Lynn White has observed, "the technological dominance of the Western culture is not merely characteristic of the modern world. It begins to be evident in the early Middle Ages, and is clear by the later Middle Ages." Further, he notes, "as early as the seventh century, Europe began to show a rising velocity in technical innovation, that in this trait it quickly outran its related cultures of Byzantium and Islam, that by the fourteenth century it had exceeded even China both in absolute achievement and pace of development."[14] In technology and science, the Middle Ages were not, as is still widely imagined, a period of stagnation nor was innovation fueled purely by influences from the outside or only by the revival of classical learning. While early medieval Europe was not as inventive as contemporary China, many major inventions were made or brought into daily use, with drastic impact on society. Even in the Dark Ages European society was technologically far more advanced than classical Greece and Rome. Incomparably superior to the early medieval world, in other respects, Greece and Rome had been technologically almost static. Inventions such as the horse collar, horseshoe, tandem harnessing, the heavy moldboard plow, and the three-field system revolutionized agriculture. These developments and the development or introduction of improved watermills, the windmill, and the crank enabled Europeans to make vastly greater and more efficient use of animal, water, and windpower and provided them the highest living standard in the world. By the eleventh century, and probably earlier, Europeans were better fed, and made more use of machines, than other peoples of the world. They could also field armies of well-mounted, armed, and armored knights. Although the internal organization of medieval states made it hard for them to make major foreign conquests—at least on land—European troops, from then on, generally enjoyed a qualitative superiority over the other soldiers of the world, other than the Japanese, and for brief periods, the Mongols and the Ottoman Turks. The later Middle Ages saw the development, or the introduction from the outside, of mechanical clocks, gunpowder, cannon, the compass, paper, printing, and movable type. European technology had clearly surpassed that of China, even by the most optimistic rating of the latter, by the late fifteenth century. And the Chinese had not developed science.[15]

The scientific revolution began in the late Middle Ages. While the Moslem world preserved much classical learning that had disappeared in Western Christendom and transmitted Hindu algebra and numerals to Europe—Moslem scholars did useful work in astronomy, optics, and chemistry—it did not develop the scientific method.

Despite the streak of antirationalism in early Christianity, the Church preserved and spread learning. Its control was loose enough to permit science to develop—indeed many important churchmen, notably Roger Bacon's patron Robert Grosseteste, nursed a considerable interest in the natural world; and the greatest of medieval theologians, Aquinas, argued elaborately that there could be no conflict between revelation and rational knowledge. The reintroduction of Aristotle's work (which had mostly been preserved in Islam) and the rise of philosophical nominalism helped produce a new system of thought. For all the absurdities of Aristotle's physics, his works promoted a more empirical approach to reality. The combination of observation, experiment, and logical analysis gradually led to the scientific method. In the fourteenth century, French and British scholars like Jean Buridan and Jordan de Nemours were already performing experiments and correcting some of the errors of Aristotle's physics.[16] (It was only much later that the Church foolishly tied itself to the Aristotelian system—which it had initially opposed—and blunderingly tried to halt the development of science.)

An important factor in Europe's development was its ability to absorb ideas and techniques from the outside; other civilizations lacked or lost this quality. The Moslems, who had taught the medieval Europeans much, had much interest in nature, and had been some of Aristotle's warmest admirers. (Westerners called the most fanatical Aristotelians, who refused to admit that the master had ever been wrong, "Averroists," after the leading Moslem commentator on Aristotle.) But the Moslem world turned away from proto-science. Its theologians increasingly became hostile to science. Indeed the part of Islam under Ottoman rule experienced stagnation and even retrogression.[17] Other parts of the world had never even made the tentative stabs toward science that the Moslem world did. Modern science was a Western creation, and for many centuries a Western monopoly. Until the end of the nineteenth century, when some Japanese and Indian scientists appeared, scientists were all Europeans, and overwhelmingly Protestant Northern Europeans at that.

THE KEYS TO EXPANSION: SHIPS AND GUNS

During much of the Middle Ages, and indeed most of early modern times, Europe was under varying degrees of siege from without—sometimes by Vikings, Hungarians, or other barbarian invaders, but almost continually by Islamic powers. First came the Arabs, then the Ottoman Turks. The state of the almost endless wars with the Moslems, and Europe's economic relations with them, were strong pointers toward the rise of Europe and its capability of expanding across the oceans.[18]

During the early centuries of Islam, the Arabs had conquered not only Spain, but most of the islands of the Mediterranean. In the latter half of the tenth century, the Byzantines retook Crete and Cyprus. In the course of the following century, paralleling the overland Christian advance in Spain, Catholic Europeans recaptured virtually all the islands in the west and center of the middle sea. The Pisans and Genoese conquered Corsica and Sardinia, and helped the Normans capture Sicily and Malta. In part these gains were due to the Christians' belated exploitation of long-standing basic advantages. The Arab-held European islands were "occupied" territory; no large Moslem community had been established, save in Sicily. The Western Europeans had a bigger population and enjoyed the advantage of the "weather gauge" much as the British later did against the European mainland. The prevailing wind was from the north; the thinly populated North African coast was a lee shore full of dangerous shallows, while the north side of the Mediterranean was comparatively densely peopled. It had many harbors and sheltered bays and safe navigational conditions.

But the Western conquest of the sea did show a new dynamism. The reconquest (or liberation, from a Christian point of view) of Moslem-occupied parts of Europe shifted easily into expansion. It was driven not only by feudal lords seeking new land and loot, but also by the growing power of the commercially oriented Italian city-states. In the Dark Ages proper, Western Europe had little outsiders deemed worth buying. Its prime exports were slaves and bullion. This period also saw the Western Europeans, or some of them, develop other products that could be successfully sold in the Moslem world. (This will be discussed in more detail in the next chapter.)

Westerners had gained control of the Mediterranean with ships little, if any better than those of the Moslems or Byzantines. They had devised cheaper, faster, methods of ship construction, laying a keel and building an internal structure of ribs instead of starting the hull first.[19] Over the next several centuries, however, Westerners surpassed everyone else by combining the "Northern" or "Atlantic" and "Mediterranean" ship-building traditions.

In the Dark Ages the Scandinavians had already developed ships that were superior in their ability to make long voyages in stormy oceans. The *knorr* or *hafskip* (not to be confused with the long ship or *drekkja* used in

Viking raids) was strongly "clinker-built" of overlapping planks and depended on a large square sail. Worked by men using surprisingly sophisticated navigational techniques, it conveyed Norse settlers to Iceland, Greenland, and finally North America. But the Norse ships could not sail straight across the ocean to Vinland and their stab across the Atlantic was short lived. Apart from the limitations of their ships and the unpredictable and exceptionally bad Atlantic weather, Norway, and still more its colonies, were poor and thinly populated. Iceland and Greenland lacked timber and were dependent on Europe for even minor items; the Greenland settlement eventually died out and the Iceland settlement may have come close to doing so. The Norse remained technically stagnant and were overtaken, even in home waters by the Germans of the Hanseatic League, using "cogs," larger, higher, decked-over ships with much greater cargo capacity, and run by small crews. During the thirteenth century cogs began sailing into the Mediterranean. The "Nautical Revolution of the Middle Ages" began. Using the economical framework-first method, the Mediterranean powers began building cogs, or in the case of the Venetians, developed the "great galley," actually a large sailing ship with auxiliary oars. Navigational techniques were vastly improved, with the introduction of the compass, marine charts, and pilot books. For the first time, Mediterranean ships could cross the middle sea safely during winter and they began sailing out of the Straits of Gibraltar to northern Europe. A further melding of Northern and Mediterranean methods produced the ships that were to cross the Atlantic, Pacific, and Indian oceans. Mediterranean ship-builders developed the cog into the multimasted carrack, which employed "carvel" construction (smooth hulls built of planks laid end to end) and combined the Northern "square rig" with Mediterranean "lateen" (triangular) sails. Improved carracks, and a smaller type, the caravel, could cross the Atlantic regularly. And, while that was not the world's biggest ocean, it was by far the stormiest and most difficult. Once it could be crossed with reasonable safety, Europeans could go just about anywhere.[20]

And their ships carried effective guns. For a long time Europeans wielded little effective military power on land in Africa and Asia, but they quickly became superior at sea. The Ottoman Turks developed huge, effective cannons for sieges, but they and the other Moslem powers failed to develop effective field artillery. They belatedly installed cannons on ships only after the Portuguese reached the Indian Ocean. With the aid of Venetian technicians, the Egyptians and Gujerat Indians hurriedly improvised some gun-armed ships, and for a time they gave the Portuguese some trouble. Then the Portuguese replaced their smaller forged guns with heavy-cast cannons. After that the Asian powers never caught up.[21]

3

The Great Frontier I

In 1952 Walter Prescott Webb, discussing the expansion of the European peoples, noted that the most celebrated frontier, that of the American West, had been just one sector of a far vaster frontier, one that comprised virtually everything beyond the world-island of Eurasia and Africa. To Webb, the European exploration, development, and closing of this "Great Frontier" was *the* theme of modern history. Moreover, it was sui generis and an unrepeatable phenomenon.[1]

Webb may have overstressed the centrality of the frontier. He underrated the impact of science and technology, and his concept, vast as it was, was too limited. He ignored the expansion of Russia and the still less well known Balkan frontier.[2] And, given space travel, there is no reason to think that the frontier is a closed book. Nevertheless, Webb performed a real service by developing this insight. Its importance is not even reduced by the recognition that many of the phenomena he described had appeared before. The "Great Frontier" *was* the greatest of frontiers.

It was not, however, the first.

The expansion of relatively advanced peoples at the expense of more primitive groups is an old story, at least as old as the development of agriculture. Farming was introduced to Europe by Neolithic migrants from Anatolia. This history of most of sub-Saharan Africa over the last 2,000 years is one of the expansion of the Bantu-speaking Negroid farmers and herders from West Africa at the expense of other groups of different races who had remained in a hunting-and-gathering culture, the Pygmies and the Bushmen, who once held virtually all of central, eastern, and southern Africa. The civilized Sinhalese migrated from northern India to Ceylon, displacing most of the primitive hunting-and-gathering Vedda natives. Iron-using Indonesian farmers and fishermen colonized Malaya and much of the island world of Indonesia at the expense of their more primitive Proto-Malay and Australoid inhabitants. The Japanese settled their island at the expense of the primitive Ainu aborigines. The history of Chinese civilization is one of steady expansion from a nucleus in the Yellow River valley. Some of this expansion took place by the conquest and Sinicization of advanced non-Chinese peoples, (analogous to the Romanization of Gaul and Spain), but much of it took place by colonization at the expense of relatively primitive peoples in South and West China and on Taiwan. The peoples of the Southeast Asian mainland—Thais, Burmese, and Vietnamese, in some cases fleeing before the Chinese advance, repeated the process at the expense of the peoples they found in the south.

FEUDAL EXPANSION

Nor was the Great Frontier the first frontier of Western civilization. In many respects it merely recreated, on a vaster scale, the medieval frontier of Western Christendom, which itself created Europe as we know it. Europe did not exist, ex nihilo; *Europe itself was created by expansion.* The medieval frontier lay in the east of Europe itself; it was the sphere of the Germans and Russians, and to a lesser extent, the Italian city-states and the Scandinavians. (It has been relatively ignored in the English-speaking world, since Western Europe took little part in it.) The latter half of the Middle Ages saw the colonization of large parts of Eastern Europe by Germans and of what is now northern and eastern European Russia by Russians, while the Italians and the Germanic Scandinavians established political and trade domination of the Mediterranean and the Baltic. The Germans and Italians, and to a lesser extent the Scandinavians and the Russians, were better organized and technologically more advanced than their neighbors.

German expansion, like later European expansion (which it anticipated in several respects), took several forms. German nobles and crusading orders, with Danish help, conquered the pagan Wends and the Old Prussians, and introduced German settlers who ultimately absorbed their surviving Slavic and Baltic neighbors. Germans peacefully settled in Pomerania, Silesia, Bohemia, and Transylvania on the invitation of the local Christian Slav and Hungarian rulers. (The arrival of the Jews in Eastern Europe was probably a related phenomenon; the Kings of Poland, realizing that they needed subjects with what were then "modern" skills, let in German-speaking Jews as a lesser evil than politically more dangerous German Christians.) Ultimately, Pomerania, Silesia, and parts of Bohemia and Transylvania were peacefully Germanized, while large minorities of Germans lived elsewhere. Prague and Budapest, for example, were largely inhabited by Germans and German Jews rather than Czechs and Hungarians until the nineteenth century. German and Swedish crusaders conquered the pagan Finns and Balts of the eastern Baltic, and settlers from their countries remained dominant minorities in Finland, Latvia, and Estonia until the twentieth century. Some Scandinavians settled in Lapland, while the Finns expanded at the expense of the Lapps. Russians colonized territories inhabited by primitive Finnish peoples.[3]

During the course of the Reconquista, the Spanish and Portuguese Christians found that areas they recaptured were often depopulated, even when they did not exacerbate this by deliberately driving out Moorish inhabitants. Conquest often had to be combined with settlement or resettlement. Although, like the overland expansion in Eastern Europe described above, this took place mainly under the auspices of feudal lords, it had a direct connection with the colonization of the lands across the Atlantic.[4]

OVERSEAS COLONIZATION

The overland expansion of Europe in the East was characteristically feudal and medieval; a simultaneous development on the seas was not. It has been well said that "the maritime empires that in modern times have become the hallmark of Europe after 1500 are foreshadowed again and again during the Middle Ages."[5] Indeed, "foreshadowed" may be too weak. The Italian city-states, especially Venice and Genoa, pioneered the "imperial" aspects of later European expansion on a small scale, taking over the seaborne trade of the Mediterranean and Black Sea, and taking control of some major islands and coastal points in the middle sea. The Italians even prefigured the later development of slavery and the slave trade in the Americas. They not only ruthlessly enslaved Greeks and other Orthodox Christians from the Balkans, but developed an elaborate trade with the Crimean Tatars in white and Asian slaves through the Black Sea. The Venetians established slave-worked sugar plantations, manned partly by black Africans on Cyprus, resembling the West Indies of the early modern era.[6] (We will return to this topic later.)

Indeed Venice, in many respects, was almost a miniature prototype of the modern British Empire. It, and its weaker rival Genoa, were perhaps initially stimulated by the Arabs' economic development of North Africa. Like the British and Dutch in later centuries, Venice and Genoa developed their commercial strength on the basis of shipping bulk cargoes over relatively short routes to and from nearby areas. Food, salt, raw materials (especially wool), and alum needed by the developing cities of northern Italy, and the textiles, weapons, and metal products of those places were the main items of trade. Venice and Genoa did not have much of a technological edge over their potential rivals, but depended on the intelligent use of what they had (which in the case of Venice included standardized ship construction and even the development of interchangeable parts and the assembly line): Italy's sophisticated commercial and financial innovations—including joint-stock companies, brokers, and insurance—and force. Apart from their slaving activities, the Venetians and Genoese were not believers in modern free-market ideas or freedom of the seas. The Venetians smashed commercial rivals by force, excluded other ships from the Adriatic, and insisted that all goods in the regions they dominated must pass through Venice. Later they monopolized all trade with their colonies.

While erecting their domination of the sea on carrying bulk, low-value items, the Italians went on to develop long-range trades in luxury items—spices, silks, cotton, rhubarb, and other "drugs" and jewels—with the Eastern Mediterranean. With the Crusades, they established trading posts—again anticipating later European powers—in the ports of the Near East. When the Latins overwhelmed Byzantium in the Fourth Crusade, the Venetians seized part of the Byzantine Empire, gaining control of Crete and many other islands in the Aegean and Ionian Seas and parts of Greece. They and the Genoese burst into the Black Sea, establishing colonies on the coast of South Russia. They traded with the Tatars for slaves and luxuries from Asia brought by the northern caravan route.

Venice's colonies were a strange combination of ruthless exploitation and careful attention to justice. Sugar cultivation had been introduced to the Mediterranean lands by the Arabs; the Venetians and Genoese now established full-blown sugar plantations, with some refineries, worked by slaves, on the islands they ruled. While some of the Greek natives were serfs (*parioi*) others remained free men, or even retained their positions as members of privileged classes. Venice established a uniform colonial administration much like that of the later Western European empires. It allowed some self-government in its colonies (that is to its Italian residents), but made use of native officials and let some Greek merchants become Venetian citizens. Other Greeks were carefully segregated from the Italian communities (another anticipation of later Western European practices in Asia and Africa, although inspired by Catholic-Orthodox hostility rather than racial ideas.)

Venice itself anticipated modern Britain in many ways. Niccolò Machiavelli and many others did not consider it part of Italy, just as many people in the modern era did not consider Britain part of Europe, because it was oriented toward the sea, and its society was too different from that of the mainland. Much in contrast to most of Renaissance Italy, Venice was a stable, orderly, and humane polity; its government, although not democratic or egalitarian in the modern sense, was widely respected as a just one. It was governed by a far-seeing, humane aristocratic oligarchy. The Venetian "nobility" consisted of successful merchants, not feudal landlords, and power was widely dispersed with obligatory office-holding and limited terms of office. The rulers took care to see that the lower classes were not too badly off. And their sense of justice extended to their colonial subjects— or at least the nonslaves among them.[7]

In the Western Mediterranean there was another frontier, dominated by Genoa and Aragon, which expanded into the small islands held by the Moors and the large but backward islands of Corsica and Sardinia. The Aragonese made extensive conquests in Majorca and Minorca and Sardinia, and the Genoese and other Italians became heavily involved in the economy of Spain and Portugal. There they supplied advanced Italian commercial techniques and investment capital that the relatively backward Iberian states lacked.

Driven partly by curiosity, and the impulses driving the Reconquista, the Portuguese and Spaniards moved out into the Atlantic. Already, in the fifteenth century, Western European expansion was well underway and taking several routes, objectives, and forms, which were complexly interrelated. The expansion of the Portuguese, who long had by far the larger role in this, took a dual route, down the African coast and out into the ocean itself in search of rumored and suspected islands. The Portuguese inched down Africa in search of fish, ivory, gum, gold, and slaves—white, brown, and black. Originally they were interested in Africa for its own sake; the idea of sailing around it to Asia for spices came later. Columbus, Cabot, and others developed the rival idea of reaching Asia by sailing west from Europe. Both routes, unintentionally, led to the Americas. (Not long after Columbus a Portuguese expedition to India, sheering too far west while passing the Atlantic Narrows, ran into Brazil.) But the Atlantic itself was believed to contain much of value; long before Columbus, Europeans had begun—or resumed—sailing to the west to look for islands. English sailors, seeking the legendary island of Hi-Brasil (which had nothing to do with the real Brazil) may have reached North America before Cabot, or even before Columbus got to the Bahamas. That did not lead to much; the expansion of the Iberians in the middle latitudes had more immediate results. The Portuguese settled the uninhabited Azores and Madeira; with Genoese help they introduced the sugar-slave plantation economy already established in the eastern Mediterranean.[8]

THE CANARY ISLANDS: PROTOTYPE FOR THE AMERICAS

The Italians also had a major role in the economic development of another group of Atlantic islands—once they were conquered.

Unlike Madeira and the Azores, the Canary islands were already inhabited, by a Caucasoid people related to the Berbers of North Africa. The Canarians had a Neolithic culture not too different from that of the Indians of what is now the Southeastern United States, although making more use of domesticated animals. It is unclear whether their ancestors had migrated to the islands before the mainland Berbers learned to use metals, or had been marooned there by Roman rulers and had lost the ability to do so. In any case, they had been effectively isolated from the rest of the world for a long time. Despite their stone and wooden weapons, the Canarians were formidable fighters. Their presence both complicated the European settlement of the islands and provided a potential profit—for slavers.

The conquest of the Canaries was a central event of Europe's expansion, foreshadowing or demonstrating many things (especially the unpleasant ones) that occurred later. Yet, until recently, it has attracted relatively little notice from scholars, although some of the great historians of that expansion tried to draw attention to it. As Samuel Eliot Morison (himself quoting an earlier historian) noted in 1942, the Canaries were a "microcosm of the early history of America."[9]

The islands were discovered (or rediscovered, since they had been known in classical times) in the fourteenth century and became the focus of rivalry between the Spanish and the Portuguese. More primitive than most peoples medieval Europeans encountered, the Canary islanders attracted some attention. "Most of what was said about American Indians was precisely foreshadowed in literature about the Canarians."[10] Norman noblemen, acting as vassals of the Castilian crown, began effective colonization in 1402, but the conquest of the islands was not finished until 1496. Coping with the Canarians' tough resistance was complicated by Portuguese attempts to horn in. Attempts to land on some islands were defeated outright. As in America, once they got ashore, the Spaniards' horses were a decisive advantage, probably more important than guns. Cavalry enabled the Spanish to quickly dominate the flat areas, but the islanders often held out in incredibly rugged mountains. As late as 1494 the people of Tenerife smashed a small Spanish army. But the Spaniards kept coming and were willing to use any method to win.

The islanders had no overall unity. Some soon became dependent on European trade goods or converted to Christianity. The people of one island could be used to conquer another; sometimes even the inhabitants of the same island could be played against each other. Pagan islanders taken in battle could be enslaved legally by the standards of the time, although unscrupulous Spaniards sometimes grabbed Christian converts too. Many slaves were removed to Spain or sold to the Portuguese islands. Epidemics to which Europeans, but not the natives, seemed immune, and slave raids gradually wore down resistance. The remaining natives were finally defeated in open battle or overcome by treachery. The Spaniards freely intermarried with the native aristocracy. Lower-class survivors who were not enslaved were divided into "encomienda"—their villages were put under the "protection" of an individual Spanish hidalgo who received tribute and forced labor from them. (This system was also used to deal with the conquered Moors in Granada and later in the Americas.) The natives were discriminated against in the allocation of land, the Europeans receiving the best areas, and were often forbidden to grow sugar, the most profitable crop. They continued to decline in numbers under the impact of disease; the European settlers eventually absorbed them.[11]

Although John Mercer, the leading expert on the Canary islanders, holds that they were not as completely destroyed as has often been assumed, he concludes that "The record shows the extermination of a people and its culture beyond anything effected by the Spaniards in the Americas."[12] (In the Western Hemisphere, the Crown and the Church seem to have exerted somewhat more restraint on the colonists.)

But the general similarity between events in the Canary islands and the Americas is clear. The only gross difference between the two situations—that the Canary islanders were "white"—was a difference that made no difference.

4

The Great Frontier II

The end of the fifteenth century was not so much the beginning of Western expansion as much of the start of a new stage, with the Western Europeans crossing the oceans, settling the Americas, Australasia, and the southern tip of Africa, while the Russians, shaking off Tatar rule, moved east and south into Siberia and the great Eurasian steppe. The countries in a more central position, like Germany and Italy, exhausted their fields of expansion, or were thrown on the defensive by the Ottoman Turks' advance into the Mediterranean and southeast and central Europe. (It should not be forgotten, although it often is, that the modern era was *not* simply one of aggression by Europeans against the rest of the world.)

The peculiarity of European expansion after the fifteenth century was not just its size, but the extreme technological and cultural disparity between the Europeans and the lands they settled. Although the Wends, Old Prussians, and Finnish peoples were few, illiterate, and backward compared to the Germans, Russians, and Scandinavians, they were Iron Age barbarians comparable to the Germans, Russians, and Scandinavians of a few centuries earlier. The cultural gap between Europeans and the peoples they met overseas was enormously greater.

The Amerinds of southern Mexico, Central America, and Peru had established civilizations, but technologically were only on a par with First Dynasty Egypt. Most Amerinds, and the Maori natives of New Zealand, like the Canary islanders, were sparsely-settled Neolithic farmers, although their societies otherwise varied greatly. (Later observers, favorable or not, were unduly inclined to homogenize the many different Amerind cultures.) Some Amerinds, in western North America and parts of the southern continent, the Australian aborigines, and the Bushmen of South Africa, were still hunters and gatherers. Only the peoples of the Eurasian steppe, and the Bantus the European settlers met in the interior of South Africa, were more advanced "barbarians" like those encountered in eastern medieval Europe.

In one important respect the peoples of Central and South America had surpassed those of the Eastern hemisphere. They had domesticated more types of plants—including corn, the potato, the sweet potato, the avocado, cacao, the tomato, manioc, squash, the peanut, the papaya, and many varieties of beans, as well as independently developing cotton. (Tobacco was also an Amerind development, of more doubtful utility.) They had also learned to use rubber. It has been said that over half the foods currently used are of American origin. But in every other aspect of technology, they were far behind the peoples of the Old World. Even the most advanced had just started using metals; all lacked iron and bronze, as well as glass, the plow, the potters' wheel, the arch, and really useful domesticated animals. Mexicans used the wheel—but only in toys.[1]

IMPACT

Another gap between Europeans and aborigines was almost as important as the technical one—the gap in disease resistance. Some might argue that it was more important. The peoples of the Old World had long been ravaged by epidemic diseases. Although medical science was virtually helpless to deal with them, repeated exposures gave Europeans, Asians, and most Africans some natural immunity. Amerinds, Polynesians, and Australian aborigines and the peoples of the Cape region of southern Africa had no such immunity. With the uncertain exception of syphilis, and probably of tuberculosis, the peoples of the Western Hemisphere had not developed native epidemic diseases of their own. They had not had dense concentrations of population long enough, nor domesticated animals, which, in Eurasia and much of Africa, appear to have acted as "reservoirs" in which diseases developed. Smallpox was the biggest killer. After the first British settlers arrived in New South Wales, smallpox swept over all of Australia except the northwest and wiped out a third of the Australian aborigines at one blow. It had almost as spectacular effects on the Amerinds; some of the badly scarred survivors, who had never encountered such a disfiguring disease before, committed suicide. But even childhood diseases could kill people without immunity; some even died of the common cold. Gonorrhea raged and caused widespread sterility.[2] Disease caused most of the steep drop in the native population of the New World, not massacre or oppression although there was, unfortunately, no shortage of the latter.

Exposure to liquor was devastating. Amerinds, and their counterparts in Siberia, Australia, and New Zealand, had nothing like "social drinking." They drank to get drunk, and intoxication often made them violent. Gangs of violent drunks raged through villages terrorizing the sober, frequently committing murder. Fatally, the Amerinds regarded drunkenness as an excuse for crime.[3] The similarity to modern Western society's stupidity, cowardice, and impotence in the face of addictive drugs need not be elaborated. The Amerinds at least had the excuse that their societies had no mechanism to deal with this sort of thing.

And the cultural gap between Europeans and natives was nearly unbridgeable.

A fairly uniform process of disease, war, dispossession, demoralization, and ultimate cultural collapse operated throughout the Americas, Australia, New Zealand, and Siberia from which only a few groups escaped. In the case of the Americas, this was often accompanied by enslavement, especially in the earlier stages of Spanish and Portuguese colonization, and to a lesser extent in the early phases of British North America.[4]

In time, the cycle of collapse gradually ended and was followed by a degree of recovery. This was partly because the most advanced nations changed their policies. Native populations began to grow and tried to reach at least a tolerable compromise with the modern world. But the remnants of native societies still suffer massive poverty, alcoholism, mental illness, and other sorts of social pathology. Even today their position is problematic. This is most notable in the case of the American Indians. In those parts of Latin America where large numbers of Indians survived, a multiracial, layered population and society evolved. On top, there was a level of more or less "pure" whites—with Peninsular Spaniards on top of the native-born "Creoles" before independence was won. Beneath them was a layer of more or less Europeanized people of mixed white and Indian ancestry—"mestizos" (in some areas called "ladinos"), and underneath them were the pure Indians, whose way of life had sometimes altered little since the conquest. In some Andean regions a distinct intermediate group of "cholos"—partly Hispanicized Amerinds—appeared. Although differences between the layers have blurred, they still exist. In other areas, and North America, it is often hard to say whether Indians, or specific groups of Indians, are best viewed as minority groups within the larger society or as enclaves of people who are still, in all but a geographical sense, "outside" it. Some Indians in the United States would seem to fit the first picture and some the latter, with a tendency to evolve toward the "minority" situation.

RACISM AND THE NATIVES OF THE AMERICAS

The history of relations between European settlers and natives was often a sorry story. But race prejudice played less of a role than is generally imagined, at least in the case of the American Indians, and probably in others. Brutal actions against natives were more often justified by the fact that they were non-Christians or culturally inferior barbarians, rather than beliefs that they were innately inferior. The idea that Amerinds were an inferior race was a relatively late development, belonging to the eighteenth and nineteenth centuries. It was always a fairly controversial idea, which many influential thinkers, notably Thomas Jefferson, bitterly opposed.

For a long time there was no racism against Amerinds for the simple reason that they were not perceived as belonging to a different race. Until the late seventeenth century, and even later, Europeans regarded them as dark-skinned white people, not a separate race. It was only then that scientists tentatively began classifying them as members of the "Mongoloid" rather than the Caucasoid race (to use slightly anachronistic technical terms), a classification that was by no means universally accepted at first. Indeed, it was widely believed, at least in northern Europe, that the Amerinds' color was due to tanning or staining rather than heredity. They were usually described as "tawny" or "olive" (or occasionally as "dirty-orange"), not as red-skinned. The odd notion that Amerinds had red skins was a later confusion prompted by garbled reports of groups that painted themselves with red ochre.

Far from deeming the Indians a separate, inferior race, Spanish leaders married Mexican and Peruvian women (of the upper classes of the conquered peoples), and their offspring married into the Spanish aristocracy. (It is worth noting that such alliances would have been inconceivable with people of Moorish or Jewish origin.) The Spaniards treated the mass of Amerinds much like the white Canarians, dividing them into *encomienda*. The English—although usually *after* hostilities had developed—tended to transfer experiences in Ireland to relations with the Amerinds, although on the whole they had more patience with the Amerinds than with Irish Catholics.

Indeed, Europeans had little desire to see the American Indians as something entirely different or new and expended much energy trying to force them within the Biblical, or classical, or some other familiar intellectual framework. It was widely suspected, at least in Protestant countries, that the Amerinds were descended from the Lost Ten Tribes of the Jews; a variant of this idea is preserved in the doctrines of the Mormon Church. (Contemporary Jews believed that at least some South American peoples were of Jewish origin.) Still other theories were current, for example, that the Amerinds were descended from colonists from the lost continent of Atlantis, or alternatively, that the Americas were really Atlantis, which had been mislaid instead of being sunk. The British showed much interest in tales that some Indians were descended from the Welsh colonists supposedly brought by Prince Madoc in the twelfth century.[5]

The early settlers in New England and Virginia shared the general view that the Amerinds were white. Unlike the Spaniards some of them were surprisingly open-minded and even admired some aspects of the Amerinds' cultures. Even those—a majority—who did not tended to assume that the Amerinds would be quickly assimilated into a transplanted English society, rather than being brushed aside or remaining as a permanent foreign or inferior element. It was the disappointment of such hopes, and the violent conflicts that developed, that later helped to promote views of the Amerinds as basically alien and inferior.[6]

It is interesting to note that for a long time the term "Indian" itself lacked any definite content, or had a meaning, or meanings, quite different from those later attached to it. It is well known that Columbus applied it to the natives of the Western Hemisphere because he thought he had actually reached Asia (or somewhere near it). But "India" and "Indian" had already become an exceedingly hazy concept, including all Asia east of Iran. (Columbus's specific objective was Japan.) The Spaniards went on to apply the term "Indian" not only to Asians and New World natives but to Pacific islanders—including both the light-skinned Polynesians (whom they perceived as "white") and the black Melanesians.[7] The conventional modern use of "Indian" to describe both the natives of the Americas and the inhabitants of the Indian subcontinent, while perhaps unfortunate and confusing enough, thus represents a sensible narrowing of earlier usages. (Interestingly, there is a loose parallel to this in the evolution of the Russian usage of the word "Tatar.")

Moreover, the term "Indian" did not always apply to all natives of the New World. Columbus used it to designate the Tainos or Island Arawaks, the first people he encountered in the Caribbean, and other noncannibal groups, but balked at calling the cannibal Caribs "Indians." The English and the French were long reluctant to use the word "Indian" (distastefully associated with their Spanish enemies) for the natives of the Americas, or else used it to refer only to the southern peoples under Spanish domination. Until well into the 1600s, they preferred the term "savage"—which then lacked the hostile connotation it acquired later, and just meant "primitive."[8]

The disappointment of hopes to convert or assimilate Amerinds, successive wars with them, the relegation of Amerinds or people of mixed blood to lower places in a developing social hierarchy, the intellectual classification of Amerinds as a separate, nonwhite race, and the pseudoscientific claptrap often connected with that classification later shoved Amerind-white relations into a "racial" framework it had not originally possessed.

The evolution of relations between Europeans and Amerinds and the ideas and vocabulary connected with it, is a vivid lesson in how ideas can change. The seemingly "obvious" fact that American Indians belong to a different branch of humanity is a modern concept, unknown in the first two centuries of European contact. As we shall see later, attitudes toward blacks, by contrast, are an object lesson in how deep-rooted and rigid ideas can be.

EUROPEANS AND AMERINDS

While the cycle of contact, decline, and recovery operated almost everywhere, there were important variations due both to differing native responses and the differences among Europeans, as well as phenomena that recurred throughout the relations between settlers and natives. Even when the native societies collapsed they did not necessarily do so quickly; and in the interim the Amerinds sometimes exerted considerable influence on the newcomers. The latter adopted native foods and occasionally other items (for example, the hammock and the birchbark canoe.)

The initial reaction of Amerind groups to the Europeans differed greatly. The New England natives were generally friendly to the Pilgrims and the Puritans—the former survived only thanks to their help—as the North Carolina natives were to the Roanoke settlers. At Jamestown, however, some of the local Amerinds attacked the English as soon as they landed. The Spanish encountered a comparable range of reactions among both civilized and primitive peoples. Until the Spanish alienated them, the Tainos were friendly, while the Mayas attacked the Spaniards right away. The Aztecs and the Incas at first, may have suspected that the Spaniards were gods.[9]

War was nowhere continuous, and far from being simply shoved aside North American Indians were often vital partners in the valuable fur trade. They offered a market big enough so that it was worthwhile to make goods especially designed for their tastes. Trade in turn quickly became an important factor for the Amerinds, so great that it is arguable that, between the impact of trade goods and disease, few Europeans ever saw Amerind societies in their "pristine" form.[10]

Trade was central in the Iroquois creation of a sort of empire or subempire which became a major force in the rivalry between the European colonies. For a time the Iroquois had the strongest armed force in Northeastern North America. Until defeated by Count Frontenac in a series of grueling campaigns, they were by far the deadliest enemies of the French in Canada—far more so that the English. Even after that, although usually nominally neutral, they held the balance between the English and the French.[11]

Some peoples, like the Navajos and the Araucanians, while remaining basically conservative in their cultural orientation, assimilated some elements of Western technology. They used this and favorable terrain to remain independent for a very long time. That was true, to some degree, of the most famous Amerinds of all, those of the Western Plains. Far from having a culture dating from time immemorial, the distinctive way of life of the

Plains tribes arose only in the seventeenth century when the peoples of the area—previously farmers or hunters and gatherers, learned to ride the horses the Spanish had brought to the Americas. It is a curious oddity that the Indian culture most often stereotyped as "the" Indian way of life (by people who imagined there was only one Indian way of life) was really a byproduct of the Europeans' arrival in the New World. The Plains Indian culture was actually younger than that of the settlers.[12]

A few groups—the "Five Civilized Tribes" (Cherokees, Choctaws, Chickasaws, Creeks, and Seminoles) of the Southeastern U.S., the Nez Percé, and the Gila Pimas, like the Maoris, the Polynesian natives of New Zealand—displayed an unusual ability to adapt themselves to modern civilization. To be sure they were not completely free of the problems of other native groups; their members tended to drift into the lower class of the dominant society. (It is an interesting comment on modern Westerners' attitudes toward their own society that cases of successful "acculturation" to Western society receive rather slight attention and even seem to cause embarrassment.)[13] The reasons for successful acculturation seem to be obscure and not fully understood. As Edward Spicer has noted, even Amerind groups with virtually identical cultures when first exposed to European contact reacted quite differently under virtually identical stimuli so any generalization is rather hazardous. However, some common factors seem to appear:

1. These societies, especially the Maori, seem to have been more stratified and complex than most at a Neolithic level. Unlike many Amerind tribes, who had very loose, or even nonexistent political organization, they could decide on a course of action and enforce it.

2. There was considerable intermarriage or other friendly contact with Europeans before they came under direct pressure by settlers. The Cherokees, for example, lived well inland, away from the frontier proper for a long time, while European settlement among the Maori was small in scale for many years before major colonization and British annexation took place in 1840. Many Maori had been crewmen on whalers.

3. There was a strong missionary influence and much Christian conversion among these groups.

4. Luck and individual leaders played an important role. In the case of the Cherokees, the genius Sequoyah (George Gist) invented a syllabary that enabled ordinary tribesmen, not just the upper class, already heavily intermarried with whites, to become literate. The Maori also showed an exceptional interest in literacy. Their numbers did fall steeply. They suffered from intertribal warfare (made deadlier by the acquisition of guns) and epidemics of sexually transmitted diseases (STDs), on top of the traditional practice of infanticide, prevented reproduction at a normal rate. But the British stopped the Maori from fighting each other, and the Maori were lucky in that smallpox, the most terrible threat to native society, never reached New Zealand before British medical missionaries vaccinated them.[14]

As a result of acculturation, the original coincidence of differences of language, religion, belief, and color that had roughly existed when the first Europeans arrived in North America had ceased to exist by the early nineteenth century (and in New Zealand ended a bit later.) By the early 1800s that always vague term, "Indian," denoted both the primitive hunters and gatherers of the Great Basin and cultured Cherokee plantation owners who were excellent representatives of the Old South. (Cherokee units would be the last Confederate troops to surrender at the end of the Civil War.)

There were important variations in the behavior of Europeans as well as native responses. Although Cortes was a relatively humane man, and the Spanish occasionally behaved well, there is little doubt that they generally behaved more brutally than the other European nationalities in this era—in as well as outside Europe. The destruction of the Caribbean islanders may have been due mainly to Spanish exploitation and mistreatment, rather than, as was usual, disease.[15]

The French occupation of Canada was less catastrophic for the natives than other European contact because the French settlement was a sparse one, particularly oriented toward the fur trade, and heavily dependent on good relations with the Amerinds. The French limited their own expansion, prohibiting settlement west of Montreal despite a wide belt of fertile land there, to preserve the fur trade. They also placed heavy emphasis on missionary activities and intermarried on a large scale with the Amerinds.[16] The New England settlers came with higher purposes than most toward the Indians and were not entirely unsuccessful in carrying them out, although they ultimately went to war with about half the New England tribes, led by "King Philip." The popular quip that the Pilgrims, "fell on their knees to thank God and then fell on the Indians" is the exact opposite of the truth. Plymouth Colony enjoyed basically good relations with the Amerinds. The other New England colonies waged only one small war, against the Pequot tribe, in the first fifty years of settlement. Quaker-dominated Pennsylvania, in its earliest stages, was another example of humane treatment of Amerinds and peaceful settlement. But William Penn's corrupt sons were responsible for some of the biggest frauds ever perpetrated against Amerinds (the so-called "Walking Purchase") and this and other factors led to bloody wars and massacres worse than anything in New England or Canada.

The nature and social background of the settlers may have been another relatively neglected factor in determining relations with the Amerinds. Both the New Englanders and their French Canadian enemies were highly disciplined groups dominated by the middle class or yeoman farmers; the French Canadians in particular were drawn almost entirely from the latter class, with none of the involuntary colonists—indentured servants and transported convicts—common in other European settlements. The more southern English colonies were created out of a more mixed human material, while the colonists of French Louisiana were largely "recruited" by emptying the jails and whorehouses of Paris. It is not surprising that the relations of such people with the Amerinds were spectacularly bad.[17] It is worth noting that the differences between colonies of the same nation were often greater than the differences between those of different countries.

INDIAN WARS

Most wars with native groups were caused by white settlers' desires for land, but there were some important exceptions. King Philip's War seems to have been caused by Indian resistance to cultural assimilation, rather than the Puritans' land policy. The latter paid for what they took, and tried to buy only unused land.[18] The Navajo Wars, and some other conflicts in the Southwest, were not caused, mainly, by the desire of whites for Indian lands, but by the ugly relationship that had developed between the Navajos and Apaches on one side and the Spanish settlers and the Pueblos and other tribes on the other. A situation of constant internecine raiding and mutual enslavement was ended when the newly arrived Americans undertook to protect the Mexicans in their recently annexed territories.[19] At the other end of the scale, the South Carolina colonists sometimes promoted wars to secure Amerind slaves; and the Seminole wars of the 1830s and 1840s were mainly caused by the desire of Southern planters to recapture runaway slaves who had fled to the Florida Indians, whose lands were of little interest to white settlers at the time. This folly cost the lives of 1,500 U.S. soldiers.[20] It should be noted that, at least in the early centuries of European settlement, the Amerinds' mutual enmities made it hard to keep on peaceful terms with all of them. Friendship with one group meant hostility with its enemies. The French in Canada found it hard to keep the western tribes at peace with each other, although their trade depended on it.[21] The "raiding complex" of the Navajos and some Plains tribes sometimes led them to attack whites even when peace had been established. Treaty-breaking was not, as some have imagined, solely a vice of whites.[22]

On the whole, the whites wished to dipossess Indians and other native groups and shunt them off to reservations, not exterminate them. But there were instances of outright genocide. The weak and primitive natives of much of California, Oregon, Patagonia, and Tasmania were practically wiped out. The vulnerability of the natives to this sort of disaster depended partly on the nature of the governments involved. Unpalatable though it may be to a certain type of libertarianism, or to those bent on demonizing the military, it was an advantage to have a strong central government and soldiers dealing with the frontier. Bureaucrats in Washington or the Colonial Office in London, and professional soldiers, were more likely to sympathize with natives than their white neighbors, or at least take a relatively dispassionate view of the situation. American officers dealing with the Indians (and British dealing with the Maori) sometimes found them more palatable than the white civilians they were supposed to protect. In the most brutal and indefensible official act committed by the United States against its Indian population, the forced removal of the Five Civilized Tribes to Oklahoma in the 1830s, the Army was the sole element of American society to behave decently. Especially after the Civil War, American officers were often far from enthusiastic about fighting Indians and they often feuded bitterly with corrupt Indian agents and others whom they blamed for provoking war. General John Pope acidly remarked, "It is with painful reluctance that the military forces take the field against Indians who only leave their reservations because they are starved there."[23] Captain (later General) Charles King, one of the most noted writers on the frontier, commented that no one would willingly have fought the Nez Percé or Dull Knife's band of Cheyenne, who, in a famous episode, had fled bad conditions on their reservation in 1878. The soldiers' attitude toward the Amerinds was ambivalent. The Amerinds' atrocities and some of their customs disgusted them, but so did the mistreatment of Indians. When Colonel Eugene Baker was blamed for massacring Piegan Indians in 1871, other officers treated him as a leper; his career was ruined. As one writer comments, "A few officers, and (General Philip) Sheridan was one, suffered no pangs of conscience over dispossessing the Indians of the West, but most recognized the great wrong that was being perpetrated on the tribes."[24] General Custer (whose reputation as an Indian-hater seems as exaggerated as his reputation as an Indian-fighter) shared this view. Even the hardboiled Sheridan argued that, while the tribes were bound to resist the loss of their land, they must be treated decently once settled on reservations, and he tried to defend their rights once they were there.[25] But the efforts of the Army, and the government in Washington, were often defeated by the latter's corruption and frontier hatreds. When a band of Anglo-Americans, Mexicans, and Papagos massacred Apaches, mostly women and children who had settled under Army control, President Grant forced a trial of those responsible by threatening to put Arizona Territory under martial law. But he could not force a conviction by jurors who were convinced that Apaches were "red devils" and killing them was not murder.[26]

THE MYTH OF EXTERMINATION

But the importance of white-Indian warfare should not be overestimated. As Wilcomb Washburn has concluded, "negotiation and purchase probably constituted the principal method by which the English acquired land in America," although war was the next most important. Nor should the amount of blood shed in battle or deliberate massacre be exaggerated. It has been estimated that in the United States during the period from 1789 to 1898 only 4,000 Amerinds were killed, as against 7,000 white soldiers and civilians, although this estimate may understate the indirect effects of the wars on the Amerinds and the number killed in massacres on the West Coast. Hollywood notwithstanding, however, massacres, either of Indians by whites or vice versa, were not common.[27] One of the strangest beliefs about white-Amerind relations is that whites deliberately, as a matter of policy, *exterminated* Amerinds. There were whites who advocated that; there were real massacres; and Amerinds were mistreated, but these evils, while considerable, did not add up to genocide.

There was less hostility between whites and Amerinds than is commonly supposed—indeed the divisions among the latter were such that it would have been hard for whites to fight or alienate all the Indians even had they tried. Indians were not so much outfought, much less exterminated, as swamped by the newcomers; indeed, when they did fight, it was often at the side of the whites. In King Philip's War, probably the most desperate struggle in American history, perhaps only half of New England's natives joined the alliance against the English settlers, while many Amerinds fought beside them. This feature of white-Amerind relations was consistent to the last. Of 270,000 Indians in the post Civil War West, under 100,000 proved hostile. In the Southwest, particularly, there was a clear-cut division between "passive" tribes—Pueblos, Pima, and Papago—who avoided war and normally fought only in self-defense, and the warlike raiders— Navajos, Apaches, Comanche, and Kiowa—who celebrated warfare as a central part of their culture. When the United States took over the Mexican Cession the former were quickly given reservations encompassing their traditional lands (which were usually of slight value to white settlers) and did not fight the United States, although they sometimes fought with the Army against their traditional Apache enemies.[28] Indian help played an important, sometimes vital role throughout the Indian wars. "Praying Indians" (Christian converts) and other allies were critical to the English cause in King Philip's War. The U.S. Army depended heavily on Indian scouts for reconnaissance; indeed much of the final fighting against the hostile Apaches was done by Apache scouts, who struck deep into Mexico to catch their relatives.[29]

Blunder and stupidity were important recurring factors in white-Amerind relations. In North America, at least, wars sometimes started or expanded by accident. One Amerind group would attack European settlers, who would counterattack some other tribe by mistake. This happened as early as the Roanoke colony and continued right up to the last wars with the Apaches. The Chiricahua chief Cochise was quite willing to live at peace with the Americans in Arizona (as long as they turned a blind eye to his continued raids into Mexico), but was wrongly blamed for a raid perpetrated by another Apache clan and dragged into war.[30] Unusually stupid or bloodthirsty frontiersmen sometimes attacked Amerinds indiscriminately, or vented their anger at the atrocities of one group on another. This occurred at least as early as Bacon's rebellion in 1676. Particularly grotesque examples occurred in Pennsylvania during Pontiac's uprising; berserk pioneers massacred peaceful Christian converts at Conestoga and Lancaster. A similar episode, triggered by Iroquois raids, took place at Gnadenhutten during the Revolutionary War. At Sand Creek in 1864 and Camp Grant in 1871, Civil War militia and civilians massacred Cheyennes and Apaches who had come to make peace, or were already under Army control.[31] Whites could not always distinguish between Amerind groups even when they tried. Often they lumped different tribes together, for example the Yavapais of the Southwest, in the 1860s and 1870s, were wrongly thought to be Apaches. Less often, whites saw differences that did not exist.

The loose social organization of many Amerinds was complicating and confusing; sometimes there was no tribal organization until one was imposed by the whites. Individual Navajo clans decided on peace and war and might ignore treaties made by others; indeed one clan, allied with the Mexicans and the Americans, consistently fought the rest. (It had made a good business out of raiding other clans for slaves.) The Apaches were not a single people but a set of clans speaking the same language, dwelling in widespread corners of the Southwest, with varying ways of life. Other tribes split under white pressure, and controversy over this or that agreement. The Cheyenne broke into "war" and "peace" factions during negotiations in the 1860s. Later the Nez Percé split into "treaty" and "nontreaty" factions depending on whether they lived on or off the reservation the majority of the nation had accepted.[32]

Especially in the nineteenth century, policy blunders, some complicated by the interests of tiny groups seeking their own profit, were a major factor and wars resulted that were totally unnecessary for any public policy. The war against the "nontreaty" Nez Percé merely replaced a small group of Amerinds, trying to become cattle ranchers on a modest extent of mediocre range, with a few white stockmen—at vast public expense and unnecessary loss of life. As Generals Pope and Sheridan bitterly noted, the failure to feed and clothe reservation Indians who had already accepted the loss of most of their traditional territory caused completely avoidable fighting.

Attempts to resettle and remold Amerinds often misfired even when carried out humanely. A characteristic failure was the attempt to resettle the Navajos and the Mescalero Apaches (although the two groups were bitter enemies) on the same reservation at Bosque Redondo, and turn them into sedentary farmers in the 1860s. Later the government concentrated mutually hostile Apache bands on the San Carlos reservation. With inadequate supplies, the Indian Bureau tried to turn them into farmers on an area the soldiers guarding them called "Hell's Forty Acres."[33]

As we have observed earlier, it was only in the eighteenth and nineteenth century, well after it had been realized that the Amerinds were not Caucasoids, did ideas of innate racial inferiority become a factor in the ill-treatment of the Indians. Given the general values and attitudes of nineteenth-century American society, Amerinds almost certainly would have been treated better had they been white, or had the racial ideology of the time suddenly evaporated; but it does not seem to have been a central factor in what happened to them. And, despite superstitions of race, standards of behavior had improved. The nineteenth century Amerinds certainly fared better than the Canary islanders of four centuries earlier.

Other groups of natives encountered by Europeans in that era fared differently. The Maori, like other Polynesians, were rated comparatively highly by Europeans. Despite the practice of cannibalism, Maori not only looked relatively like Europeans, but had certain affinities of attitude with them. This, their adaptability, and the strong missionary influence in New Zealand helped prevent the development of much racial prejudice. Australian aborigines and South African Bushmen and Hottentots undoubtedly suffered in the eyes of whites because of the darkness of their skins as well as their greater cultural backwardness. On the whole, however, the gap in culture and disease resistance, rather than racial ideas, were the decisive factors in the Americas and other areas where white settlers encountered primitive peoples.

However, this was *not* the case in the next situation we will examine.

5

Slavery, the Not-So-Peculiar Institution

Chattel slavery in the Americas, and the trans-Atlantic slave trade that supplied it, were without doubt the worst episodes in the history of the modern West's relations with other peoples. From a narrow American point of view it is safe to say that Negro slavery was the most destructive institution to exist on American soil. Even in a narrow presentist perspective it is impossible to find anything more productive of social disruption and emotional recriminations than what pre–Civil War white Southerners delicately and defensively called the "Peculiar Institution." Perhaps one of the most demoralizing, or at least confusing elements, has been the refusal of many people to recognize that, in truth, slavery was not so peculiar after all.

For slavery, and related matters, remains the focus of exceedingly strange attitudes for present-day Americans. The amount of guilt (real, imputed, or feigned) and obsessive exaggeration attached to these issues is readily apparent both in the pronouncements of scholars and everyday remarks. Two writers on the subject declare, *"Perhaps no single institution has shaped the character of American history as much as slavery, and no single feature of thought has been as important as white racism."* Another historian says, *"The racism that developed from racial subordination influenced every aspect of American life* and remains powerful." Even the conservative political commentator Rush Limbaugh has described slavery as *"this country's original sin."* Similar statements have been made by candidates for office like Pierre (Pete) DuPont.[1] (All emphases are mine.)

Andrew Hacker, in a highly touted recent book, declares that "Race has been an American obsession since the European sighted 'savages' on these shores," and that "Throughout this nation's history, race has always had *a central role*." "What other Americans know and remember is that *blacks alone* were brought as chattels to be bought and sold as livestock. As has been noted textbooks now point out that *surviving slavery took a skill and stamina that no other race has been called upon to sustain*. Yet that is not what others choose to recall. Rather, there remains an unarticulated suspicion: might there be something about the black race that suited them for slavery."[2] (My emphases.)

If such attitudes exist they might be a consequence of people like Hacker who irresponsibly assume, and lead others to believe, that the long history of slavery encompassed only the Americas (or even only the United States), and that only black Africans and their descendants (or, one might say, their obvious descendants) were enslaved—a view promoting ignorant self-pity on one side and ignorant contempt on the other. Yet even a writer diametrically opposed to Hacker's views concurs in one respect, as would many other people, declaring that "Race is the great American dilemma. This has always been so, and is likely to remain so."[3]

We have become so accustomed to statements of this sort that at first sight they no longer seem as remarkable—even bizarre—as they really are. As we shall see, many of these notions, insofar as they light on the realm of concrete fact, are incorrect. The institution of slavery was not a sudden innovation designed to "get" the black race (as many blacks and some whites imagine) nor (as some whites may privately suppose) did whites refrain from enslaving other whites out of feelings for "fellow whites," or a higher sensibility, or because whites were too tough or freedom loving to be made into chattels. All these ideas, we shall see, turn out to be quite comical. But even the forms of argument are strange. To argue that slavery or racism were the most important features of American history, or influenced all aspects of American life, is to lose all sense of proportion, indeed all normal criteria of what is central or not. Negro slavery was one institution the United States shared with the very different societies of the Caribbean and Latin America rather than Western Europe, Canada, and Australia. It is self-evident that it has not proven much of a bond or common shaping factor. It is manifestly unlikely that an institution largely limited to one backward region of the United States could have had such a central influence.

To suggest that race has always been a regnant obsession of Americans, North as well as South, is at best to project a contemporary state of mind (or neurosis) onto the past. Whatever should have been the case, it is clear that race was not a central national concern from the end of Reconstruction up to the 1950s (or even later.) Indeed, it would be surprising had this been the case, during, say, the Great Depression, or the World Wars, when people of all colors had other things to worry about. The late Ralph Ellison's lament that the black was the "invisible man" is a truer characterization of how white Americans saw, or did not see, blacks. Outside the South, at least, until quite recently, it could be truly said that blacks were out of sight and out of mind. Until well after World War I, there were few blacks outside the South, and those few were concentrated in a very few cities.

Nor is it clear what is the sense of saying that slavery was an "original sin." It is not clear what it could mean to say that this or that country has an original sin, and strange indeed to suggest that of the United States is one actually shared by virtually all previous civilized societies; even black slavery (if the issue is misleadingly confined) was shared by most of the countries of the Western Hemisphere. The usefulness of importing concepts like "original sin" into discussing history and social life is less than self-evident.

THE HISTORICAL BACKGROUND

Slavery, of blacks or others, was only one form of bondage inflicted on the lowest social classes. Most readers of this book, whatever their skin color, are descended in large part from serfs or slaves or both; it is the degree, recentness, and color coding of those involved that differ. In the Middle Ages, most Western Europeans were serfs; indeed, in some places free men hardly existed for a time outside the ranks of the nobility. Serfdom, imposed later and in a harsher form east of the Elbe, persisted in Central and Eastern Europe into the nineteenth century. The serf had more rights than a slave, and theoretically was bound to the soil, rather than being a piece of property, at least in Western and Central Europe. (Russian "serfs" were actually slaves and were openly referred to as such until the eighteenth century.) Even in Western and Central Europe, serfs were sometimes sold apart from land, and their masters regarded them with about as much contempt as slaves. A medieval German proverb ran, "a peasant is just like an ox, only he has no horns." It is only a foreshortened and misleading view of history that conceives of society as polarized between free men and slaves, or equates "white" with "free," or "black" with "slave," except in a particular period. The not too remote ancestors of most Europeans and white Americans were neither free nor slave. We might note, in passing, that serfdom, although the primary form of bondage for Western mankind, encompassing a majority of the population in the very centers of Western culture, is far less studied and discussed than slavery, although the latter, in the post–Roman West, was limited to relatively small numbers of people, or minority groups on the fringes of Western civilization. The reader who doubts this is invited to compare the shelf space libraries devote to serfdom and the space they give to slavery. That should be kept in mind even when we concentrate our attention, as in the rest of this chapter, on the worst form of bondage, chattel slavery. This chapter is thus skewed—even if it is skewed in a wholly conventional manner.

The plantation of the pre–Civil War South was not a unique house of horrors but stood at the end of a long and dismal road that had begun long before Rome. Chattel slavery is one of the oldest features of civilized society. Originally it was probably a "progressive" development, replacing the slaughter and sacrifice of war captives. Generally speaking, however, it has usually been only a minor phenomenon from an economic point of view. Most slaves, in most societies, have been domestic servants rather than a major element of the work force. Roman society of the late Republic and Empire, and the modern Americas, were major exceptions to this rule, as were nineteenth-century Madagascar and Thailand. The peculiarity of modern slavery in the Americas was not, as is sometimes claimed, its cruelty, but its racial character (although even here it was not as unusual as is sometimes said) and that character developed only gradually. It represented the combination of the traditional slavery that had come down from Greco-Roman antiquity in the Mediterranean countries, with a relatively new element of racial prejudice.

There has been a long, confused argument among American historians about "which came first," slavery or racial prejudice, a subject on which, interestingly, one finds the most curious and contradictory remarks from people who are otherwise lucid thinkers.[4] In fact, both slavery and racism originated independently, long before the first white settlers set out for the Americas. Gradually, these originally unrelated ingredients fused and became mutually reinforcing, to the point that it was hard for many to realize that they had ever been separate and distinct at all.

MEDIEVAL SLAVERY

Slavery in most of Europe died out during the Middle Ages, as former chattels and once free peasants melded into the newer class of serfs. (The very term serf derived from "servus," the older word for slave.) That process took longer, and finished later, than is generally realized. The slave trade—or trades, for several different ones existed—was often a profitable business. English and Celts, in their wars for Britain, often enslaved each other and sold their captives across the English Channel. It is said to have been the sight of Angles being sold in a slave market that inspired a Pope to send a mission to convert the Germanic invaders of Britain to Christianity. Vikings often sold their captives as slaves. "Thralls" were an important source of labor in Viking Age Scandinavia; enslaved Irish and Britons may have formed half the original population of the Icelandic republic. As late as the Norman Conquest, at least a tenth of the population of England were slaves.[5] Curiously, a few centuries later, the descendants of Northwest European slaves decided that providence had uniquely chosen black Africans to be slaves. And a few centuries after that, many of *their* descendants were somehow convinced that there was something uniquely horrible about that.

Slavery did die out north of the Alps and the Pyrenees. But it persisted in the Mediterranean countries throughout the Middle Ages, especially in the Iberian Peninsula and southern Italy. Slavery lasted in Sicily, Spain, and Portugal until the early nineteenth century. Gypsies were kept as slaves in part of what is now Rumania until the 1850s.

During the early Dark Ages, slaves were one of the few items Western Europe could export. Later, when Germans and Christian Slavs captured still pagan Slavs and Balts, they sold them to Moslem markets; our word "slave" derives from "Slav." The Moslem world employed large numbers of slaves; it opened a major slave trade across the Sahara desert. Slaves were almost as big an item as salt and fish in the early trade of Venice and remained an important commodity for that city and Genoa throughout the Middle Ages. As most of Eastern Europe became Catholic, the eastern frontier dried up as a source; but the slavers exploited other venues. The continual wars between Moslems and Christians were a steady source of slaves for both sides. The appetite for slaves grew, especially after the Black Death created a shortage of labor. The Italians imported not only captured Moslems and a trickle of blacks from the Mediterranean, but a growing stream from the east—Tatars and other peoples from the Russian steppe, Central Asia, and the Caucasus, and even Christians. Despite a widespread modern belief that scruples prevented medieval Europeans from enslaving other Christians, Orthodox Christians and occasionally even fellow Catholics were deemed fair game. Many Greeks captured in the wars in the collapsing Byzantine Empire were enslaved along with other Balkan peoples and Russians. As noted earlier, the Italians established sugar plantations, operated by slaves, in their eastern colonies. They also used slaves in mines. At home, slaves were usually used in workshops. Other local slave trades developed; the Aragonese in their wars in Sardinia often enslaved their captives. Although Catholics, the Sardinians were deemed barbarians. The lawless character of life at sea was such that slavery even reappeared on a tiny scale in Western Europe; English seamen sometimes kidnapped young Icelanders and took them home.

Both the slave trade and the sugar plantations with which it was already associated tended to migrate westward. During the fourteenth century, the Papacy, hoping to reunite the Churches, took an increasingly dim view of the enslavement of Orthodox Christians, especially Greeks. (Later on however Protestant Europeans taken in the religious wars were enslaved, usually becoming galley oarsmen.) The Turkish conquest of Constantinople ended the Black Sea slave trade, or rather diverted it to supply Turkish markets. These things seriously cut into the supply of white slaves. It might be suggested, tongue in cheek, that by disrupting the traffic in Caucasoid slaves, the Papacy and the Ottoman Turks made possible the race problem in the Americas.

Slaves for the Mediterranean area and the newly colonized Atlantic islands, which became sites for profitable sugar plantations, were obtained by capturing Canary islanders and white Moslems (and some Jews) from what was left of Moorish Spain and North Africa, and purchasing blacks brought overland across the Sahara. The "Atlantic" slave trade was initially largely white, but the supply of white chattels was declining; as the Portuguese crept down the Atlantic coast they, although interested in many items, obtained more and more black slaves.[6] Although hard to get to, disease-infested, and dangerous, West Africa was the last great source of slaves in the Eastern Hemisphere. There, slavery was already a common institution.[7] As the supply of Caucasoid slaves dried up—they seem to have been preferred when available at all (contrary to what might have been supposed later by believers in the peculiar fitness of blacks for slavery, or people obsessed with the unique victimization of blacks)—the traffic in slaves become increasingly a traffic in nonwhites. At first it was a mixture of black Africans and Amerinds, and finally comprised blacks alone. The "modern" slave trade was simply an outgrowth of the medieval one, without any sharp breaks or innovations.[8] The descendants of white slaves, like those of the relatively few blacks in the Mediterranean countries, were eventually quietly absorbed in the mass of the population. That, and the immense size of the traffic in African blacks, helped to almost obliterate the memory of the earlier traffic in white slaves.

A somewhat similar, slower process took place in Islam, where both white and black slaves had existed side by side for centuries. White slaves grew increasingly rare, and blackness became increasingly identified with slavery. This change was necessarily slow since for many centuries the ruling group of Mamluks in Egypt was drawn from white slaves from the Black Sea, and that of Ottoman Turkey depended on the *devshirme*, the enslavement of Christian children from the Balkans who provided officials and Janissary soldiers.

When the Spanish and Portuguese reached the Americas and the African coast, they naturally took the practice of slavery with them. As C. Duncan Rice has commented, "The use of slaves to colonise the Americas was not an aberration. It is nothing like as surprising that Europe's new colonists first farmed and mined through slavery as it would have been if they had not." As he grimly noted, "There is a ghastly inevitability not only about the emergence of the Atlantic slave trade, but the whole planting of slavery in the New World." Robert McColley, examining the question from another angle, commented, "It would be amazing had slavery not appeared in early Virginia."[9] There was no clear point at which the transplantation of this ancient evil was decided on or could have been averted. It may be remarked, too, that while large-scale slavery may be historically rare, so is any serious condemnation or opposition to slavery. Indeed, it is surprising that even in the sixteenth century a few enlightened men, like Bartolomé de Las Casas and Sir Walter Raleigh, had serious doubts about slavery even for Africans, and that slavery only gradually developed in what later became the southern states of the United States and seems always to have been unpopular and uncommon in the New England colonies.[10]

AMERIND SLAVERY

Slavery in the Americas was, at first, not simply a racial matter. Despite a widespread supposition to the contrary, blacks were not the only slaves in the Americas. The Spanish and Portuguese enslaved great numbers of Amerinds. To a lesser extent, although more than is usually thought, English settlers in the seventeenth and eighteenth centuries, especially in the South, enslaved Amerind war captives when they were still regarded as dark-skinned whites. Such enslavement was regarded as justified since the prisoners were heathen and primitive. The slave trade was particularly important in South Carolina, whose traders fomented wars among the Indians to get prisoners and raided the missions set up by England's Spanish enemies with the dual purpose of smashing Spanish control and capturing slaves. They largely depopulated Florida. Many slaves were exported from the South, but even there, in some places, Amerind slaves were as important as blacks. But after 1730 the supply of Amerind slaves fell off. Because of their lack of disease resistance, their ability to escape, and perhaps also for subtler cultural reasons, they tended to make poor slaves. (They commanded only half the price of blacks.) Moreover, there were always grave misgivings about the moral propriety of treating them as property; by the end of the colonial era, Amerind slavery had died out in British North America.

Under the influence of reformers like Las Casas, the Spanish outlawed Indian slavery at an early date, although some colonists evaded the law by getting Amerind slaves from Brazil. Finally the Portuguese followed their example. But these laws were never completely enforced. In frontier areas of Latin America, such as eastern Peru, Amerind slavery persisted until well into the twentieth century. In New Mexico it was only abolished well after the United States annexed the area. (It is a little-known fact that the last slaves in the United States were not Negroes but Navajo Indians.)[11] As late as the 1860s, perhaps as many as 6,000 Indians, mostly Navajos, were held as slaves in New Mexico. They cost much less (commanding some $400 a head), but had more rights than black slaves in the South; they could not be traded once acquired, were freed after marriage, and their children were born free. Federal agents only liberated them after the Civil War. On the whole, however, Amerind slavery was a relatively minor phenomenon, unsupported by the deep conviction of racial inferiority that underlay the enslavement of black Africans and their descendants. Yet, it is worth discussing because occasionally one still finds the idea, or rationalization, among white Americans that whites "respected" Amerinds because they supposedly fought back and could not be enslaved, but despised blacks because they submitted. Oddly, this sort of nonsense is also found among "progressive" social scientists and Marxists who would like to explain racial hostility simplistically as a function of or byproduct of economics. The inimitable Marvin Harris has explained that a virulent prejudice developed against blacks because they alone could be enslaved.[12] This is a childish simplification of a long and ugly evolution.

EUROPEANS AND BLACK AFRICANS

A deep-seated bias against black Africans seems to have been common in Europe long before the Age of Exploration, encounters with Africans on a large scale, or the development of the slave trade or any economic incentive for prejudice. This attitude seems to have been nonexistent in antiquity. No association of blacks with slavery existed, or could exist, for the vast slave population of the Roman Empire was almost wholly white. Contrary to impressions, due apparently to bad movies, there were few blacks in the Roman Empire and few of those were slaves. Nor were blacks seen as especially backward. Greeks and Romans did not think much of other peoples, but the blacks they encountered seemed no worse, and less annoying, than the white barbarians beyond the Rhine and Danube. For long after Rome blacks were dim figures from the rim of the world, or beyond—the Scandinavians even seem to have thought that they were blue! A belief that blacks were inferior or bad appeared in medieval Europe—it can be seen in the *Song of Roland* and its origins are still something of a mystery. It may have been acquired from the North African Arabs, and ironically reinforced by the vague association of black Africans with the white African enemies of Christian Europe.[13] The association of blacks with the Moslem foe was registered in the old English and German terms for Negro—"blackamoor" and "Mohr." But there are other (not necessarily contradictory) explanations. There is a widespread tendency, in many cultures, to value lightness of skin color and associate it with superiority and/or a ruling group. In some spectacular cases, lighter-skinned conquerors established their rule over darker natives—most notable were the Indo-European invaders of India. An element of this, although the differences between the peoples involved were less dramatic, may have occurred in medieval southern Europe. The nobility in many of the Mediterranean countries tended to be derived from Germanic tribal conquerors; as a result prestige tended to attach to blond hair and other "Nordic" features otherwise not too common in those lands. A more common association of paleness and superiority results from occupational differences. In preindustrial times the vast majority of people were peasants or other outdoor workers, and, unless they were black Africans or the exceptional sort of Caucasoid whose skin would not tan, were darkened by exposure to the Sun. A relatively pale skin was the mark of the upper or middle class, not only among Europeans but among Chinese, Japanese, and Polynesians. Up to the twentieth century, at any rate, these groups avoided becoming tanned. The idea that a tan was healthy or attractive would have struck Westerners, up to the end of the Victorian Age, as absurd. (Modern medical research suggests that they were right.)

Alternatively, it is widely believed, the "black" skin of Africans had unfortunate connotations, for Europeans, like most peoples (including black Africans), associated darkness and blackness with evil, light and whiteness with good, leading quickly and easily to the belief that those with "black" skins were inferior or evil.[14] (Just why dark brown sub-Saharan Africans and their descendants, who range from dark brown to yellow, are perceived as "black" is a problem in itself.) This thesis appears to be supported by the fact that the Japanese, who had a comparable color symbology and prized lightness of skin before they came under Western influence, exhibited similar contemptuous reactions toward both dark-skinned people from southern Asia and to the first Africans they met.[15] However, all this leaves the lack of prejudice in Classical Greece and Rome unexplained. The ancient Greeks often spoke admiringly of the "blameless Ethiopians."

In any case later Europeans thought little of blacks even before they took to the oceans and treated black slaves differently from other slaves. In Renaissance southern Italy, for example, blacks were the only slaves not allowed to ransom themselves.[16] The development of large-scale plantation agriculture in the Americas, and the trade that supported it, both fed on and reinforced this preexisting bias, although that bias did not "cause" slavery.

THE SLAVE TRADE AND AMERICAN
PLANTATION SLAVERY

At first the Portuguese mariners traversing the West African coast raided for slaves; but they soon found it much safer, and far more profitable, to buy them from the local rulers who could provide a steady supply of chattels ranging from prisoners of war to criminals. It was the beginning of an ugly business in which almost all Western European countries—even such an unlikely power as Prussia—became involved. Slaves from the nearby mainland provided most of the work force for the previously uninhabited Cape Verde islands, and then for the American tropics.

The Spanish, for various reasons, did not go slaving in Africa on their own. The *asiento*, or contract, to supply their colonies with slaves became an important prize, held, over the centuries, by various private and official groups ranging from Genoese, Portuguese Christians and Jews, to Britain and France. But there were never enough slaves to suit the colonists, so poaching on Portugal's West African preserve and smuggling slaves became an important factor in international politics. The first Elizabethan ventures in the Americas were a series of ultimately unsuccessful attempts to horn in on this trade. Eventually the northern European powers established their own slaving stations in Africa.[17]

Some of the British Caribbean colonies, like Barbados and St. Kitts, were founded by white small farmers, but large slaveholders, raising sugar and tobacco, soon drove them out of business. The small farmers moved to the North American mainland and were followed by some plantation owners—South Carolina was founded by settlers from Barbados. In effect, slavery in England's southern mainland colonies was an offshoot of the tropical slave system—and, at first, a feeble one. The islands, for many generations, were far richer than the mainland, which had far fewer slaves. The latter had been founded on white labor, very largely that of indentured servants. Although blacks were brought to Virginia as early as 1619, their numbers were few, and their status was at first uncertain; slavery was a blank spot in English law. Indeed, many English colonists, and their descendants, seem to have been uncomfortable with the *word* slave, preferring to use the euphemism "servant" even for chattels. (Pre–Civil War advertisements often speak of "servants" or "Negroes" for sale, although by then there were many free blacks.) A few blacks in early Virginia gained their freedom and became landholders; but blacks were treated differently from white indentured servants from the start. By the 1640s, when there were only few hundred blacks in Virginia and Maryland, slavery was securely established.[18]

The Atlantic slave trade led to the biggest forced migration in history until the partition of India in 1947. Nine to ten million Africans were hauled across the Atlantic in horrible conditions; on the average 10 to 20 percent of each shipload of slaves died en route. (Mortality among the seamen on slavers, it should be noted, was about as bad.) Once in the Americas the survivors and their descendants lived very different kinds of lives, depending on the type of work they did, and the time and place in which they lived, so that no real generalization about the impact of slavery is possible. It is fairly clear that the vast majority were worked very hard. In some situations owners found it profitable to work most of their chattels to death in a few years. Sugar plantations in boom times and rice plantations, especially when they were first laid out, were scenes of staggering death rates, leading an eighteenth-century poet to describe Barbados as "the sad place, where sorrow ever reigns, and hopeless wretches groan beneath their chains." Even in the nineteenth century, when treatment of slaves was more humane, a white Mississipian told Frederick Olmstead, "I'd rather be dead than a nigger on one of those big plantations" where owners regularly overworked their slaves.[19] This sort of life, or living death, was not the fate of all slaves. Domestic servants, and skilled or semiskilled workers like carpenters, were far better treated. So were field hands on small plantations and farms where the owners often worked alongside their slaves. Even on big plantations masters had good reason to preserve their slaves in most circumstances; some even ceased to care about making profits, and a few even left their slaves largely to their own devices. A situation in which people were property, and left to the tide of economic forces and the personal whims of their owners, produced a fantastic variety of circumstances. Slavery ranged from a living hell to a relatively more tolerable life, equivalent at its best, perhaps, to that of an oppressed and degraded peasantry in most societies.[20] The few slaves living in the northern English colonies were the best off; those who lived in New England were the luckiest. Slavery was not popular in New England, and slaves had the right to civil marriage, trial by jury, and such protections as the law gave indentured servants. The great Puritan theologian Cotton Mather boldly stressed that even a black might be the "elect of God"; he deemed slavery wrong and held that blacks were equal to whites. Perhaps only his unfortunate bent for witch-hunting prevented him from becoming a modern hero.[21]

The safest generalization about the evil of slavery is that it meant the near-total subjection of people to another's will. Whether or not a slave suffered any harm from his master, he had no defense against him. That, rather than fashionable attempts to determine the average number of whippings on the average plantation, would seem to be the decisive condemnation of slavery.

COLOR SUPERSTITIONS

As has been said, slavery both fed on and intensified prejudice against blacks. By 1700 this ugly prejudice had crystalized into a definite mythology, elements of which have persisted, in an increasingly tenuous form, right up to the present, when in fact some have been inverted into *compli mentary* stereotypes about blacks. The mythology was a vital component not just of slavery but of race relations in America after its abolition. Composed of falsehoods, false generalizations, and occasional facts (usually removed from context) it exaggerated the mental, and even the physical, differences between Caucasoids and Negroids. Some southern doctors, in the nineteenth century, went so far as to claim that it was not only Negroes' skins that were dark; "tinctures of darkness" pervaded even internal organs like the brain. More factually, it was pointed out that their brains were, on average, smaller than those of Caucasoids. That was true, but the actual difference in size (which was often exaggerated in the nineteenth century) of some fifty cubic centimeters was slight. And, within large limits, brain size is not related to intelligence. (It is worth noting in this context that Eskimos and some other groups of Mongoloid race average larger brains than Caucasoids.) In general, head size and cranial capacity seem to be correlated with climate and the requirements of thermal regulation and vary greatly within racial groups; Amerinds living in the tropics have smaller heads than those living north and south of them.

More general beliefs were that Negroes smelled differently and worse than whites. They were intellectually and, usually, morally inferior to whites. They were unintelligent and uncreative; any exception was due to white blood. They were lazy, dishonest and unreliable, violent and obsessed by sex; but they were also more passionate, and on that account were sometimes seen as both depraved and attractive. (It is worth noting that similar beliefs, although generally not so intense, associating "inferior" foreigners or minority groups with sensuality, appear in many societies. In Europe, for example, ideas of this sort were attached to Gypsies and even to Jews.)

It was admitted, however, that blacks had some good, or at least useful, qualities. They were strong, more resistant to heat than whites, and also resistant to some tropical diseases (there was some truth in this belief). Since blacks were closer to nature and the animals than whites, they had a great sense of rhythm.

There was also certain ambiguities and counter-stereotypes. While regarding blacks *in general* as shiftless and unreliable, upper-class whites could also express confidence in, even admiration for, their personal servants.

Sexual relations with blacks were unthinkable for white women, but possible, although disapproved of, for white men. Ideas about interracial sex and interbreeding were (and probably still are) particularly tangled and emotional. There was even a bizarre notion—technically called "telegony"—that if a white woman once had a child by a black her later children, even if fathered by a white, would be black, or in some other way "tainted." Race mixture was bad, for while instances of intelligence among blacks were attributed to white ancestry, in a curious way "black blood" had a magical power. It was stronger than "white blood"; a modest amount of Negro ancestry made a man "black," and mulattoes, while deemed more intelligent than pure Africans, were also deemed more untrustworthy. In the pre–Civil War South a person of completely European appearance could thus be classed as a "Negro" for social purposes, leading to the oddity of a society based on "white supremacy," equal rights for white men, and black slavery, holding slaves who were blond and blue-eyed.[22] (This curious obsession, however, seems to have become fully developed only after the Civil War. The so-called "one drop rule"—that any Negro ancestry whatever made someone a Negro—seems not to have existed in the slavery era.)

Important contributing elements to the beliefs in black inferiority were associated with mistaken, or at best confused, notions about Africa and

Africans; notions, which for a variety of reasons, people are often reluctant to discuss frankly even today. Those who believed in blacks' inferiority often wondered (and though usually sotto voce still do) why the "Negro race" had not achieved anything comparable to the other "major races" of mankind and pictured precolonial black Africans as extremely primitive inhabitants of dank, unpleasant jungles. In point of fact they often exaggerated the backwardness of Africans, especially West Africans and Ethiopians. Those peoples may not have been in the advance guard of human progress (as some contemporary blacks would like to pretend), but had highly organized societies, which were very far from being the most backward cultures on Earth. They were, in fact, quite literally "mediocre" (in the technical sense) on any cultural scale that could be drawn up. Apart from the handicaps imposed by the African environment we have noted earlier, the habit, persisting in modern textbooks, of designating Caucasoids, Mongoloids, and Negroids as the three "major races" of humanity obscures the fact that the last group was not comparable in numbers, or amount of territory occupied, to the others. Until comparatively recently the full-sized Negroids (as opposed to Pygmies) inhabited only a relatively narrow strip across Africa; and even today, black Africans and their overseas relatives comprise only about 15 percent of the human race. Nor were they particularly associated with "jungles" however loosely defined. The full-sized black Africans were traditionally inhabitants of the open grasslands and deserts, not forest areas, which were the habitat of their dwarfed relatives, the Pygmies. It is only within the last two or three thousand years that they moved into jungle areas; even then (like peasants in Southeast Asia) they generally disliked the jungle proper, living in clearings or on riverbanks and leaving exploitation of the remaining woods to the Pygmies.

The most basic fallacy, however, lay in the assumption that the then current cultural attainments of black Africans, whatever those were, represented the limits of their capabilities, and that their current backwardness, compared to Europeans, exactly reflected inherent and permanent differences between the capabilities of the two groups. Two thousand years earlier Greeks and Romans could have used such arguments to "prove" that the Northern Europeans were inherently inferior and would never amount to much. That cultural differences did not correspond to racial ones was also demonstrated by the range of cultural levels found among the Amerinds. Racially, the latter were a fairly uniform group from Alaska to Cape Horn, yet they ranged in cultural level from primitive hunters and gatherers to highly organized civilized states. (Incidentally, it is a curious reflection on the attitudes of many whites, that, at least in the twentieth century, few suggested that the Amerinds had been culturally backward, compared to Europeans, because they were genetically inferior; and many who accepted environmental or other nonhereditarian explanations in relation to Amerinds, easily reverted to genetic explanations when Africans or their descendants were involved.)

Some notions about the inferiority of blacks were purely mythical; some merely reflected their inferior social position and the easy but silly supposition that this corresponded to their innate abilities. Those born and held as slaves, with a few exceptions, were bound to be ignorant, subservient, and would lack the will or the ability to conform to the standards of free persons.

The stigmata of slavery were not unique to black slaves in the Americas. Traditional or at least recurrent notions fused with the preconceptions about the innate inferiority of blacks. "In general, however, slaves were despised and regarded as typically cowardly, unreliable, stupid and foul. They yielded to panic and were not in command of themselves as the proper man was." The description is of the view of slaves in Viking Age Scandinavia. Europeans enslaved by the Barbary pirates behaved similarly.[23]

Neither the social conditioning of slavery, nor the attitudes it produced in whites and blacks, disappeared with the freeing of the slaves; some of the social effects of slavery are still with us. To some extent the social pathology of American blacks—high rates of crime, alcoholism, drug addiction, mental illness, and family breakdown—may be due to the heritage of slavery and past discrimination, although a bizarre welfare system and other government policies may have enormously intensified these problems. It is interesting to note that the descendants of the Burakumin, a Japanese group once stigmatized and segregated as inferior outcasts, although racially identical to other Japanese, exhibit social pathologies similar to those of American blacks generations after their outcast status was formally abolished.

Most of the queer beliefs about blacks were shared by slave-owning societies throughout the Americas, except for those relating to interracial sex and its results. In Latin America, and to some extent the British and French Caribbean islands, race mixture and its products were more acceptable, although people of pure African descent were no more highly regarded. Spanish and Portuguese emigrants were mostly single men. Fewer family groups, and far fewer single women, went to their colonies than to English North America, so many white men had only slaves for sex partners or wives; this was also true in the British West Indies. Moreover, the lower position of women in Iberian society, which was partly responsible for the differential emigration, meant that white wives had no power to discriminate against black mistresses and their offspring. "Mulattoes" in Latin America and the Caribbean became a separate and superior category from "Negroes," while in North America they were merely a subcategory. *After* the abolition of slavery, this led to a very different sort of relations between the races, especially in Brazil.[24]

It must not be imagined, however, that interracial sex was less frequent in North America than in the rest of the Americas.

Although a quasi-hidden aspect of Southern society, racial mixing was not insignificant. An elaborate terminology developed to describe its products. "Mulatto," although often used loosely to describe anyone of visibly "mixed" origin, strictly speaking denoted a person half white and half African. A "mustee" (used, however, only in few places) was a cross between a black and an Amerind. A "quadroon" was only one-quarter and an "octoroon" just one-eighth African. A "griffe" (or "griffin" in the case of a woman) was the offspring of a mulatto and a pure African and was one-quarter white. "Fancy girls"—beautiful women, usually octoroons, specially trained as mistresses, were the costliest of all slaves, fetching prices of $5,000 or more. But they were one feature of slavery that made even pre–Civil War Southerners swallow hard and were rarely alluded to in public—save by abolitionists.[25] As a result of all this mixing, a great majority of American "blacks," perhaps three-fourths to four-fifths, are part white in ancestry, and the black population as a whole, viewed as a single gene pool, is 20 to 30 percent white. Thanks to this mixture and the quaint practice of "passing for white" the American "white" population is 1 percent "black" in ancestry. The "black" genes are rather widely spread; it has been estimated that 23 percent of white Americans have some genes from sub-Saharan African ancestors.[26] It may be that most old-stock white Americans—the so-called WASPs—have a small amount of African ancestry. It is thus a little late for the strange but widespread assumption that "whites" and "blacks" in America are fully distinct groups, whose racial superiority or historical "guilts" or "credits" for oppression can be neatly apportioned.

ABOLITION

Some Europeans had always disliked slavery. In the eighteenth century a serious protest developed against slavery with the beginning of the modern current of humanitarian and democratic ideas. As far as slavery and blacks were concerned, that current was mainly religious in origin. The secular thinkers of what is—perhaps somewhat ironically—called the Enlightenment were, generally speaking, anything but friendly to blacks and actually originated scientific racism. Rather, in this era, it began to be felt that slavery could not be reconciled with Christianity; previously, while Christianity might not have favored slavery, it had not strongly opposed it.

This, and *not* the introduction of slavery in the Americas, was a great turning point in history and a radical departure—one authority describes the abandonment of slavery as an "extraordinary decision."[27]

The development of antislavery sentiment, and the relative weakening of the economic interests involved in slavery, spelled doom for the institution. Slavery may or may not have become somewhat less profitable than it had been—although it was not on the verge of financial collapse—but the Industrial Revolution made it less important in the scheme of things. While industrialization in Britain rendered the once mighty West Indian interests less significant, the northern and western parts of the United States grew faster than the South, changing the balance of power within the country. The working out of the clash between humanitarian and democratic ideas and the traditional racial ideology, and the economic interests connected with each side, forms the pattern of the history of American race relations up to the Civil War.[28]

THE CONFLICT OVER SLAVERY IN THE UNITED STATES

Many American revolutionaries had perceived a contradiction between their beliefs and the institution of slavery so the revolution and its aftermath led to the abolition of the slave trade and of slavery in the North. There, no major economic interests were involved, and there were no large number of blacks to be feared if they were "uncontrolled." Men like Rush, Franklin, and Hamilton expressed doubts about the innate inferiority of blacks while slave-owners like Washington and Jefferson hoped for the abolition of slavery. Jefferson's considered opinion was that blacks were decidedly inferior to whites—although he conceded doubts about that—but he detested slavery. He would have liked to prohibit it in all territories of the new United States. Although one of the great plantation owners of Virginia—he owned 188 people—Washington remarked in 1786 that it was "among his first wishes to see some plan adopted by which slavery in this country might be abolished by law."[29] For a time this seemed to be a possibility, especially since slavery was not particularly profitable then. Slavery was banned from the Northwest Territory, and the treatment of slaves in the South became somewhat more humane. Laws were passed—and occasionally even enforced—that made killing a slave murder. Some historians, like Winthrop Jordan, think that for a time abolition was tantalizingly close in Virginia and Maryland, an event that would probably have undone slavery as a whole and saved the United States from civil war.[30]

But the invention of the cotton gin and the boom in cotton ended the downturn in the profitability of slave labor. And the fear of what masses of uncontrolled people of an "inferior" race would do was far more important to Southern whites than to people in the North. E. Merton Coulter, an historian of the Confederacy, once suggested that slavery was less the ultimate cause of the Civil War than "the Negro himself. It was the fear of what would ultimately happen to the South if the Negro should be freed. . . . It was not the loss of property in slaves that the South feared so much as the danger of the South becoming another San Domingo (Haiti) should a Republican regime free the slaves." That, rather than a fanatical attachment to property rights, bound the nonslaveholding majority of southern whites to the plantation owners and to the Confederacy.[31] Most Southerners, therefore, resolved that what Gunnar Myrdal later called the "American Creed" did not apply to blacks. Or it applied only partially; the treatment of slaves improved, and it became understood that a gentleman did not mistreat his slaves. The overt contradiction between white Americans' general beliefs and the treatment of blacks was more or less suppressed. The more fanatical proslavery ideologues like George Fitzhugh ultimately found it necessary to repudiate the ideas of the American revolution, but most white Southerners preferred and managed to live with the contradiction. The Confederacy was a democracy, even if for white men only, and was led by conservatives like Jefferson Davis rather than the fanatics who deemed slavery a positive good.

THE SLAVE SYSTEM IN THE PRE–CIVIL WAR SOUTH

By the Civil War slavery was a settled institution; it had changed little since the 1830s. Ownership had become highly concentrated. Only one-fourth of Southern whites owned slaves; and most of them had only a few—72 percent owned less than ten people. Few Southerners owned plantations of the sort pictured in *Gone with the Wind*, though some were incredibly wealthy. Two men owned over 1,000 slaves, although owners of more than 100 were rare. Most slaves lived on the big plantations.

Cotton was the staple crop, but many plantations still raised tobacco. Sugar and rice plantations, which involved the most back-breaking labor, were concentrated in Louisiana and South Carolina respectively.

Slaves performed a great variety of tasks. Although most were field-hands, slaves were also used as lumberjacks, miners, and stokers and many were specialized sorts of domestic servants. There were slave artisans and skilled workers—cobblers, weavers, carpenters, blacksmiths, brickmakers, and masons. There were even slave mechanics, locomotive engineers, and ships' pilots—one of the latter, Robert Smalls, became a hero during the Civil War when he brought the steamship *Planter* over to the Union.

Although there were exceptions, most of these people worked extremely hard. On most days they worked from dawn to dusk (with a rest period after lunch) and as much as sixteen hours a day during growing and harvesting seasons. Normally they had Sundays and holidays off and often worked only a half day on Saturday. (Some masters gave all of Saturday off.) Children were given small tasks as early as the age of five; by ten or twelve they were listed as "fractions" of full-grown fieldhands. Masters usually left slaves to their own devices when work was finished; but the slaves had housekeeping tasks of their own and had to tend the private gardens most masters allowed. Masters sourly observed that (rather like later Soviet collective farmers) the slaves worked far more energetically on those plots than in the masters' fields.

A few masters—Jefferson Davis was the most famous—depended on slave supervisors rather than white overseers and followed a policy of giving their slaves maximum autonomy to accomplish assigned tasks, but few dared to do this. Work was the main focus of the tug of war between master and slave and the slave's sly resistance to his condition. A few slaves, mostly skilled workers, took pride in their enforced tasks, but most had little reason to do so. Escape and outright rebellion were rare (for reasons we will discuss shortly), but slaves made ample use of all the devices ever thought up by soldiers, prisoners, and serfs for malingering, gold-bricking, and sabotage. Masters came to expect shirking; as President Washington dryly noted, slaves would never work hard, save under the eyes of an overseer. Some ingenious men avoided work for years by pretending to be crippled; others *did* cripple themselves. Not unlike members of the lower classes in other societies, but to an even greater extent, slaves energetically feigned stupidity. They broke or misused equipment and wasted supplies. Some masters gave their slaves only crude, clumsy tools, lest they be broken. Petty theft from the masters was normal; slaves considered that "taking," stealing was robbing from each other. Their passive resistance was not without effect. Most masters realized that there was a limit beyond which their slaves could not be pushed; if their hours were lengthened too much, the slaves would just work more slowly.[32] They knew that despite divisions among the slaves—most slaves hated "drivers"—they stuck together and despised informers. Despite their commitment to the Negro's intellectual inferiority, an idea the slaves deliberately cultivated or made use of, many masters came to concede a certain malicious cleverness to their slaves. And all were well aware that slaves could not be trusted.

This point must be stressed for some have claimed that slavery was so crushing that many or most slaves, like some German concentration-camp prisoners, were broken in spirit, developing a "Sambo" personality that neatly fitted the masters' stereotype of the ideal slave. This overrates the oppressiveness of slavery, or underrates the slaves, or both. Whatever some optimistic Southerners pretended after slavery ended, those who owned slaves, like George Washington, had no such illusions. They knew that their slaves were not content and that what they saw was a mask. "The only way to keep a Negro honest is not to trust him," ran one proverb.[33] Even the old-fashioned historian Coulter, while overemphasizing slave loyalty during the Civil War, conceded that "The wise Southerner never felt quite sure of what went on in the minds of his slaves, but he believed that eternal vigilance was the best policy."[34]

One reason that slave rebellions were rare in the Old South (despite periodic "panics") was that, unlike the French in Haiti, American slavemasters did not drive their slaves to desperation with cruelty. And while slaves might outnumber whites in limited areas, they must have known that there were far fewer slaves than whites in the South as a whole. But the main reason was that Southern whites took a no-nonsense approach to security precautions. Normally a white man, either master or overseer, was always on the plantation. Slaves and storehouses were usually locked up at night, and their cabins periodically searched. The law insisted that slaves must leave plantations only with a pass, but many masters tried to prevent their getting out at all. They kept them away from free blacks or lower-class whites—whose relations with slaves were usually bad anyway—and often insisted that they choose mates only from the masters' own chattels. If the owner was careless the official slave codes were rigorous. (They also applied, partially, to free blacks.) These prohibited gatherings of more than five slaves off a plantation. Except in Kentucky, they forbade slaves learning to read and write. Slaves were forbidden to have guns, horses, mules, dogs, or alcohol and were not allowed to administer drugs or medical care to whites.

Although all of these rules were broken by individual masters when it seemed convenient, they generally held good, and the codes were enforced by a system of official slave patrols, for which white men were sometimes drafted. They patrolled the roads at night to catch any slave without a pass and periodically ransacked slave quarters; they were also notoriously more ruthless and brutal than the owners themselves. Crimes against whites received short shrift—rebels, or those who murdered or raped whites, often did not live long enough to reach trial and were lynched or burned at the stake.

Backing official force was a variety of punishments for disobedience. Slaves could be locked in private jails, clapped into stocks, or put in irons. Branding and castration were rare, but did occur. Normally, the most extreme punishment was flogging with a whip, or sometimes a leather strip specially made so that it would not cause scars.

It should be noted that corporal punishment of all sorts was still common in the nineteenth century. It was only then becoming disreputable even for white men. (Flogging was abolished in the United States armed forces only in 1861; and the substitutes that were reintroduced in the Army of the Potomac during the Civil War were, if anything, even worse.) The general consensus of historians of slavery is that, if only for practical reasons, gross brutality was not common among pre–Civil War Southerners; and the attitude of ex-slaves toward their owners, which will be discussed later, seems incompatible with such a situation. The abolitionist James Redpath, who traveled widely in the South and did not start off with any admiration for slaveowners, was surprised that they behaved so well.

In the background the owner held the fear of being sold away to the Deep South. Lesser controls also existed. The master could seize his slaves' private plots (although that usually increased his costs for feeding them), demote domestics or artisans to fieldhands, and forbid dances. But many masters found it desirable to use carrots as well as sticks; they gave slaves gifts or money for unusual or additional work, allowed dances, or gave passes to leave the plantation.[35]

Slaves' daily lives varied considerably. They were generally fed enough food (often from communal kitchens), but their diets tended to be monotonous and ill balanced, albeit often through the general ignorance of nutrition. Their diets may not have differed much from that of lower-class whites and was almost certainly better than that of the European lower classes.[36] Except for domestics, they were badly—often inadequately—clothed. Slaves wearing little more than rags were common.

Some slaves were comfortably housed even by the standards of Northern whites, but most lived in crude one-room log cabins that were often cramped and dirty. Often the one room was shared by two families. Slaves' health was not good. Infant mortality was very high, and mental illness was common—descriptions of slaves teem with overt neurotic symptoms.

The uncertainty of the more intimate parts of their lives must have been a major factor in this. Contrary to a once widespread myth encouraged by abolitionists and later by sensational novels like Kyle Onstott's *Mandingo*, slaveowners rarely deliberately "bred" their slaves. Normally they let the slaves choose their mates, although most insisted that slaves marry only among the master's own chattels. North American slaves had much more regular family lives than those in other slave societies. But their family structure was nevertheless weak compared to that among whites. Some masters left the private lives of their slaves alone, others tried to enforce Victorian ideas of propriety among them, punishing fornication, adultery, and wife-beating. But in any case the authority of fathers was weak. Often, neither parent (working full time) had much to do with raising their children, who were exposed to their parents' humiliation, even public punishment. As we have noted elsewhere, many masters and overseers did not resist the temptation to make sexual use of slaves. Most slaveowners tried to avoid breaking up families, or selling small children separately from their mothers. Both these things were strongly condemned by the otherwise proslavery Southern churches. But splitting of families was nevertheless common, if only because of forced sales to pay debts or the breaking up of the estates of deceased slaveowners. Slaves generally thought this the worst aspect of slavery; and escape attempts were often prompted by separations even more than flight from overwork or fear of punishment.[37]

The subjects of this dismal system had one big protection. Fortunately for the slaves they had become costly items. By the time of the Civil War the average field hand commanded a price of $1,500; artisans as much as $3,000. Owners calculated that a newborn baby was worth $100 as soon as it was born; a child of nine or ten (who could already do some work) cost $400 to $450 apiece.[38] (All these figures must be multiplied by at least *ten*, to be understood in terms of contemporary price levels.) An enormous amount of capital was tied up in the slaves, and one important reason masters usually refrained from mistreating slaves was that they were just too costly to be abused.

THE AFTERMATH OF SLAVERY

The defeat of the Confederacy and the abolition of slavery did not abolish the ideology of racial inferiority, one which was widely if less intensely believed in the North as well as the South. Nor could it suddenly turn a largely illiterate, ignorant, and disorganized peasantry into a group capable of participating on an equal footing with the white majority. The attitudes of many ex-slaves to work, and the mutual deception between whites and blacks in the South, did not make things easier. These features should not be overstressed, however; those who commanded ex-slave black troops in the Civil War were struck by the fact that they were well disciplined and well behaved. To the surprise of Union observers, ex-slaves demonstrated little vindictiveness or hostility toward either whites in general or their ex-masters. Their predominant emotion toward whites had been fear, not love or hate, and afterward was distrust. They did not even seem to hate their masters, rather they hated the system that bound them.[39] Observers were struck by the fact that, although very ignorant, they seemed to have a thirst for education. General Oliver O. Howard, the head of the Freedman's Bureau, thought that they seemed to be more eager for it than white children. He deplored the fact that schools for them were but a "drop in the bucket."[40] Unfortunately, burning down black schools and violence against the white Northern school teachers who taught in them was one of the favorite activities of the Ku Klux Klan.

Most white Southerners accepted the end of slavery, but they emphatically did *not* accept the equality of blacks or daily social contact. The latter, it should be noted, was not something that much interested blacks at the time, although they resented the stigma implied by legally enforced separation of the races. The topsy-turvy situation of disenfranchisement of ex-Confederates and black voting was not so much insufferable as inconceivable to Southern whites. Even that most reasonable of ex-Confederates, Robert E. Lee, remarked, "My own opinion is that, at this time, they cannot vote intelligently, and that giving them the right of suffrage would open the door to a great deal of demagoguery and lead to embarrassments in various ways. What the future may prove, how intelligent they may become, with what eyes they may look upon the interests of the state in which they reside, I cannot say more than you can."[41] (It is amazing that a man of his background was willing to concede the possibility that they could ever vote sensibly at all.)

The general view of race relations in the South was reflected in the "Black Codes" rammed through by the first postwar Southern state governments. These more or less explicitly aimed at permanently reducing the freed slaves to propertyless rural workers. The codes restricted blacks' occupations and their purchase or rental of land and bound them to their places of employment. Some crimes were designated as felonies only when committed by blacks, and some black crimes received stiffer penalties. General Howard shrewdly reflected on the attitude more typical of the South than Lee's: "they will not be brought in a day to love the thing they hated." He remarked, "The negroes were generally very ignorant and not wisely led, and even if they had been the wisest of rulers, the opposition of the whites to being ruled by their late slaves would naturally have been very fierce." Even Howard thought that black suffrage should be limited by educational qualifications.[42]

With the Confederates beaten and slavery ended, Northerners were mostly indifferent to what went on in the South. Most felt that, while Negroes should not be slaves, they were vaguely inferior; and some fully shared the Southern view of them, which they could now express without incurring the taint of treason. The general view, which was probably shared by Abraham Lincoln, was that their "basic rights"—rights of property and to equal treatment before the law—ought to be recognized, but they need not be granted the vote. (Most Northern states, before the Civil War, had denied blacks that privilege.)

Voting—and this was in accordance with ideas generally accepted in the nineteenth century and which also applied to white women—was deemed a privilege, not a basic right, and could be restricted or not as the relevant community which then meant the state, *not* the nation) chose. Complete social equality was still further from their minds, while breaking up plantations to provide the freedmen with land was seen as a violation of property rights.

It is likely that Lincoln shared this view of the matter. His political calculations seem to have been based on turning the South over to civilian rule as fast as possible, while drawing prewar Southern Whigs into the Republican Party. He hoped to make them the dominant element in the South, thus helping ensure Republican control of the whole nation. Had his plans succeeded, they would not have produced equality for blacks, but might have left them better off than they were in 1865—or 1877. But neither his successor nor Congress really tried to follow his plans.

It was the Black Codes, and President Andrew Johnson's acquiescence in them, and the brutal violence of proto-Klansmen against the freedmen that angered most Northerners, for a time, into supporting the Radical Republicans and black suffrage.[43]

Congress, however, imposed the Radical Reconstruction program only on part of the South. And these state governments, while not nearly as bad as Southern myths (ironically often elaborated by Northern historians) later pretended, were weak and corrupt, and their real defects tended to obscure such constructive achievements as the creation of free public schools in areas which had never had them. They were the products of an artificial situation and depended on continued Northern intervention to prop them up.

The white Southerners who, rather than the blacks, largely ran these governments were themselves weak and divided. The Republican Party in the South was an unnatural coalition of prewar Whigs, wealthy merchants, and plantation owners who had generally supported the Confederacy and poor Unionist hill people. The latter had often fought heroically for the United States, but commanded little influence and less respect among Southern whites in general. The two groups had little use for each other and less for blacks. The idea of a reforming coalition between poor whites and blacks was a fantasy created by later writers such as W.E.B. DuBois and unfortunately had no basis in the real situation of the 1860s. Racial dogmas were too strong; and lower-class whites had not really rejected the rule of the plantation owners. (When they finally did so, many years later, they were *harsher* toward blacks than the upper-class "Bourbons.") In the nation as a whole Radical Reconstruction was tied to the weakening and increasingly corrupt "Stalwart" faction of the GOP. Many radicals lost faith in blacks, or turned to other, more fashionable causes. The weakness of the blacks' position was such that the brutal violence used against them may not really have been needed. It is doubtful that Reconstruction could have ended any better than it did. Blacks were disenfranchised; the slave system was transformed into a sort of caste system, although simpler, less rigid and less lasting than that of India. The social situation was simply too unfavorable to the ex-slaves. Only the further working out of the "American Creed," growing literacy and the growth of a middle class among blacks, and the migration of many out of the South—to places where they could vote— gradually put blacks into a position from which they could secure equal rights.[44]

Reconstruction had not been entirely in vain, however. It had eliminated the obnoxious Black Codes, leaving the way for blacks (and the South as a whole) to improve their economic situation. The Fourteenth and Fifteenth Amendments to the Constitution left white Southerners in an awkward position. Blacks might be denied their rights as citizens, but only by evading the Constitution. The law was on their side, if it was ever enforced. The preservation of the status quo in the South was henceforth married to illegality. It was the reformers who stood for law and order.[45]

The treatment of slaves and their descendants is not a pretty story, but it should not be seen, as is currently fashionable, completely out of historical context. It bears repeating that most societies have held slaves. The notion that everyone living in a society is actually *part* of it, and, moreover, entitled to freedom and equal rights, is a very recent idea even in the Western world. Most Western Europeans were serfs until the fourteenth or fifteenth centuries; most of the people of Europe east of the Elbe remained serfs until the same era in which slavery was abolished. Before, and after, slavery most Europeans lived in societies that were steeply stratified and hierarchical. Most people had few rights and were often harshly treated.

Moreover, that was true, to a far greater extent than is generally recognized, of those colonies that became the United States. Many white emigrants to the Americas, including British North America, were indentured servants, unfree or semifree for their term of service, or convicts who were being exiled instead of imprisoned. Indeed, Georgia was actually founded as a sort of liberal penal colony, in which, at first, black slavery was prohibited. The loss of the Thirteen Colonies as an outlet for "transportees," and the need for a substitute, was a major factor in leading the British government to colonize Australia.[46]

Unfortunately, such facts have been obscured by different groups for different reasons, including the silly ideas that white Americans like to entertain about each other. Traditional patriotic history tended to idealize the American colonists and was often written by men who probably did not care to recall that some of their own ancestors had been semislaves and jailbirds; that feeling may still influence some old-stock white Americans. (It is only recently that it has become fashionable for people to boast about *how badly off* their ancestors were.) The so-called "consensus historians" of the post–World War II era may not have been influenced by such attitudes, but liked to stress the extent to which the American nation had been "born free," having left behind many archaic and oppressive European institutions even in the colonial era. In a general sense, they were probably right, but their case was arguably exaggerated. Later still, those nursing ethnic grievances, or who for some other reason liked to give the impression that old-stock Americans, or white Americans in general, were all exploiters or were guilty of some crimes their ancestors had allegedly committed, liked to forget the indentured servants and convicts. And many Americans descended from later immigrants, who were purely voluntary, simply found it hard to imagine that many of their predecessors had to be dragged here. Some liked to blubber about the sufferings of their own immigrant forefathers, who had suffered the indignity of crossing the Atlantic in the steerage class of steamships—unlike the ancestors of the WASPs who had wallowed in the luxury of much longer crossings under sail. Unfortunately, perhaps, no stereotype of American race relations is repeated more often than the absurd claim that, while the ancestors of white Americans came freely, blacks had to be forced to come here.[47] Only the second half of this cliché is well founded.

Against the true historical background, black slavery is less singularly outrageous. The point is worth making because, as is the case with the relations between European settlers and aborigines, fashionable patterns of thought insist on painting matters as even worse than they were (especially when dealing with slavery in the United States) and of enlarging the importance, unusual nature of, and historical impact of black slavery, as well as severing it from the earlier history of slavery. This curious insistence can be seen in the comment by the intelligent writer C. Duncan Rice that "what was uniquely wicked about the white colonists of the Americas was not that they enslaved their fellow-men, which was commonplace, but that they came to restrict their activities to Indians and latterly to Africans, that is to alien races who had not previously done them any harm. The construction of a race system based so strictly on race was a new development." While Rice may have had his tongue planted firmly in his cheek, it is easy to find similar views elsewhere, intended dead seriously.[48] Actually, it is quite usual for there to be a considerable ethnic difference between master and slave.[49] And it is a bit strange, as well as not quite accurate, as we have seen, to upbraid Europeans for enslaving *only* strange-looking foreigners.

More serious confusions, however, are common. As Ronald Segal and others portray it, the slave trade was not just a slave trade, but a "racial war," as though there had been no slave trade before Europeans contacted West Africa.[50] In point of fact, however, the slavers did not raid Africa for slaves but traded for them with local rulers and merchants. As Rice comments, "it is impossible to make a sound analysis of the history of the slave trade without accepting the fact that it depended on wicked Western merchants who were prepared to buy their fellow men; but also on African merchants who were prepared to sell them." The slave trade was a commercial deal, albeit an evil one, between equal partners.[51] (The famed TV show *Roots* and some other portrayals of the slave trade imply that Europeans raided far inland to secure slaves. This rather perversely lends a tone of Vikinglike daring to what was just a sordid business transaction.)

In fact, Europeans were not then powerful enough in relation to Africans for it to be any other way. A perhaps related myth emphasizes the horrific impact of the slave trade on the development of Africa. In this view, West Africa was no more, or little more, backward than Western Europe at the start of the modern era. The slave trade, by allegedly perverting commercial development and provoking wars between African states, caused Africa to fall behind. One writer comments that the belief in African backwardness was a "myth which served to justify the cruelties of the slave trade and to assuage the guilt of the European nations involved in the largest forced dislocation of people in history."[52]

Alas, however, sub-Saharan Africa was backward compared to Europe, even though, as far as West Africa, the most advanced sector, was concerned this may have been exaggerated a bit in the past. (Ethiopia was clearly a civilized society, although very backward.) Although the development of states and urban conglomerations had begun in West Africa, most of the cultures of that area were preliterate and technologically well behind the Europeans and Asians. Cannibalism, human sacrifice, and other unpleasant customs such as clitoridectomy were common. The barbarism of most black

Africans was not invented by Europeans, even if they sometimes exaggerated it and falsely attributed it to some inborn inferiority. In fact, the extent to which black Africa trailed behind Europe and Asia is readily explained by the relative isolation of Africa from the principal cultures of the Old World; nor, as we have observed, is the area particularly favorable for development,.

Moreover, there is little evidence that the slave trade permanently injured those Africans who stayed at home. The number of people taken was not enough to reduce Africa's population or retard its growth. Curiously, it was precisely those areas that were most deeply involved in the trade that became the most advanced and densely populated areas below the Sahara.[53] Ethiopia, which was not involved in the Atlantic slave trade, was saved rather than harmed by Europeans; a Portuguese expeditionary force helped save it from being overrun by Moslem vassals of the Ottoman Turks.

A particularly widespread myth about slavery arose after World War II. This myth portrayed slavery in the American South, and also in the British and Dutch Caribbean colonies, as far worse than slavery in any previous era or in Latin America. It was held that because of the influence of Protestantism, or a more highly developed capitalism and profit orientation, slaves were treated much worse by the Northern Europeans than by Latin American owners. Precisely because slavery in the Mediterranean countries had a continuous existence, institutions and rules to ameliorate their lot were, allegedly, comparatively well developed. Supposedly, laws in Latin countries recognized the slave's humanity, while in English-speaking America the black was allegedly viewed as an object. This notion seems to have appeared in the nineteenth century, but it became widespread thanks to the work of twentieth-century writers, such as Arnold Toynbee, Frank Tannenbaum, and Stanley Elkins. As one writer put it succinctly, "American slavery was profoundly different and more vicious in its effects than its counterpart elsewhere in ancient and contemporary time."[54] While such invidious generalizations cover a lot of ground, it is doubtful that the plantations of the Old South and the Caribbean ever saw anything approaching, much less worse than, the Roman games or the Mediterranean slave galleys of early modern times. Toynbee and some others of this school propounded the odd notion that Northern Europeans and/or Protestants, and English-speakers in particular, were more "racist" in general than other Westerners; a theory difficult to reconcile with the well-known fact that modern Hawaii and New Zealand are the least racist spots in the world.[55]

Moreover, research over the last twenty-five years has shown that the favorable contrast of Latin America, at least with the American South, is almost entirely false. In fact, it is probably the reverse of the truth. It is fairly clear that this notion was based largely on a misunderstanding of slavery in Latin America and especially on a rose-colored view of slavery in *parts* of Brazil originated by the Brazilian writer Gilberto Freyre.

In point of fact, the laws in the American South, as well as the laws of the Ibero-American world, defined slaves as both humans *and* pieces of property. Some of the laws in Latin America that earlier scholars thought were designed to protect black slaves were actually meant to protect Indians, not blacks, and anyhow were rarely enforced. Laws to protect Negro slaves did exist in North America and occasionally were enforced.[56] There was little difference in attitudes between the Protestant and Catholic churches; in fact, outside the Southern United States, it was the Protestant denominations that tended to produce abolitionism. Even within the South, they were a strong force for better treatment of slaves.

The actual treatment of slaves in the Americas did vary widely. Those in the Caribbean islands, whatever the nationalities of their masters, seem to have been far worse off than those on the mainland of the Americas, probably because of the differing economic situations. Cuban slaves may have been worst off of all. On the whole, blacks in the southern United States seem to have been better off than those in the rest of the Americas. Slaves were probably treated more harshly in Brazil, the main center of slavery on the southern continent. Mortality rates there were high. The decisive evidence seems to lie in mortality and population growth rates. Although the area that became the Southern United States absorbed just a small fraction (about 5 percent) of the New World's slave imports, American blacks formed a much larger part of the black population of the Americas. As Carl Degler wrote, "The endurance and even expansion of United States slavery (after the abolition of the slave trade) without any substantial additions from importation, is unique in the world history of slavery." The family life of blacks was more stable than in other American slave societies. It should be stressed, however, that this may well have been due to the working out of market forces; not necessarily to any greater humanitarian bent in the Old South,[57] although that may have existed.

Yet another myth exaggerates the economic value of slavery and its importance to the Western world, suggesting that profits from slavery in the seventeenth and eighteenth centuries financed the industrial revolution and thus created its present prosperity. As Gary Nash puts it, the "slave trade and slavery were crucially important in building the colonial empires and in generating the wealth that produced the industrial Revolution."[58] This notion is a curious counterpart to the nineteenth-century Southern apologists who presented slavery as the indispensable basis for their society.

Slavery and the slave trade *were* profitable and important. The West Indies, which were little but conglomerations of slave plantations, were Europe's most profitable colonies in that era and a prime objective in its wars. It has been estimated that 300,000 British died in military campaigns in the West Indies from the midseventeenth century through the Napoleonic Wars. (During the latter struggles, more British soldiers died in the

West Indies than in Wellington's Peninsular campaign.) The West Indian islands were so valuable that William Pitt's decision at the end of the Seven Years War to demand the cession of Canada from the French, instead of some islands, was violently criticized. After the war of the Spanish Succession, the *asiento*, the contract for supplying slaves to the Spanish colonies, was regarded as a principal prize of war. (By then, however, part of its value was that it offered a wonderful opening for smuggling other goods into the otherwise closed Spanish Empire. By what we would regard as perverse turn, the Spaniards forbade what we would consider honest commerce while opening the door for slaves.) A third of Britain's merchant marine was engaged in carrying slaves or slave-made products, and great ports such as Liverpool grew up on the slave trade.

However, slavery was not enormously more profitable than other investments, for it was also a risky business. As C. Duncan Rice and others have shown, it was simply too small a slice of the British and European economy to be a decisive force. The profits generated by slavery, even if they had been totally reinvested, would have formed no more than 1.8 percent of Britain's total national investment in the eighteenth century. They were just too small to provide the financial basis for the Industrial Revolution.[59] Like the Hobson-Lenin theories of imperialism, this particular effort to ascribe the advance of the Western world to "exploitation" is a failure, and for very much the same reason. The primary focus of the European economic effort was at home, not overseas. It was home production and bulk trade with nearby relatively advanced economies that was the base of British prosperity and development. And the scientific and technological advances that underlay that certainly owed nothing to exploitation of any sort, whether of slaves, colonial subjects, or of the European lower classes, who were certainly far more important economically than the former groups. (We will ignore, here, the troublesome fact that gross exploitation in many societies did not produce progress.) The curious recurrence of obsessive efforts to prove that prosperity and progress are "really" the result of exploitation, brutality, and crime, rather than creative endeavors, is certainly one of the curiosities of modern history. As an intellectual oddity, it may be exceeded only by recent efforts to argue that freedom in America was not contradicted by slavery but was based on it. As Gary Nash put it, "the promise of American colonial society was intimately and unforgettably intertwined with the exploitation of African labor and Indian land." Whereas earlier generations of "liberal" historians sometimes tried to write off the old South as "un-American," through a curious reversal these historians visualize all of the founding era of American history through the prism of the eighteenth-century Southern plantation, holding slavery to be an indispensable part of American freedom.[60]

The absurdity of such arguments should be obvious; the New England colonists, not to mention those of Canada, Australia, and New Zealand, managed to stagger along without slaves, which, in fact, were not an important factor in the South until very late in the seventeenth century. As late as 1700, there were just 18,000 slaves on the North American mainland in a total colonial population of 300,000. And, right up to the Civil War, the backbone of the South was the white yeoman farmer. The latter may have hoped to become a plantation owner, and may have thought slavery vital to maintain the submission of an "inferior race," but he did not gain economically from it. Far from it; the presence of slaves helped drive nonslaveowners off the best land and depressed the wages of white workers in general. In the short run, slavery generated wealth, for some; in the long run, it helped make the South the poorest, most backward part of the United States.[61]

It goes without saying that slavery was an evil. It was, also, in no sense a "necessary" evil.

6

The Colonial Empires and Race

It has been noted earlier that it is incorrect to picture either European expansion or racism as a single, undifferentiated phenomenon. European colonial rule in Asia and Africa was a very different development from either plantation slavery or the white settlement of areas thinly populated by primitive peoples. Further, it generally developed much later. Europeans did not rule any sizable area of Asia until the British conquest of Bengal and the Dutch conquest of Java. In most of Asia, and nearly all of Africa, the colonial era was very much a phenomenon of the nineteenth and twentieth centuries. Imperial rule coincided with an era when liberal and humanitarian ideas were more widespread and influential than ever before. Unfortunately, so were racist notions, at least about Asians. (Opinions of blacks had sunk as low as they possibly could.) The era of colonial rule coincided with the heyday of pseudoscientific racial theories, and these had a considerable, negative impact on the relations between European rulers and their colonial subjects.

But race was not a key or arguably even a decisive feature in the age of empire in Asia or even Africa. Unfortunately, here, as in the discussion of other historical questions, race and racism have become entangled with other problems—in this case the reputation of empire, or more precisely, that of the European overseas empires. For, curiously, less moral obloquy has attached to the somewhat similar empire built by Japan, and the great land empire built by the Russians in the same era, and still less to the vast number of empires that have existed throughout history in every part of the world that has reached the stage of civilization and state-building. No one would think of talking about the Incas, or Rome, or Majapahit, or Asoka, or even Genghis Khan, the way contemporaries routinely moralize about the now equally departed empires of Western Europe, although some of these earlier realms would seem to have had far more drawbacks and far fewer redeeming features. Thinking about the European overseas empires is confused with what Geoffrey Fairbairn describes as "guilt feelings . . . about what the democratic West really stood for and stands for, vis-à-vis the non-European world.

There is no evidence that the rule of the white imperial administrations was less humane toward the subject peoples at large than any, or almost any, independent government has proved to be; and their rule was certainly found much more agreeable by the vast masses of minority peoples of various kinds. This is not in any way to suggest that European imperial rule in Asia and Africa created a humanly attractive relationship between peoples; it most certainly did not, and it did have its atrocious moments. But . . . the guilt-neurosis which has become embedded in so many educated Europeans' attitudes toward words like nationalism and imperialism *is* a neurosis in the sense that it is not grounded in substantial fact.[1]

TRADE AND EMPIRE

Europeans went east in search of trade—not unmixed with piracy. Their earliest ventures in Asia and Africa were often predatory, but fairly limited in territorial aims. The Portuguese, the first to reach the Indian Ocean, ruthlessly smashed the existing Arab-dominated trade, combining rapacious profit-seeking with the eternal war with Islam. Following the pattern of the previous rulers of the sea, they seized strategically located bases, mostly on small islands. They constructed a trade monopoly of the most critical and valuable items, like spices. They did not have enough shipping to replace local merchants entirely, but made them obtain licenses to stay in business and excluded them from some areas. They avoided major land conquests. That was not simply a matter of choice, for they, and other Europeans, found it hard to muster much power ashore. They could not transport or supply a large force in the east, and even if better-armed, Europeans did not have a decisive advantage on land. (Indeed, one of the seeming paradoxes of the early modern era was that while they were expanding dramatically in the Americas and the Indian Ocean, Europeans were falling back under Turkish pressure in the east of Europe itself.) The Spanish and Dutch followed the pattern set by Portugal, while the British were, if anything, particularly uninterested in conquest.

It is interesting to note that for several centuries the pattern of eastern trade did not alter much in terms of what was exchanged. It remained a small fraction of the West's commerce. As late as the 1770s less than 10 percent of the British merchant fleet sailed to the Indian Ocean. The Europeans sought, for the most part, luxury goods, or what were then rated as luxuries—above all, spices, Indian cotton and cotton goods, silk, coffee, indigo, jewels, opium and other drugs, Chinese porcelains, and copper. They found it hard to pay for these things, for Asians generally did not wish to buy European goods. To pay for imports from Asia, Europeans depended on sales of silver and gold (mostly obtained from the Americas) supplemented with such items as Asians found interesting—mostly base metals and metal goods. Asians had to obtain one luxury item—Mediterranean red coral—from Europe, but showed a gradually increasing interest in European manufactures—glasswares, toys, utensils, naval stores, armor, and above all guns. In contrast with the period after the Industrial Revolution, Europeans found it hard to sell textiles; Asians rejected all but some woolen and linen goods. While some groups made great profits in Asian trade, right up to the mideighteenth century, many Europeans were gravely worried at the loss of gold and silver to the east. And there was bitterness at the way *Asian*-manufactured goods—textiles and porcelain—hurt *European* producers.

Then things changed drastically. Opium (bought in India) began replacing silver as a means of payment in East Asia; and in the 1790s, machine-made British textiles began ousting Indian products from their own markets. This coincided with a drastic change in political relations between Europeans and Asians.[2]

CONQUEST ASHORE

The first European power to make real territorial conquests in the east had been the Spaniards in the Philippines. But the situation there was unusual; indeed Spain's role in Asia remained limited, its colony there an offshoot of Mexico. Those Filipinos who had not been converted to Islam were at a low level of political organization. Legazpi's expedition, crossing the Pacific westward from Mexico, obtained a quick and largely bloodless submission of most of the local tribes. Small Spanish forces, supported by local auxiliaries, subdued the rest of the pagan Filipinos, but the Spanish never conquered the Moslems of the South. They converted most Filipinos to Catholicism, the sole conversion of most of a nation to Christianity in Asia. In other ways the Philippines remained a wholly atypical colony. Few Spaniards settled there permanently, and most of them stayed in Manila. They concentrated on trade with China, which depended heavily on cooperation with Chinese merchants at Manila. Only the Church showed much interest in the Philippine hinterland. The colony's life revolved around the trade bringing luxury goods from China, and the yearly "Manila galleon" from Manila to Acapulco—the longest trade route in the world until the Industrial Revolution. The Spanish government often pondered abandoning this fragile creation, but the merchants and the Church always mustered just enough strength to prevent it.[3]

The efforts of the Dutch, or more exactly the monopolistic-chartered East India Company, which, like its English and French counterparts, conducted not only trade but war and diplomacy in the east, proved more typical. Using new types of rigging, the Dutch sent superior numbers of more efficient, medium-sized ships with much smaller crews to deal with the clumsy Portuguese galleons. Smashing the hold of Portugal (then controlled by their Spanish enemies), the Dutch grabbed the very source of the most valuable trade item, the "Spice islands" of the Moluccas. When the Bandanese proved refractory, the Dutch massacred them and moved in more obedient subjects from other islands. They closely regulated the growing of spices to maximize profits; they bullied the rulers of other islands to stop their growing of spices or make them sell only to the Dutch. Neither the Dutch, nor anyone else in that era, believed in free trade; although England was a fellow champion of the Protestant cause and an ally against Spain, English merchants intruding in the Dutch sphere got equally ruthless treatment.

The Dutch set up a major base and trading post at Batavia (now Djakarta) on Java, which gave them the "weather gauge" and a permanent strategic advantage over the Portuguese. Their position there was at first precarious—outside the limits of the post, the Dutch found it almost as dangerous as New York. Gradually, however, the East India Company was drawn into the conflicts among the Indonesians, whose wars often endangered trade. They often sought Dutch help against their rivals, paying for Dutch help with permanent economic concessions, which usually involved monopolies of selling manufactures, opium, and all imports from China. To secure Batavia, and food-growing areas to supply it, the Dutch took advantage of the natives' conflicts to expand the area under their direct control. The slow process of expansion throughout the Indonesian archipelago was not finished until the end of the nineteenth century.

A parallel process led to the British conquest of India. The collapse of the Mogul empire, which had been created by invaders from Central Asia in the sixteenth century, produced a power vacuum into which the British and French East India Companies moved. In the 1750s, the British Company intrigued with Indians to replace the unpopular Nawob, or Viceroy, of Bengal, by then a practically independent ruler. When the plan miscarried, the Nawob retaliated by attacking the Company trading post at Calcutta (a new city which had risen around it). The Nawob's atrocities against his British prisoners in the "Black Hole of Calcutta" and the Company's successful cover-up of its earlier actions enabled it to get the support of the British government in the war with the Nawob. The British conquered Bengal with a largely Indian, but British-led, trained, and equipped army. They found that, led by men like Robert Clive, even a small European-type army could smash gigantic Indian-style forces, or indeed similar armies in the rest of Asia and Africa. The latter might vastly outnumber a Western force, but usually consisted mostly of hastily mobilized peasants who merely hampered the few real trained troops at hand.

The East India Company turned from a commercial establishment into a colonial government—indeed it ultimately largely abandoned commerce. Initially it ruled badly. It paid dividends from outright plunder, and its employees often took a cut on their own. For its first decade and a half British Bengal was a "robber state." Overtaxation and sheer bungling caused famine. Pushed by the great statesman Edmund Burke, the British government began to supervise and reform the Company. The same forces that had led to the conquest of Bengal drew the British into further expansion. Finally they adopted a policy of conquering the whole subcontinent, although much of India (the "Princely States") remained loosely supervised protectorates until the British left. (The independent Indian government then seized the Princely States.) Some of the Indian wars, which were entangled with the Revolutionary and Napoleonic Wars in Europe, were anything but walkovers. French advisers reorganized and retrained some Indian armies; the Indians even devised new weapons, reviving the war rocket in an improved form eagerly copied by the British. But Britain normally controlled the surrounding seas, while the French were based in relatively poor areas of South India. In the end, the British were victorious.

The Company's reformed regime seems to have been no worse than that of the native rulers it replaced. (In 1858 the Company was dissolved and replaced by an outright colonial regime.) Eventually British rule became beneficial. By the late nineteenth century the British had brought modern education, technology, and elements of a modern economy to India. They had introduced modern government, laws, courts and police, formed a modern army, and given India the best transportation system in Asia. The subcontinent was politically and economically unified. A Westernized class of Indians emerged. (It was British-ruled Indian Moslems, along with Volga Tatars under Russian rule, who created "modernist" interpretations of Islam.) Once the British were firmly established, they attacked some of the most horrible features of Indian society. They abolished "suttee" (sati), the Hindu custom of burning widows alive on their husbands' funeral pyres, ended slavery, and smashed "thuggee" (thagi), a bizarre religious cult that had ritually murdered up to 50,000 people a year.

In Indonesia the era of ruthless exploitation, albeit with some variations, lasted much longer, surviving the dissolution of the Dutch East India Company. Under the "Culture System," Indonesians were forced to grow certain crops, and the colonial government sent tax revenues collected in Indonesia home to the Netherlands. But by the late nineteenth century, the Dutch too supplemented crude exploitation with civilized practices.

Despite the claims of some later nationalists, the initial phases of plunder do not seem to have had a permanent impact on the countries involved. Although the Europeans gravely injured native merchants and trade in Bengal and Java, there is no reason to think that the natives were anywhere near launching an industrial revolution parallel to the one in Europe.[4] The technological developments of the Industrial Revolution took place in Western Europe and North America and did not even spread to other parts of the West quickly. Nor did colonial exploitation guarantee development in Europe; the Spanish empire amply showed that prolonged and highly profitable colonial exploitation did not produce technological and economic progress in an imperial society unsuited to generate it. Even contemporary observers were struck at how, in the words of a Venetian observer, "The gold that comes from the Indies does on Spain as rain does on a roof—it pours on her and it flows away."[5] The overall importance of Asia to Europe's economy remained small. Trade with the Americas remained larger in volume and far more valuable.[6]

MODERN COLONIAL EXPANSION

By the nineteenth century, much of the world had remained stationary compared to the West. The Moslem world, the area with the longest, most direct contact with the West, reacted hardly at all to the growing challenge. Japan, whose social and political structures resembled those of later medieval and early modern Europe, had closed off Western contact and remained isolated until the 1850s. The technological gap between Western Europe and the other civilized parts of the world, comparatively small in 1500, had widened into a yawning gulf.

In the nineteenth century, Western control spread to most of Asia and Africa. Several factors caused this expansion. Turbulence in areas bordering those already ruled by Europeans often provoked intervention by the imperial authorities, and a variety of objectives led to European expansion. Sometimes the drive was economic, Europeans (and Americans) desiring trade forced Asians and African rulers to permit commercial access. The biggest, and ugliest, instance of this was the Opium War, during which Britain seized Hong Kong from China to serve as a permanent base. In some cases a business firm had enough influence on a home government to get it to intervene in its favor, even if the resulting colonial venture was unprofitable for the nation as a whole—as it usually was. Few colonies had the mineral resources or prospects for the specialized plantation agriculture that made them profitable. Nor was actual European rule necessarily needed to permit trade or investment.

In general, the primary causes of nineteenth-century expansion were political. The rivalries of the European powers were transferred to a global stage and played out in the partition of Asia and Africa. The scramble for

Africa after 1875 was the biggest example of this. Each European power sought to match or block its rivals and seize areas that *might* be useful—lest its competitors get there first. In the 1890s a similar process, started by Japan's defeat of China, led to the establishment of bases and spheres of influence there. Some colonies were taken because they were, or might be, of strategic value in war. Britain's later expansion was particularly characterized by such preemptive motives. Cyprus, for example, was taken from Turkey to serve as a base against Russia. The British established their suzerainty in Malaya in the 1870s because they feared the Germans might obtain a base there that could threaten Britain's China trade. Once the scramble for a region began, it tended to be played out to the end. But sometimes a canny or lucky local government, as in Iran or Thailand, used a buffer position between rival empires to save itself.

Prestige and internal politics played a major role in French and German expansion. Notions of military glory were still alive and fame could be won cheaply in "little wars" in the colonies. Colonies were often prestige items that symbolized or contributed to great power status. The French conquest of Algeria began as a futile effort to revive Bourbon prestige; later in the century the Third Republic sought to salve national humiliation after the Franco-Prussian War by expansion in Africa and Indochina. Sometimes politics forced action by governments with no real interest in colonies, as in Germany. There the Conservative and National Liberal parties pushed a reluctant Chancellor Bismarck into annexing areas in Africa and the Pacific.

German colonial expansion and its consequences offer a particularly good example of the process. The clear-sighted Bismarck had no use for colonies himself. As a cool-headed Junker, he wanted real assets for the Prussian state and cared little about glory and less about the benefits to capitalists or natives. In 1868 he noted that the notions that colonies were economically useful were "based to a large extent on illusions. For the costs of founding, supporting and keeping the colonies are much bigger than the profits for the mother country, as the examples of England and France prove. Another argument against colonies is that it is hardly just that the whole nation should pay for the advantage of some commercial and industrial enterprises." Moreover, it would cause "unwanted conflicts."[7] A fashionably anticolonial commentator in the 1950s could hardly have done better. Germany's colonies proved worthless, and, in an interesting example of the sort of interaction just described, provoked British annexations in the Pacific. The British were pushed on by the Australians and New Zealanders, who (rightly) saw the Southwest Pacific islands as the "Green Armor" needed to protect their countries. They were of strategic value to them, as World War II showed, but not to Germany.

Other groups also exerted political influence in favor of expansion. Humanitarian and missionary sentiment played an important role, especially in British policy. Many urged European control of Central and East

Africa as the only sure way to crush the Arab-dominated slave trade. Antislavery policies contributed to British annexations in West Africa and the establishment of protectorates over the coasts of Arabia.

An important factor in making colonial expansion acceptable was its relative ease. Sometimes Asians and Africans did defeat Europeans, but for the most part Western technical superiority was overwhelming in the nineteenth century. Once a foothold was established, conflicts among the local peoples could be manipulated. Neighbors often, even usually, hate each other more than strangers, and in many empires, the various subject peoples continued to hate each other as much, or more, than they did the ruling nationality. Few Asian and African states were held together by anything like national sentiment. It is no accident that the East Asian lands, where loyalties that at least resembled nationalism existed, largely escaped *Western* conquest, or that in those cases where true nation-states were annexed—notably Burma and Vietnam—the peoples involved, or at least the majority nationality, tended to have particularly venomous relations with the imperial power. Often, submission was gained with little or no bloodshed. The acquisition of Malaya and much of Africa took place with little or no fighting.

When resistance or uprisings took place in the nineteenth century, it was largely by unpopular or "reactionary" elements. The classic instance of this was the Indian revolt of 1857. The modern-oriented minority of Indians, who later formed the nucleus of Indian nationalism, then backed their British rulers.

Once again, the process of contact between peoples had obliterated the original coincidence of *all* the differences between them. Some Indians had absorbed important elements of Western culture—usually to be sure, they did not abandon all of their own. Ultimately, however, the very creation of Westernized or partly Westernized groups, which were receptive to modern Western ideas like nationalism, democracy, and Communism, spelled doom for the colonial regimes. Such elites were small and had uneasy relations with most of their compatriots, but they were closer to them than the European rulers. Ultimately they were strong enough to make it increasingly hard to maintain colonial rule without resorting to repressive measures that were unpopular in the Western democratic countries. Western influence and modernization had some unpleasant psychological effects— many Western-influenced people became disaffected from their own culture, or felt caught between old and new. It is the reaction to this, rather than to real or imaginary exploitation, that accounts for much hysterical anti-Western sentiment.

The multicausal explanation of imperial expansion has been well documented by studies drawn from European archives.[8] But such analyses have often been less popular than another explanation, most impressively presented by the British radical John A. Hobson and Lenin, that expansion was caused by the desire to find places for overseas investment. In his book *Imperialism* (1902), Hobson claimed—amid cranky ramblings about the decadence of Britain's aristocracy and the sinister activities of the Jews— that profits on investments at home had declined. It had become far more profitable to invest in underdeveloped areas, exploiting cheap labor and raw materials, and this caused expansion in Asia and Africa. Hobson was not hostile to capitalism as such; he emphasized that most businessmen based in Britain did not gain from imperialism. Only a minority of investors and speculators did. Imperialism should be ended by social reform at home and curbing the activities of investors abroad.

Lenin realized the usefulness of Hobson's ideas for Communist purposes. Modifying Hobson's work, his essay *Imperialism* (1916) performed several crucial functions. It rationalized away several gaps in Marxism and supplied a basis for Communism in what were later called underdeveloped countries. But, together with Hobson, Lenin's notions convinced many people who refused to "buy" Communist doctrines as a whole, and laid the basis for the "Third World" ideology of the post–World War II era.

Lenin pronounced imperialism the incurable final stage of capitalism. Imperial expansion had prevented capitalism from collapsing and blocked Marx's "law of increasing misery of the proletariat" from operating. The high rate of profits on overseas investment and the low cost of raw materials from colonies kept capitalism alive. Some of the "superprofits" of empire were used to "bribe" part of the proletariat at home, creating a "workers' aristocracy." That was the source of the reformist socialism Lenin hated. And the escape route Hobson envisaged did not exist; social reforms and redistribution of income could not take place, nor capital be directed into agriculture and other needy segments of the economy. Imperialism would go on, ultimately causing war between the imperialist countries. But those wars, and the revolutionary reactions they would provoke among exploited colonial peoples, would ensure capitalism's downfall. After 1919, when Lenin saw that Communist revolutions in the West were not imminent, revolution in the colonial world became a vital element in Communist strategy.

Lenin accomplished a major shift in terminology. In the Hobson and liberal view, imperialism was caused by capitalism, but was not an inevitable product of it. In Communist, and much leftist usage, capitalist investment abroad *is* imperialism, even if it never led to political control.

Hobson's belief that Britain invested heavily overseas was correct; and quite a few later economists thought it exported too much capital for its own good. But neither capital exports nor trade explain the late nineteenth-century expansion in Asia and Africa. As Walt Rostow has written, "nothing in the capital markets of the Atlantic world or their trading patterns justified much ado about colonies on strictly economic grounds, from, say, 1873 to 1914."[9] The pattern of foreign investment bore little relation to that of colonial control. Over half of Britain's overseas investments went *outside* the British Empire; the largest single recipient of British capital was the United States. Latin America, as a whole, also took more investment than any colony. Most British investment (and trade too) *inside* the Empire went not to the underdeveloped lands of Asia and Africa but to the "white dominions," the white settler colonies of Canada, Australia, and New Zealand, and to South Africa, where settlers were a large minority and which economically resembled the former colonies. General Wolfe, Captain Cook, and the settlers who followed them did infinitely more for Britain and its economy than the conquerors of the nonwhite empire. The fraction of British investment and trade that was channeled into the nonwhite colonies went largely to India and Ceylon, where British rule had long been established. Except for Malaya and the Transvaal, areas acquired after 1850 proved of little economic interest.

Nor is there much evidence that businessmen were often interested in expansion. Britain traded with and invested in underdeveloped lands to a larger extent than most industrial countries—in fact, it was the only colonial power to invest significantly in its colonies before World War I—but it was not an exception to the rule that developed countries mainly invest in and trade with other developed countries. Contrary to the Hobson-Lenin thesis, investment in colonies was not consistently more profitable than at home. Nor did "trade follow the flag." Britain's share of its empire's trade decreased between 1854 and the Great Depression, and protectionist policies then increased it only slightly. In the 1930s the empire took fewer than half its imports from Britain and sent it only 42 percent of its exports.

Other countries fit Hobson's model even less. Of 45 billion francs invested abroad by France before 1914, just 4 billion went to French colonies. Nearly three times that went to Russia, the biggest site for French investment. The French empire as a whole was a dead loss economically; it exported less than it imported. The Germans, Italians, and Portuguese were even less interested in their colonies, which were valueless. (Libyan oil was found only after World War II.) Nor did colonies perform a major supply function. Britain drew only 8 percent of its strategic raw materials from its colonies in the era between the World Wars. As World War II showed, the Western world as a whole could get along quite well without any access to its Far Eastern colonies. It is one of the great ironies of modern history that the West became dependent on underdeveloped countries for a major raw material, oil, only after the passing of its colonial empires. And oil came mostly from areas that had never been colonies at all.

Colonies did make some noneconomic contributions to the power of some countries. They provided bases (which however served mostly to defend the colonies themselves) and some military manpower. The Indian Army was a major addition to British power; North African, West African, and other colonial troops were heavily mobilized by France in both World

Wars. If a form of exploitation, this was one that those who approve of the Allied cause in those wars are in a poor position to criticize.

The Boer War, a favorite target of anti-imperialist critics, was not popular among businessmen and bankers. Most British investors in the Transvaal mines were content with Boer rule; the British desire to take over the Boer states was prompted by political leaders who feared the Boers controlling most of the wealth of Southern Africa, and perhaps backed by Germany, would threaten Britain's control of the Cape. Cecil Rhodes, the greatest of all "capitalist imperialists," was motivated by similar political considerations and a belief in the need to extend "Anglo-Saxon" domination.

Lenin's version of imperialism was even more faulty. The "law of increasing misery" was false, and "superprofits" did not explain why the workers of countries without colonies, for example Scandinavia, were better off than workers in countries with big empires, like France. There was no correlation between the development of reformist socialism and control of colonies. (British socialists were reformists, like the Scandinavians, while the French socialists, whose country owned the second largest empire, were among the few socialist parties to convert en masse to Communism.) The twentieth century showed that workers in democracies, but not Communist countries, had considerable power to secure wage increases and social reforms. Lenin claimed that backward sectors like agriculture in capitalist economies could not be modernized, but the dismal history of Communist agriculture showed that the joke was on him. Nor did the desire for colonies cause either World War. The most advanced capitalist countries were the most reluctant to fight in 1914, and later were the most willing to give up their colonies.[10]

The notion that the West developed by "plundering" the underdeveloped world has about as much economic reality as the Nazi view that the Jews thrived by exploiting the Aryan race. The sad fact was that Asia and Africa were too poor to have much worth stealing. Even Hobson's most articulate modern follower, John Strachey, thought that the alleged economic benefits of empire went to no more than 10 percent of Britain's population. The economic relationship between advanced and backward parts of the world are not consistent with this picture. The most advanced Asian and African lands, like Taiwan and Malaysia, have the closest economic ties with the West, while many developed countries have only marginal economic contacts with Asia and Africa.

CONSEQUENCES OF EMPIRE

Empires, then, were not vital, or in general, profitable, to the advanced Western countries. What were their effects on the subject peoples?

Gross exploitation existed, but was generally a passing feature of the first stages of imperial rule. Besides Bengal and Java, very oppressive situations developed in the first stages of Belgian rule in the Congo/Zaire. (It should be noted, however, that the cruelties in the Congo took place when King Leopold treated it as a private estate; things changed drastically when the Belgian government took over.) Most colonial governments in Africa initially demanded forced labor on public works and roads, while white settlers in Kenya and Rhodesia used forced labor for private purposes. (Forced labor ended at an early date in British colonies, but existed to some extent in French areas until 1946.) Confiscation or forced sale of land and cattle often occurred during the European settlement of Algeria and Rhodesia/Zimbabwe. But such gross evils were ended long before the end of imperial rule. Basically, colonial economic and governmental relationships could not be considered particularly exploitative. Wage rates in colonies were low, but reflected the local value of largely unskilled labor. Mining operations did extract irreplaceable natural resources, but such resources usually had not been recognized or used as such until the Westerners arrived with advanced technology.

Colonial governments, except in their final stages, were basically authoritarian. But the colonies of democratic countries were supervised by the home governments and staffed by officials expected to live by humanitarian, if paternalistic standards. The British Colonial Service and the Indian Civil Service (the latter had an Indian majority by the 1940s) had particularly outstanding records. After the initial period of conquest, the British administration compared favorably with the postcolonial rulers. According to the sociologist Stanislav Andreski, an observer of Africa, "Neither the British nor the French colonial rule was particularly oppressive in areas where there were no substantial settler populations. Especially during the last decades of its existence, the British colonial administration was the most benevolent government which the African countries ever had, or will have in the foreseeable future. . . ." Even exploitation was not without recompense; in the Congo/Zaire "the Belgians were appropriating the largest share of wealth, but to judge by the condition of the country since their departure, their services were worth it."[11] Those colonies dominated by minorities of European settlers (Algeria, Kenya, Rhodesia/Zimbabwe) posed the most difficult problems during decolonization, but they also generated more economic development.

European colonial governments never maintained the forces necessary to sustain really oppressive rule. The British never had more than 75,000 British troops in India, and usually fewer. Their African colonies contained a garrison of only 12,000 black soldiers under white officers.

Colonial governments generally did not deliberately seek to Westernize their subjects. Indeed, they sometimes even catered to their subjects' prejudices in a lickspittle way—the British let the Moslem emirs of Northern Nigeria exclude Christian missionaries from the region, much to the irritation of later generations there, who had no desire to become Christians, but recognized the benefits of missionary schools. Nevertheless, they ended suttee, intertribal wars, cannibalism and human sacrifice and forbade the African custom of killing twins. They halted the Arab slave trade, which might have depopulated East Africa, and ended piracy in Arabian and Malaysian waters.[12]

More positively, Western rule was the entering wedge for modern ideas and institutions, science and technology, education , business methods, and political ideas (if not practices) to be transmitted into non-Western areas. In Africa, literacy reached vast areas for the first time. Western rule introduced the prerequisites and sometimes the actual start (as in India and Zimbabwe) of industrialization. Transportation systems, some technical training, and modern economic organization were introduced everywhere Europeans went. Save for Japan, which already resembled the West in many ways, the countries of Asia and Africa that remained independent (e.g. Ethiopia and Afghanistan) generally lagged behind former colonies both economically and politically.

It is, however, true that colonial economic development was "unbalanced." In part, this was simply a result of the sudden introduction of modern developments in societies where they had not grown naturally. But the imperial governments did make what we can now see were mistakes. British rule in India affords perhaps the best example of such miscalculations. British policies saddled India with the difficult problem of absentee landlords. The educational system produced an overabundance of lawyers and white-collar workers and too few technicians, scientists, and engineers. The abolition of internal warfare, together with improved sanitation and health measures, without birth control, unleashed a population explosion.

It may, of course, be said that the concept of empire was intrinsically objectionable to democratic sensibilities. But this condemnation of imperialism is a twentieth-century Western idea, and there is no warrant to project current moods onto earlier centuries. Europeans conquered other Europeans, and Asians and Africans subdued other Asians and Africans (and occasionally Europeans, as did the Ottoman Turks.) Why, then, should it seem particularly objectionable for Europeans to rule Asians and Africans?

EMPIRE AND COLOR

When the Portuguese first reached Asia, they often had a very low opinion of the peoples they met. (To be sure, the feeling was mutual; Asians, or at least the upper classes, considered the early modern Europeans they saw dirty, rude, and uncultured—with reason.) As in the case of the Amerinds, however, such contempt was based largely on religious and cultural differences rather than on color.

For one thing, as in the case of the Amerinds, ideas about race were rather different from what they were later. The Europeans who reached East Asia in the sixteenth century described the Chinese and Japanese as "white."[13]

That, arguably, made more sense than the later fashion of describing them as "yellow," and in any case the slight difference between their skin color and features and those of Europeans did not seem striking to men who landed in East Asia after months, even years, passing through regions inhabited by Africans and South Asians with really dark skins. And some of the more intelligent Europeans admired aspects of Chinese and Japanese culture. Both Jesuit missionaries and many figures of the Enlightenment went remarkably far in this direction. In the eighteenth century the original admiration for China declined—partly due to distrust and dislike of the Jesuits, their most vocal Western admirers, and partly to closer contact with the Chinese and disgust at their corruption and tyranny.[14] The Portuguese developed contempt for the Indians (even Indian Christians) they ruled, while the Spaniards looked down on Filipinos, in ways somewhat parallel to their attitudes toward the Amerinds they controlled.[15] But no elaborate racial theories or rigid patterns developed. Other Europeans in the east seemed to care little about color up to the nineteenth century. There was, for a long time, no block to social relations with natives, especially women. Often native mistresses and wives were a social asset; they were jocularly called "sleeping dictionaries."

The British conquerors of Bengal, although often ruthless and amoral, treated their Indian collaborators as equals and often married Indian women of classes comparable to their own. In the succeeding era, this willingness to associate with Indians disappeared, although the British rulers were unquestionably more humane. As John Strachey, a descendant of a distinguished British-Indian family, put it, "Decency and distance had succeeded pillage and intimacy" and "the fatal doctrine of racial superiority came more and more to dominate the imaginations of the British in India." Strachey's own ancestors married Bengali and Persian women; but such marriages would have been unthinkable to their Victorian descendants. He comments that "This terrible withdrawal of genuine human community went far to undo—in some respects it more than undid—the good which the immense improvement in British conduct might have done for the relations of the two great peoples." An observer in 1850s India commented, "if a man who left this country thirty years ago were to visit it now, he would scarcely credit the changes he would universally witness in the treatment of the Native, high and low. The English were not then absolute masters everywhere. Now they are, restraint is cast away . . . and they displayed a supercilious arrogance and contempt of the people."[16] Part of the change has been credited to the arrival of large numbers of English women in India; they discouraged intermarriage and the keeping of Indian mistresses and finally all close social relations with Indians. A degree of influence may have also been exerted by the Indian caste system; the British, as the latest conquerors of the subcontinent, merely inserted themselves as another new ruling caste and imitated the extreme social differences among the Indians themselves. That caste exerted some influence is suggested by the fact that the British tended to pick up the Indians' own contempt for Untouchables—although the traditional Hindu rationalization for the treatment of Untouchables was contemptible by either rationalist or Judeo-Christian standards. It is also noticeable that the British in Burma, which did not have a caste system, associated more freely with natives than their counterparts in India. And—precisely because nineteenth-century Europeans were more humane than their predecessors—many Indian customs were increasingly seen as intolerable and a badge of inferiority.

Probably more important in producing a swelled-head syndrome among the British was the simple intoxicating experience of easy domination over masses of Asians. A doctrine of contempt for Indians as innate inferiors developed. They were often treated in a humiliating and contemptuous fashion in any sort of personal contact. Strict social segregation developed; even upper-class and Angicized Indians, no matter what their personal worth, were excluded from British clubs and any sort of off-duty contacts. The few British (generally enlisted men and other lower-class persons) who married Indians became social outcasts. Their offspring were segregated. Eurasians were treated as a slightly better class of Indian; some jobs (for example on the railroads) were reserved for them.[17] A similar pattern of behavior developed among the other Western powers in Asia (including the Americans in the Philippines) and in colonial Africa, where older ideas of black inferiority, albeit in a milder form than in the age of slavery, persisted. There were variations in national behavior; the Dutch treated Eurasians as Europeans and were perhaps more polite to the Indonesian aristocracy than most colonial rulers. (It should be noted that their more humane treatment of Eurasians ultimately backfired as far as the latter were concerned, making them more hated by the natives than half-castes in other colonies.) The French were widely believed to be freer of color prejudice than other Westerners and there seems to have been a limited amount of truth in this idea.[18] Russians, for reasons peculiar to their national history, had little racial prejudice against Asians.[19]

The ideology behind prejudice against Asians was contradictory and vaguer than that revolving around blacks, and the emotions involved were less intense. Asians, after all, lived in literate, highly organized societies. They might be seen as inferior, but no one could dismiss them as mere savages. The peoples of East Asia were regarded as submissive, impassive, hard working, and unemotional, but also as treacherous, cunning, and clever, although less intelligent and creative than white people. They suffered from obscure physical inferiorities to Europeans. (As late as the start of World War II it was widely believed that the Japanese made poor pilots because their eyesight was poor and they lacked a sense of balance. During 1941 and 1942 that notion died very quickly, along with a lot of Western airmen.) A somewhat similar stereotype of Indians existed, although the

British tended to regard the inhabitants of the subcontinent as alternately hysterical and lazy rather than stolid and unemotional. This belief was somewhat counterbalanced, however, by the recognition that the men of the Indian Army were tough, courageous, and dependable fighters. There was a vague association of Chinese, and to a lesser extent other Asians, with "vice." That was encouraged by the prevalence of opium addiction in nineteenth-century China and the behavior of womanless Chinese male immigrants in the American West (who were mostly unwilling indentured workers, very unlike either European immigrants of that day or the Chinese immigrants of today).

Asians were held to be brutal, submissive to tyranny, and indifferent to other people's lives and their own. Again, this view contained a limited degree of truth, although, once again, attitudes and cultural orientation were mistaken for inborn "racial" features. Most Asian cultures *were* brutal and tyrannical by nineteenth-century Western standards, as were most societies in all times and places. Some customs the Europeans encountered in Asia, notably suttee, were horrible by any standards. The treatment of women even in China and Japan was disgusting even by earlier European standards, much less Victorian ones. There was little liberty in precolonial Asia and Africa. Democratic ideas came with imperialism, however unfashionable and distasteful many people may find that fact.

An ugly prejudice against Asians, as well as Africans, undoubtedly existed. It is doubtful, however, whether racism was a *determining* and decisive factor in the relationships between the empires and the subject peoples. Nor was racism simply a rationalization for imperialism or a "functional" justification for it, although this has been a common belief among both liberals and Marxists. As Harold R. Isaacs succinctly put it, "The 'racial' mythologies built around differences in skin color and physical features were among the prime tools of power used in the era of the Western empires." UNESCO claimed (inaccurately) that there was no racism until the colonial expansion of the Europeans, "when it became necessary to excuse violence and oppression by decreeing the inferiority of those enslaved and robbed of their own land, denying the title of men to the cheated peoples." Marxists merely defined racism as nothing but a functional myth calculatingly spread by a ruling elite.[20]

Actually, there is no evidence that racism was either developed for or fulfilled any function for European imperialism. (It should be noted that the UNESCO outburst quoted above neatly encapsulates the view that there was something uniquely wicked about *European* imperialism, or possibly even that there was no other sort of imperialism. And it is unclear just who the "excuse" was supposed to impress. The idea that Europeans saw what they were doing as oppressive seems to be yet another shaky assumption.) Prejudice against blacks was undoubtedly "functional" for slave traders and slave owners, although it developed well before an economic interest in it appeared. The latter was only an intensifying factor. But in the case of the colonial empires, racism was not necessary, or even useful, to the rulers.

The appearance of elaborate pseudoscientific theories "demonstrating" the superiority of the white race to all others came at the same time as the height of European imperialism. That was no accident. But the development of the theories followed the fact of European rule; they were not ideological constructs necessary to justify conquest, or indeed primarily formulated for that. As we have noted, British and Dutch rule in part of India and Indonesia preceded the development of racism against Asians; if racial justifications for conquering and ruling Asians were needed, Robert Clive and Warren Hastings were unaware of this. Even in the nineteenth century, imperialists did not actually base their claim to rule explicitly on white superiority, however warmly most of them believed in it.

France, the power with the greatest psychological need for an ideological justification for imperialism, emphasized its "civilizing mission" and the ultimate aim of assimilating the subjects to French culture. The British, although less given to high-flying theories, also stressed the superiority of their civilization and the benefits of their rule. They were sure—and not without reason—that they had brought peace, order, justice, and modern development—not violence and oppression, to India and other colonies. As the Colonial Secretary, Joseph Chamberlain, put it in the 1890s, the British were "trustees of civilization." He remarked that "I do not say that all our methods have been beyond reproach; but I do say that in almost every instance in which the rule of the Queen has been established and the great Pax Britannica has been enforced, there has come with it greater security for life and property, and a material improvement in the condition of the bulk of the population." (Interestingly, he also boasted that Britain *alone* had made colonies pay.)[21]

In fact, neither Britain nor France could have afforded to base their claim to rule on racial superiority, for the simple reason that both the biggest colonial empires had many white, as well as "colored" subjects. Most of the people of French North Africa were white, albeit darker than the average Frenchman. Britain ruled not only black Africans, Indians, Ceylonese, Burmese, and Malays, but white Maltese, Ionian and Cypriot Greeks, Boers, and Arabs. Although English and French Canadians and the British colonists in Australia, New Zealand, and South Africa fell into a different category, they too came under the purview of the Colonial Office. *Their* expected obedience to the Queen and Parliament could hardly be justified on the grounds of racial inferiority.

Indeed, the true relationship between empire and pseudoscientific theories seems to be quite different. As Douglas Lorimer has shown, there was little if any direct connection between the racial theorists and ardent imperialists in Britain. (On the continent, as we shall see in the next chapter, racial thinking tended to focus on other whites.) And the theorists came into prominence at an interval in the mid-nineteenth century when expansion was not particularly popular. The white settler colonies were then expected to become independent, while India and the tropical colonies were deemed a burden. (Indeed, many Britons, up to the 1880s or even later, tended to think of the white settler colonies as "*the* empire" and regarded India and other nonwhite territories as exceptions. There is reason to think that that attitude never quite died out, especially among the lower classes, who cared little about places like India, but had warm feelings for Canada or Australia where they had relatives.) The growing appeal of such theories may be related to changing class relations within Britain itself, and the growth of pessimistic views of the world—a constellation of fears that free trade, liberalism, and education would not, as earlier Victorians had hoped, lead to the reclamation of the poor at home and freed slaves in the West Indies, and the advance of the backward peoples of the world. This may be associated with the observations of Robinson, Galbraith, and Denny that relate late Victorian expansion to similar fears—a general insecurity and a feeling that the earlier liberal confidence in self-government and free trade, and working with local foreign collaborators, could not be trusted to preserve Britain's position and prosperity.[22] Racial theorizing and imperial expansion thus did not generate each other; both were products of the same mood.

Moreover, racial doctrines and the social segregation characteristic of the era do not seem to have been of any actual value in maintaining colonial rule. Rather, the reverse was the case. The development of nationalism in Asia and Africa was doubtless inevitable, but the snubs administered to educated Asians and Africans can only have speeded their alienation from their Western rulers. The racial arrogance of the European rulers was not needed to justify their own self-confidence and the will to rule, as the French demonstrated by crushing several Arab uprisings. It just annoyed precisely those of their subjects who were most Westernized. There is little evidence that the Western colonial empires actually treated their subjects more brutally because of the racial doctrines; nor do they seem to have treated the nonwhite subject peoples very differently from white ones. But they hurt many people's feelings and could only distort the rulers' view of the world. Poisoning the relations of Europeans and their subjects, racial ideas did nothing but harm to both. Had the European powers turned their colonial subjects into helots, using them as only cheap labor and crushing all attempts to develop modern education, a civil service, or a middle class, then racial theories and discrimination might have made a brutal sort of sense. But none followed such a policy. All allowed the development of a middle class and trained at least some native civil servants and technicians (although perhaps not as many as might have been desirable) while following social policies and cultivating attitudes bound to alienate them. In this respect, the ancient Romans, who courted the upper classes of conquered peoples and made "useful" individuals throughout the empire Roman citizens, showed more sense than modern Westerners, as even some Victorians saw. And, in fact, very late in the day, between the World Wars, the Western authorities began to stamp out the grosser forms of discrimination and segregation.

Racism aside, as we have noted before, empire was not an attractive relationship between peoples. But there is little evidence that imperial rule in Asia and Africa was bad or inhumane compared to the behavior of most governments in most times and places, that it was worse than the indigenous regimes it replaced, or even that it compared unfavorably with most of the regimes that followed it. It would be necessary to show at least one, if not all, of these things to justify the strange attitude of guilt over empire that exists in the minds of many Westerners.

Nor has the aftermath of empire suggested that its racial aspects prey much on the minds of the former colonial peoples of Asia and Africa. Late in the colonial era, and periodically during the period of decolonization, there was much anxiety among liberal Westerners, such as Pearl Buck and Gunnar Myrdal, that resentment against imperial rule and racial discrimination would permanently poison the relations between the West and the nonwhite world in general. It was feared that the Japanese, or some subsequent aggressors, might make use of "PanAsian" or more general hostilities toward whites by "colored" peoples. That overrated the intensity and importance of such sentiments. The rapid and generally peaceful nature of decolonization, the fact that the Cold War cut right across racial issues, and perhaps above all the parochial hatreds that divided the non-Western world rendered this fear an unreal one. When the British or Belgians left, Hindus, Moslems and Sikhs, Tutsis and Hutus found they no longer cared much about them—but they continued to hate each other. The "imperial" thread of race relations continued, but in a fashion no one had predicted—through the formation of large immigrant communities in Europe, mostly derived from the former colonies. But that had little to do with international relations; like the subject of the next chapter, it concerned Europe itself.

7

Pseudoscientific Racism and Its Consequences

Here and there we have referred to the pseudoscientific racism that developed in the eighteenth and nineteenth centuries. Contrary to what is sometimes claimed, the intellectual origins of modern racial theories do not lie in biblical rationalizations but in scientific or pseudoscientific ones. The doctrines that appeared among the so-called "Enlightenment" thinkers of the eighteenth century, such as Voltaire, were developed and rationalized by medical men, biologists, and anthropologists in the following century. In fact, racism was closely tied to the rise of anthropology. Perhaps no other scientific discipline had quite so disreputable an origin. The early scientific study of man was highly confused and fumbling. Whether that was due to the intrinsic difficulty of the subject, or merely because those attracted to it were less capable than those working in the "hard sciences," is an interesting problem.

The intellectual impulse for racial theories was a complex one. The interest of most European nations in their historical origins, and the myths revolving around those origins, the urge to rationalize and intensify existing beliefs of racial and even class superiority, and even the early discoveries of linguistics, all played a role.[1] It should be noted that a strong bias toward emphasizing heredity, or "blood" (as it was traditionally put), has been common in most societies; it was accentuated by the role of the aristocracy in medieval and early modern Europe. Even primitive social organizations, which do not recognize hereditary privileges, are based on kinship; and few societies have been as indifferent to descent as twentieth-century America. Obsessions with genealogy may well be silly, but it should be remembered that they are historically more "normal" than our own attitudes.

ENLIGHTENMENT AND PSEUDOSCIENCE

The Enlightenment and the general advance of a scientific outlook in the eighteenth century is usually seen as a movement to free man of religious superstitions. In part, it was that. Unfortunately, it was also a movement *toward* new superstitions and involved discarding certain beliefs that, while they may have been nonrational and religious in origin, happened to coincide with the truth rather better than the fumbling early scientific investigations of man. While the Judeo-Christian tradition had upheld the essential unity of the human race and the equality of men in "the sight of God" (if not in social relationships) the weakening of the tradition allowed the gross exaggeration of differences among men, to the point that "poly-genesis"—the theory that the various human races had entirely separate origins—became popular for a time. Although this extreme current could not be sustained, the element of exaggeration of human differences became securely embedded in "scientific" thinking about race. Evolution would be interpreted as supporting the importance of race. (Darwin's personal views on the subject were ambiguous, but generally antiracist.)

Voltaire's, and others', hatred of the Church and the Jews was such that their very insistence that mankind was of a single descent, and that racial differences were of no great moment in the sight of God, was enough to make them rush to the other extreme. While other Enlightenment figures, notably Rousseau, opposed racism, their ideas had less influence. Even the cooler thinkers of the Scottish branch of the Enlightenment, like Hume, were remarkably ready to generalize about people on the basis of very limited information. Hume declared that "There never was a civilized nation of any other complexion than white, nor even any individual emi-nent either in action or speculation."[2]

Within France, a political/ideological dispute entangled issues of race and class. (It should be remembered, again, that "race" did not yet have the restricted meaning it has today.) Some defenders of the privileges of the nobility, notably Henri de Boulainvilliers, argued that they were the just rights of conquerors, for the nobles were descended from the Germanic Frankish tribesmen who had given France its name; the common people of France were descended from the inferior Gallo-Roman conquered people. This absurd antithesis between a "Frankish" ruling class and Gallic com-moners was widely accepted by partisans of both classes—although, as so often in discussions of race, it was bad history. Many Franks must have been absorbed into the native lower class, while the Gallo-Roman upper class had continued to hold high places in the Frankish kingdom. And there had been much movement up and down since then. Many noble families were known to have been raised from commoners in the Middle Ages"—and none were certainly known to be of Frankish descent. But that did not stop what became known as the "controversy of two races," which led to the odd result of a French upper class identifying itself with a purported Germanic superiority, which was increasingly rationalized in pseudoscientific terms.[3]

As this insane debate was played out in the French Revolution, there was a growing interest in the scientific study of man. There was special interest in the brain and skull and fascination with "craniometry" based on the not entirely correct assumption that the shape of the skull was an especially stable and important hereditary feature.

The impact of this pseudoscientific racism on attitudes toward non-Europeans can easily be exaggerated. It rationalized and furthered the idea that European whites were permanently and innately superior to Asians, Polynesians, Amerinds, black Africans, and Australian aborigines, ranking nonwhites in approximately that order as far as their intellectual, cultural, and moral attributes were concerned. Nasty though these ideas may have been, their effect outside Europe was doubtful. While often seized on by apologists for slavery, "scientific" racism could not actually worsen the position of blacks, for their reputation was already as bad as it could get. And the strength of other influences insured black emancipation in the Americas at the same time that the pseudoscientific racial doctrines were growing in strength. They were a nuisance to abolitionists, but not a decisive factor in the dispute over slavery. The doctrine may have had more effect on attitudes toward Asians, but that effect is hard to trace, and the arrogance and conceit induced by actual European domination in Asia was probably more important than any theory in inducing notions of racial superiority. In any case, racial theories were not very long lived in their influence. As noted before, no Western power actually based its claim to rule on them. By the 1930s, well before the end of European rule in Asia and Africa, the imperial powers repudiated such ideas.[4] The main impact of pseudoscientific racism was not on relations with nonwhites, but lay in Europe itself. The key element in this development was a specific doctrine, the myth of the Aryan race and Nordic superiority.

THE INDO-EUROPEANS AND THE ARYAN MYTH

The Aryan race myth has been often analyzed; but the pattern of thinking involved is of permanent interest, since it is characteristic of other ideologies of ethnic grievance and self-assertion. The Aryan myth arose from the discovery, in the early nineteenth century, that most Europeans, and many other peoples in the area stretching south and east to Bengal, spoke related languages descended from a single ancestral tongue. The original speakers of this language were called Aryans. (Modern scholars prefer to call them "Indo-Europeans." The term "Aryan" properly refers only to those Indo-Europeans who invaded India.) The original Indo-European speakers were probably the first people to tame the horse. Thanks to this they were able to spread from their original center, which was probably in the south Russian steppe or southern Poland, through almost all of Europe, part of the Near East, and Northern India, imposing their languages on the conquered peoples and mixing with them.

It should be noted that some scholars have recently advanced an entirely different analysis. They think that the original Indo-European speakers lived in eastern Anatolia, and that the expansion of their languages began much earlier, during the Neolithic period, and was associated with the spread of agriculture from its point of origin in the Near East.[5] The fact that archaeologists and linguists can disagree on such basic matters, after over a century more of intensive research, with far better tools than any available in the nineteenth century, suggests the silliness of basing political ideas on what little was known of prehistory in the Victorian age.

In a confusion of language, culture, and race characteristic of the period (and to an increasing extent, the end of the twentieth century as well), many nineteenth-century thinkers envisaged the original "Aryans" as a distinct and superior racial group and credited them with the development of civilization in both Europe and India. The modern Europeans, however, or some particular racial or national group among them, were viewed as the purest or "true" descendants of the Aryans. The most familiar version of the Aryan myth, since it was adopted by the Nazis, though it was not exclusive to them, identified the Aryans with the "Nordic" type or subrace, that is, the tall, fair-haired, blue-eyed, and dolichocephalic type common in northern Europe. It was widely believed that the people of Northern Europe and perhaps Central Europe had once all been fair-haired Nordics, all brunettes there resulting from foreign admixture. Alternatively, many thought, the Nordic/Aryans had, in some remote era, migrated into Europe from the eastern steppes, absorbing or driving out a native European population that was originally predominantly Mediterranean in type. (Both these theories were probably wrong. The population of Northwest Europe was probably predominantly, but never exclusively, "Nordic," from the time the area was settled after the glaciers retreated, and there was no evidence for the vast migration from the east.) The French Count Joseph Arthur de Gobineau, a successor of Boulainvilliers, played a particularly important role in publicizing the Nordic/Aryan myth, although his ideas were later given a twist that would have horrified him. Gobineau's influential, pessimistic racial theory of history, selectively quoted, influenced much nastier people. Gobineau maintained that the mixture of original "pure" races had originally been necessary to produce civilization—the white race, alone, could not have done so. (A curious idea later racists, not surprisingly, did not pursue.) But the *continuation* of mixture must inevitably cause universal decadence. Gobineau did not think much could be done about all this; but other people reached a different conclusion.

Gobineau, and later the Nazis, regarded the Scandinavians, and to a lesser extent, the Germans and the English, as the last relatively pure survivors of the superior Aryan race. Later in the nineteenth century, however, French and Italian racial theorists tried to identify the Aryans with the "Alpine" and "Mediterranean" types or subraces, that, by no vast coincidence, happened to be most common in their respective countries. (If the original Indo-European speakers lived in Poland or south Russia, as most scholars think, they probably were predominantly Alpines.) The Franco-Prussian War led some French theorists to argue that the Germans, or at least the Prussians, weren't really Aryans, but superficially Germanized "Slavo-Finns." There were endless arguments about the racial merits of Nordics, Alpines, and Mediterraneans, although such issues seem to have obsessed the Romance-speaking peoples less than Northern Europeans.

All this was a tissue of absurdities. No national group consisted or ever had consisted purely of any of these types, while all the different types could be found within members of the same family. Mixtures of the types (of which "ideal" examples were rare) could be traced indefinitely far back; James Mellaart found skeletons of Mediterranean and Alpine types commingled at the neolithic proto-city of Catal Huyuk in Turkey.

Tacking together vague theories, mistakes, scientific linguistics, and an occasional stray fact, the Aryan theorists argued that the development of civilization was due to the leavening effect of the Aryans even in the Mediterranean and other areas where they formed a small proportion of the population. The Nazis and their predecessors thus claimed that, even though the ancient Greeks and Romans had been largely Mediterranean in type, their ruling classes, descended from the Aryan conquerors from the North, were really superior Nordics. This supposed Nordic Aryan minority was responsible for the rise of Greek and Roman civilization; its absorption by the mass of inferior Mediterranean types led to decay. The Aryan enthusiasts could point to some slight apparent basis for this idea; the ancestral Greek and Italic-speakers arrived from the north, and, if not "Nordics," were probably fairer on average than the native populations of Greece and Italy. There is some evidence that as late as classical times fair skin, blond hair, and blue eyes were common among the Greek and Roman upper classes, and much more so than the Greek and Roman population at large. (The Nazis would so harp on the Nordicism of the Hellenes that some German soldiers arriving in Greece during World War II were disappointed to find that the real Greeks were mostly small, dark, and distinctly unfriendly to their "Nordic German brothers.") When all these theories were formulated, the actual origins of Greek civilization on Minoan Crete, which probably long predated the expansion of the Indo-European speakers, were not yet known. The Aryan theorists rose to the occasion and did not let later inconvenient discoveries trouble them unduly.

According to them the Germanic invasions during and after the fall of the Western Roman Empire refreshed the "blood" of the upper classes and ultimately produced the Italian Renaissance. Similarly, a Scandinavian ruling class had galvanized a mass of inferior Slavs and enabled them to build a formidable Russian state. (In fact, much of the modern Russian aristocracy was of Tatar origin.)

Preposterously, Central European Aryan theorists, and later the Nazis, would insist that the Slavic-speaking peoples were not really Aryans, although the Slavic languages were actually closer to the original Indo-European speech than the Germanic languages. Yet they also accepted the Finns, Estonians, Latvians, and Lithuanians as Nordics or the closely similar Baltics, although the first two nationalities did not speak Indo-European languages at all, while the Baltic languages of the latter were fairly close to the Slavic tongues.

This method of annexing the achievements of other peoples and making them redound to the glory of one's own ethnic group—or the group one chooses to identify with—has been widely imitated.

The "true" Aryans were held to be superior not only to nonwhites, but to other elements of the white race, particularly to Jews and other "Semites," who became increasingly the focus of attention as an enemy. The very term "anti-Semitism," introduced by Wilhelm Marr in the 1870s, was part and parcel of the racial concept. The Aryan race myth was not always and inevitably anti-Semitic, for some believers in it held that the Semites too were a superior race, and as good, or nearly as good as the Aryans (Count Gobineau, for example, was not unfriendly to the Jews), while some others believed that European Jews were largely European in descent and thus really "Aryan," rather than "Semitic" in ancestry. It is worth noting that there were other strange notions distinguishing between various types of Jews and/or degrees of Jewish influence. The variability and complexity of nineteenth century ideas is suggested by George Du Maurier's famous novel *Trilby*. Its Eastern European Jewish villain incorporates virtually every anti-Semitic stereotype of the era. But a Sephardic Jewish character is portrayed favorably, and the hero of the novel has some "Jewish blood," which is a good thing; "fortunately for the world, and especially for ourselves, most of us have in our veins at least a minimum of that precious fluid."[6]

The association of the Aryan myth with the Nazis should not obscure the fact that many people of democratic and humane temperament (including Winston Churchill, Theodore Roosevelt, and Ernest Renan) believed in it for a time. It was widely accepted in Europe, including Britain; even some Jews swallowed it.

In the long run, however, the Aryan myth was tied in with the development of racial anti-Semitism, the idea that the Jews were a distinct racial group, which was permanently hostile and inferior to other peoples.[7]

It should be noted that the Jews' own ethnic pride often led *them* to imagine that they were indeed a distinct group, almost unmixed descendants of the ancient Hebrews, an assumption their persecutors found it convenient to score off. Actually, of course, as the Ethiopian Jews show unmistakably, and a careful examination of European Jews would indicate to an unbiased observer, Jews have mixed to some degree with other peoples wherever they have gone. Genetically, the German and East European Jews appear to be primarily the product of a medieval mixture of Jewish immigrants from the Mediterranean lands with the French and Germans, and later with the Slavs. The believers in the anti-Semitic version of the Aryan myth carefully averted their eyes from the fact that quite a few European Jews were "Nordic" in appearance. In a further irony, both they, and most Jews, identified "the Jews" with the Ashkenazim (German- and Yiddish-speaking Jews) of Central and Eastern Europe. Although the Ashkenazim constituted a majority of the world's Jews, the Sephardim of the Mediterranean countries more authentically preserved the traditional customs, and probably the original physical type, of the Jewish people.

Increasingly bad-tempered exponents of the Aryan myth, of whom the most influential were Richard Wagner, Houston Stewart Chamberlain, Vacher le Pouge, and Paul de Lagarde, focused on the antithesis of Aryans and Semites; and the writings of the insane philosopher Friedrich Nietzsche (who was not anti-Semitic) were often twisted to bolster their ideas. Both directly and through even cruder popularizers, such as Adolf Lanz von Liebenfels, who befriended the young Hitler, they influenced the Nazi movement. The amazing influence of Wagner, one of the great musicians of the age and the greatest opera composer of all time, was particularly unfortunate. He was the center of a cult among the European upper and middle classes, comparable in influence only to the Beatles in our own time. Unlike them, he had vast philosophical pretensions. He exerted particular influence in Germany, in confounding everything "Germanic" and "Nordic" with German nationalist manias. Max Nordau wittily described his feats: "He has an inimitable mastery of chauvinistic phraseology. Was he not able to convince his hypnotized hysterical following that the heroes of his pieces were primeval German figures—these Frenchmen and Brabanters, these Icelanders and Norwegians, these women of Palestine—all the fabulous beings he had fetched from the poems of Provence and Northern France, and from the Northern saga, who (with the exception of *Tannhauser* and the *Meistersinger*) have not a single drop of German blood or a single German fibre in their whole body? It is thus that, in public exhibitions, a quack hypnotist persuades his victims that they are eating peaches instead of raw potatoes."[8] Wagner promoted the strange German tendency to identify closely with the Scandinavians and ancient Germanic tribes like the Goths, who were only remotely related to the modern German-speaking peoples, and to think of their doings as the "deeds of Germans in foreign countries." This was particularly odd since the German language makes a much clearer distinction between "German" (Deutsch) and "Germanic" (Germanisch) than English does.

Another German peculiarity was an effort by Aryan theorists there to either attack Christianity (as an expression of the "Semitic spirit") or "de-Judaize" it. Fantastic efforts were made, particularly by Wagner and his son-in-law, Houston Stewart Chamberlain (an Englishman who became a German citizen), to show that Jesus and the early Christians were not of Jewish origin. Christ was not the Jewish Messiah, but a stalwart Nordic hero who had unaccountably wandered down from Scandinavia, or the stage of one of Wagner's operas. (Although the Nazi leaders did not really believe this idea themselves, they would find it tactically most convenient.) Chamberlain's book *Foundations of the Nineteenth Century* became a bestseller. He was almost as influential as Wagner, and was praised by such worthies as Kaiser Wilhelm II and Bernard Shaw. He lived long enough to join the Nazi party. The increasingly fierce anti-Jewish slant was also accompanied by a growing stress on the inferiority of the Slavs.

It should be stressed that while the stress on "scientific racism" originated on the political right, it was by no means limited to the right. Many socialists, in the late nineteenth and early twentieth centuries, were racists. Marx strongly believed in white superiority and was contemptuous of Jews, Karl Kautsky, his successor as the leading "Marxist" theoretician, shared the former belief for a time. The author of the era who most closely anticipated Adolf Hitler's schemes of expansion, Josef Reimer, was a socialist. Reimer insisted that only the Germans and some Western European nationalities who could be assimilated to them, and emphatically not the Jews and Slavs, were suited to shape the socialist future.

ANTI-SEMITISM OLD AND NEW

The Nazis' racial concepts basically differed from the traditional hostility to the Jews common in Europe, but there were connections between the two.

As the only non-Christians in Christendom, outside of Spain, the Jews had been a sort of natural target. The dominant religion was an offshoot of Judaism, but no Jews, and few Christians, took pleasure in that fact. Christians felt that their faith superseded the older one; there was something wrong if the Jews refused to convert. And, although the idea was really incompatible with the central elements of Christian theology, the Jews were often blamed for their ancestors' supposed role in the crucifixion.

A perhaps more important role was played by the peculiar social position of the Jews. They were often, to be blunt, more civilized than the peoples among whom they settled; and they often occupied much, perhaps most, of the position of an urban middle class in primarily agrarian societies whose upper classes and peasantry were solidly Christian. In many cities of medieval Western and Central Europe, and in much of modern Eastern Europe, they formed a substantial part of the urban population. They may have had a very disproportionate role in the early stages of the development of capitalism in Europe. Their position was not too dissimilar from that of many other minority groups in Asia and Africa—Chinese in Southeast Asia, Indians in Burma and Africa, Christian minorities in the Middle East, and Moslems in Ethiopia—and it was noticeable that these other groups often experienced similar episodes of persecution and worse. The situation of the Jews and similar middle-class groups was a powerful generator of social and economic hostilities.

Christians also picked up other, older anti-Semitic ideas, which had originated among the Jews' pagan Greek and Roman enemies, a source of hostility that influenced many medieval thinkers such as Thomas Aquinas. Jews were pictured as arrogant, clannish, greedy and cheap, and also, perhaps more accurately, as implacably obstinate. During the peak of anti-Semitism in the Middle Ages, further, more violent ideas were added, for example, that Jews murdered Christian children as part of religious rituals and were responsible for spreading the Black Death. There were notions that Jews differed physically from Christians; it was claimed that they had a special unpleasant odor (associated with the Devil) and even that they had horns.

However, these supposed characteristics were not hereditary and disappeared when Jews converted to Christianity. Anti-Semitism among Christians remained sporadic, if sometimes very violent. And it varied greatly between sects and nationalities, and in different historical periods. The Jewish experience in medieval and early modern Europe ranged from some of the worst massacres in Western history, during the Crusades and in the seventeenth-century Ukraine, to toleration, and occasionally even prestige and power, as for the "court Jews" of eighteenth-century Prussia. While the Orthodox churches were generally quite hostile to the Jews, Protestants were rarely anti-Semitic. The Catholic Church cycled between toleration and persecution and was often bitterly divided on the subject. And individual Catholic nations differed drastically; Italians were rarely anti-Semitic, while the Spaniards were bitter enemies of the Jews. (But they treated Protestants no better.) Violence against Jews, it should be noted, generally stemmed from inflamed secular elements in society and was generally not encouraged by the Church itself. Those Jews who lived in the part of Italy under the rule of the Papacy, though treated in a demeaning manner, were secure from physical attack. And, outside Imperial Russia, which preserved many of the worst medieval traditions, the traditional forms of anti-Semitism tended to decline during the modern era.[9]

RACIAL ANTI-SEMITISM

The racial anti-Semites made the Jews' supposed objectionable features permanent hereditary characteristics. They discarded the specifically Christian charges against the Jews. Indeed, while conserving and expanding on the pagan element of traditional anti-Semitism, the Nazis stood Christian anti-Semitism on its head. They blamed the Jews not for failing to embrace Christianity, but for creating it. Although Hitler was cautious about discussing this fully in public—Germany, after all, was a nominally Christian country—it was the Jews' creation of the Judeo-Christian tradition that was their chief crime. That tradition cut across far too many Nazi ideas. (The "antinominian" features of Nazism are not a fashionable topic for discussion.)

The Nazis combined the Aryan race myth with the thesis of a vast Jewish plot to conquer the world. They made much of a bizarre document, *The Protocols of the Elders of Zion*, that claimed to reveal the conspiracy. Forged by the Russian secret police early in the twentieth century, it got little attention until after World War I; then it was publicized throughout the world. (Later, the Protocols were revived by Arab propagandists—Gamal Nasser, who ruled Egypt from 1954 to 1970, praised them—and again by the Black Muslims.)

In the ultimate Nazi formulation, the Jews (whom the Nazis usually personified as "*the* Jew") were not just an inferior race, but a "counterrace" embodying pure evil, as the Aryans embodied pure good. They were unnatural, their characteristics not merely different but diametrically opposed to those of all other peoples; they were a race of physically disgusting vampirelike parasites, which behind the scenes, ran both capitalism and Communism. Although basically weak, they seemed to have virtually occult powers, which, curiously, enabled them to dominate immensely greater numbers of the supposedly superior Aryans (a point the Nazis never quite explained). Should they triumph, Hitler warned quite seriously in *Mein Kampf*, their rule would lead to the extinction of the human race.

Despite the Jews' distinctiveness, and the fact that only they would be slated for complete extermination, the Jews, in the Nazis' minds, were closely connected with the merely inferior races, the "untermenschen," (subhumans), who actually comprised most of humanity—the Slavs and the nonwhite peoples, and to Communism. Nothing in Nazism was purely political. Everything was a subdivision of biology. Communism was a Jewish plot. That odd idea was common between the World Wars, but Nazi anti-Communism was a truly weird, apocalyptic doctrine quite different from that of even the most reactionary enemies of Communism. As we noted earlier, the Nazis held that only a Nordic ruling class had made Russia a formidable power. In their view, the Bolshevik Revolution had been an uprising by the Jewish-led Slav majority against this group. Communism was the most extreme and horrible form of Jewish rule; but, while it threatened the rest of the world, it could not last. And it actually presented an opportunity for a National Socialist Germany. For the Jews, who were fundamentally inferior, had destroyed the only real obstacle to Germany's drive eastward by killing off the Aryan ruling stratum. Hitler viewed the USSR as a rotten structure that would quickly collapse under attack. Communism (or more precisely Marxism, since the Nazis did not distinguish clearly between Communism and Social Democracy) in Germany itself was an uprising of the racially inferior strata there that was the result of foreign mixture. It cannot be too strongly stressed that, while some Nazi ideas represented a revival of some features of medieval demonology, the Nazis prided themselves on being "scientific." In 1942, Hitler modestly compared himself to the great disease fighters of the nineteenth century. "The discovery of the Jewish virus is one of the greatest revolutions that could have taken place in the world. The battle in which we are engaged today is of the same sort as the battle waged, during the last century, by Pasteur and Koch."[10]

NAZISM IN POWER

But by the time the Nazis attained power their ideas had clearly descended to the level of pseudoscience. Toward the end of the nineteenth century, the findings of biologists and anthropologists began to cast doubt on the extent of racial differences, and also to some extent, the role of heredity in human affairs in general. (That heredity had only a limited explanatory power might have been suspected by any observer of the royal families of Europe.) Some of the scientific measurements on which earlier theories had been based were discredited or rendered less important; for example, Franz Boas showed that skull shape was not always a stable hereditary feature. With this, and perhaps less rational turns in intellectual fashion, the belief both in the Aryan race myth and the superiority of the white race began to fade, outside of central Europe.

There, cranky racial ideas remained more influential. Some peculiarities of Germany's cultural atmosphere, and the ugly ethnic conflicts in the neighboring Austro-Hungarian empire, played a major role. There was a heightened animosity between Germans and Poles, while in Austria-Hungary relations between the dominant German minority and the empire's Slavic and Jewish populations were bad. Many Austro-Germans feared Slavic numbers (in alliance with Russia) on the one hand, and were jealous of the successful Jewish minority on the other. Hence there was a good market for theories of racial superiority, although more among Austro-Germans—like the young Adolf Hitler—than in the German Empire. Before World War I Germany did not diverge greatly from the general trend of European development. With the defeat of Germany and Austria-Hungary in that war, an explosive situation, peculiar to Germany and Austria, developed. The humiliation of defeat, the subjection of many Germans to Polish and Czech rule, the development of a strong Communist movement in Germany, and the failures of the Weimar Republic all provided raw material for a violent radical mass movement, which mixed nationalism, anti-Jewish and anti-Slav racism, and other ideas—Nazism. The moral deterioration of German life (another important but unfashionable subject for study) made a group led by perverts, drug addicts, pornographers, and convicted criminals (and, in the case of Hitler, not even a German), whose personal qualities, much less ideas, would have excluded them from German public life before 1914, acceptable participants in politics.

To what extent the mass of Germans believed in the anti-Semitic and anti-Slav aspects of Nazi doctrine is unclear. But once the Nazi leaders were in power no one dared question their ideas openly. They were in a perfect position to carry out the dictates of the racial ideology in which they firmly believed—believed in spite of the fact that few Nazi leaders were exemplars of the "Aryan race." Only the SS leader Reinhard Heydrich (who seems to have been part-Jewish) was "Nordic" in appearance, while Hitler himself was probably part-Czech.

THE DESTRUCTION OF THE EUROPEAN JEWS

The Nazis' most spectacular crime was the destruction of the European Jews; but it must be emphasized, again, that this was not an isolated episode and was closely tied to other Nazi actions. Even the methods used were tried on other, smaller groups first.

Hitler approached the destruction of the Jews in a step-by-step manner; perhaps he thought that even many Nazis would find it hard to work up to the proper state of mind where genocide would be acceptable. (It also helped put the victims off guard.) Before World War II, the Nazis harassed and segregated the half-million German Jews, ruining them economically, but letting them leave Germany, which most did. Unfortunately, many, like Anne Frank and her family, emigrated to neighboring countries that were subsequently occupied by Germany. Nazi policy changed with the conquest of Poland, the principal center of European Jewry.

Some Jews were sent to forced labor camps; most of the Polish Jews were jammed into ghettoes, which were just small parts of the traditional Jewish quarter of Polish cities. Eventually some of the remaining German Jews were shipped there too. A process of slow starvation began; had the conditions established in 1940 lasted long enough, the Jews might have been wiped out without any further steps by the Nazis. The final phase of Nazi policy began with the invasion of the USSR in June 1941. Four SS *Einsatzgruppen* (task forces) of a type first used in Poland to wipe out the Polish upper class began the outright extermination of the Jews in Soviet territory. By February, 1942, with the aid of Romanian troops, local auxiliaries recruited in Latvia and Lithuania and the Ukraine, and occasionally Waffen SS and regular Army troops, the *Einsatzgruppen* killed half a million Jews and many thousands of other people, including Soviet political commissars and prisoners of war with Mongoloid features. The victims were hardly aware of the danger—like many other inhabitants of the Soviet Union, some Jews had actually welcomed the Germans as liberators, which sorely puzzled the Nazis—and were taken by surprise. Told they would be relocated, they were taken to preselected sites and shot, or sometimes poisoned in mobile vans by exhaust fumes from diesel engines. In 1942, the *Einsatzgruppen* were reinforced by police units to continue the campaign. Meanwhile, a parallel series of actions had destroyed the Jews in the German-occupied parts of Yugoslavia. The fascist Ustache puppet regime the Nazis had installed in Croatia massacred the Jews and Serbs in its territory, while the Serbian Jews were shot in "reprisal" for Communist and Chetnik resistance actions. Having killed most of the Jewish men in this way, the SS brought in a gas van and wiped out the rest of the community.

But, apart from the fact that many Jews in the east had been missed, the Nazis found the *Einsatzgruppen* and gas vans unsatisfactory. Their actions were becoming too well known, the surviving targets were now alert, and the local non-Jews, even if at first indifferent or even in favor of the killings, were fearing that they might be next. The tactics were not suited for application in the rest of Europe; and the SS was perturbed by the effect of the killings on the men of the *Einsatzgruppen*. Except for a few sadists, even most of these well-indoctrinated Nazis were demoralized by the constant killings and the disposal of the dead. So the Nazis shifted to a more impersonal, efficient means of killing, one again already tested against non-Jews.

Since 1939 the Nazis had murdered mentally ill and retarded "Aryan" Germans in gas chambers; this program eventually killed 80,000 to 100,000 persons. Having decided that gassing in large static chambers was effective, in 1941–1942 the Nazis set up a chain of six special extermination camps in the conquered east, of which Auschwitz became the most famous. Jews from all over occupied Europe were rounded up, told they were to be "resettled" in the east, sent to the camps, and murdered.[11]

THE SLAVS

Although only the Jews were slated for, or suffered, total destruction, their fate was, as we have already noted, tightly interwoven with those of their Slavic neighbors.

The Nazis thought that a sizable fraction of the Czech people were of German descent, and could be "re-Germanized"; this and their dependence on Czech industry caused the Nazis to show some restraint in the Czech lands. But even the most pressing practical considerations barely curbed the Nazis' hatred of the Poles. Poland was split into two areas; part annexed to Germany, the rest treated as occupied territory and called the "Government General." Many Poles were deported from the annexed area to the Government General in the middle of a dreadful winter in 1939–1940, and were deprived of all rights. The Nazis deemed few suitable for Germanization, although the SS valiantly expanded this group by kidnapping Polish children of Nordic appearance and taking them to Germany. *Einsatzgruppen* of the sort later used in the USSR wiped out the Polish upper class and intellectuals to "decapitate" the nation. The Polish educational system was destroyed; and all Poles from 18 to 60 were subject to compulsory labor service, with many arbitrary killings in reprisals for resistance, or just anyone who was believed likely to resist. The needs of the war effort forced the Nazis to postpone their plans to uproot all industry; but they planned to rename the Government General the "Vandalengau" after the war and annex it to Germany. Ultimately, most of the surviving Slav population would be deported to the interior of the conquered USSR and Poland would be resettled by Germans.[12]

The most important areas of the new Nazi empire were to lie in former Soviet territory. Hitler resolved in 1940 to annex the Baltic countries to the Reich; their peoples would be Germanized. No such happy fate was envisaged for the other peoples of the Soviet empire. Like the Poles, they were to be thinned out and enslaved. The head of the SS, Heinrich Himmler, remarked in January, 1941, that 30 million Slavs would perish in the course of German plans for the east. All education, health services, and sanitation for the Slavs would be eliminated; as unskilled laborers they would serve German colonists, who would eventually swamp the Slavs. The Ukraine and the Crimea would be the main focus of the settlement effort.

In 1942 the SS formulated "General Plan Ost" for the first stages of colonization. It envisaged building a system of "Siedlungsmarken"—settlement marches   in Soviet territory. A system of military strong points would be surrounded by new villages for German agricultural colonists. These marches would be the nuclei for further settlement, although the Nazis saw a serious problem in finding enough settlers.

When they had invaded the USSR they had implemented the first stages of their program in a bloody, and ultimately self-defeating fashion. Over the not very strong objections of the German Army and some Nazis who thought that at least some Soviet nationalities ought to be treated as allies, they treated all but the Balts with varying degrees of hostility. The *Einsatzgruppen* massacred not only Jews, but other selected categories of the Soviet population. Ordinary Soviet war prisoners, taken in the first campaigns, were deliberately starved to death. At least two and probably three million died. Hitler ordered that when Moscow and Leningrad (Saint Petersburg) were surrounded, no surrender of those cities would be accepted. Instead, they were to be razed to the ground when they were taken, along with their population. (In a fit of generosity, he offered the site of Saint Petersburg to the horrified Finns, who declined it.) The Germans maintained the unpopular Soviet collective farms as instruments of exploitation and formed new state farms using forced labor in occupied territory.

The Soviet regime had already revived slavery on a basis of collective state ownership; the Nazis quickly built a parallel system on a racial basis. After they had destroyed the prisoners taken in 1941, the Nazis suddenly realized that they had a severe labor shortage. The remaining prisoners were turned into slave laborers, and a ruthless program of rounding up civilians from occupied Europe to supply more slaves was set up under Fritz Sauckel, the Gauleiter of Thuringia and "Plenipotentiary General for Allocation of Labor." In Eastern Europe this took a particularly violent form. Whole villages were rounded up, and the buildings then burnt down. By late 1944 there were 7.5 million civilian slave laborers as well as 2 million war prisoners working in Germany. Although peoples of virtually all European nationalities were seized as forced laborers, Slavs formed a majority of them and were the worst treated. Some half million of the luckier ones were given to German farmers; although not treated as "private property," their condition somewhat resembled that of American slaves. The ones used in cities and industry were the worst off. Overworked, starved and brutalized, deprived of winter clothing, often shoeless and dressed in rags, they were housed in conditions resembling badly run kennels. They suffered a high death rate. Nevertheless, they kept the German economy running. Production designers broke down even complex devices like the Messerschmitt 262 jet fighter and the V-2 missile into simple subassemblies, which could be handled by unskilled slave laborers. (The V-2 rocket was largely built by slaves in a bizarre underground concentration camp at Nordhausen.) Slaves did most of the tremendous task of clearing rubble in bombed cities and railroad yards and building fortifications. This grotesque modern slave system functioned until Germany was overrun in 1945.[13]

The development of racism in the Western world had ended in a curious paradox. Only once did a serious political movement centering on a racial ideology come to power in a major country. And its destructive impact was directed, not against "colored" victims, but against other whites.

8

Race-Structured Thinking Today

As we noted earlier, racism of the traditional sort—that is, a belief in white superiority—seems to be dead or dying in the Western world today. Yet "race-structured" thinking, perhaps even new forms of racism, are, unfortunately, a major factor. Many instances of this, and many erroneous beliefs that are ingredients for such obsessions, have been noted throughout this book.

Since the 1950s American society has passed from a situation where racial discrimination was legally enforced in the South, and existed spottily elsewhere, through a brief period in which discrimination was being rapidly ended in the name of equal treatment for all. From there, however, it changed, even faster, to a situation where supposedly benign forms of discrimination were mandated. Earlier ideals of "color-blindness" were discarded in favor of a hyperconsciousness of color once limited to the South. It seems that even issues of political and social policy, far removed from color at first sight, cannot be discussed without injecting race.[1] The insidious virus of race-consciousness is alive, often fostered by those who are, or claim to be, noisy enemies of traditional sorts of racism.

It may be useful to remind ourselves just how extreme the situation has become. As early as 1967, Ronald Radosh reports that white radicals at the New Politics Convention abjectly accepted responsibility for the "centuries of oppression" inflicted on blacks; one blurted out, "After 400 years of slavery . . . it is right that whites should be castrated."[2] We are now told that ours is a white, male-dominated European culture that "deserves to die." It is widely argued that freedom of speech should extend only to "victimized minorities," since the white majority does not need such protection. A law professor declares that all standards have been established by white males and may not be applicable to blacks and women.[3] In the 1970s, Senator Walter Mondale, later vice president of the United States and a presidential candidate, declared that the United States was rapidly coming to resemble South Africa. Two decades later, a highly touted author Andrew Hacker, commented that the "American version of apartheid, while lacking overt legal sanction, comes closest to the system even now being reformed in the land of its invention." The famous liberal writer, Murray Kempton, in a slap at the labor movement, commented that the "AFL-CIO has lived happily in a society which, more lavishly than any in history, has managed the care and feeding of incompetent white people."[4] A religious writer, Jim Wallis, blubbers that "The United States was established as a white society, founded on the genocide of another race and the enslavement of yet another"; whites "built their new nation's economy on the backs of kidnapped Africans." What has not changed is the systematic and pervasive character of racism in the United States and the conditions of life for the majority of black people."[5] A black Detroit city planner declares, "As a people we have more soul, we are more spiritual than others. Our technology will be tempered by that soul. If white folks leave us alone and give us the resources, we could solve our own problems."[6] A well-publicized book blandly assures us that "It goes without saying that a profound hatred of African people . . . sits at the center of American civilization."[7] Studs Terkel's interviews with ordinary people, while perhaps selective, disclose similar remarks, for example "the white man has destroyed the earth."[8]

Some of the remarks quoted above were made by whites, some by blacks. It is of doubtful comfort that many of both races swallow the same absurdities.

How did this tangle of exaggerations and lies, of reverse and inverted discrimination, of psychopathic hatred for Western culture in general, and the United States in particular, develop? The question is a serious one, for this state of mind is not only bad in itself, but an obstacle to understanding the true social crisis of the United States, the social disintegration most obvious in, though not necessarily limited to, the underclass. Whether this rotting of the social structure is due to blundering changes in social, legal, and educational policies in the 1960s, as has been eloquently argued by Charles Murray and Myron Magnet, or is an effect of economic structural change, as has been most ably argued by William Julius Wilson, is a matter of debate. But both sides equally reject the proposition that any current, continuing racism, is responsible for the development of the underclass, which has grown enormously precisely since the barriers to black advancement have fallen.[9] The muddled thinking about race, and the problems of the underclass, do have roots in earlier developments, particularly in the civil-rights movement, and in the way they are often presented to the public.

THE BLACK SITUATION IN THE EARLY TWENTIETH CENTURY

The writer has no intention of trying to recapitulate the history of the civil-rights movement. It must be noted, however, that even that well-known story is often distorted in popular commentary. The version of its history often fed to the public is curiously foreshortened, and the vision of the social situation in the United States strangely simplified and warped. It is common to see accounts that disregard the considerable differences that once existed between North and South. It is widely assumed that the civil-rights movement and all significant progress for black Americans was purely a post–World War II phenomenon, that race relations were basically static and unchanging before then, and that progress was either a gift from above by the Supreme Court, or the product of a sudden, almost magical and spontaneous upsurge by Southern blacks without precedent or preparations, or some combination of the two. That is not a realistic description of what happened. It does less than justice to many who labored hard for civil rights for generations, under much worse conditions than their successors, with results that might later have seemed unspectacular, but were nevertheless important.

It should be noted that even in the South, the permissible view of Negroes, among whites, was not uniform. It ranged from the incredibly hate-filled "Negrophobic" view typified by the Klan, most common among the lower classes of the Deep South, which regarded blacks as vicious animals (and spilled over, to some extent, into hatred of Catholics and Jews) to views most common in the upper classes and the Upper South, that blacks were good-natured slobs, who must be "kept in their place" but should be treated "fairly," though emphatically not equally. There were many gradations between these views. And some Southern whites knew or suspected that black inferiority was a myth. But, until after World War II, only an exceptionally courageous few would openly say so.

Even in 1900 the situation of black Americans was neither uniform nor static. In the South, they were an oppressed lower caste overhung by the threat of violence from two sides; they not only suffered at the hands of whites but from each other. (Enforcing the law against blacks who committed crimes against other blacks was a liberal innovation of the early twentieth century. Memories of the earlier situation, where the law was invoked only against blacks, were a major factor in shaping black attitudes toward law enforcement later on.) At the opposite pole, in some smaller Northern communities, the "few resident Negroes were highly regarded and occupied positions of virtual social equality with their neighbors," although most Northern whites regarded them as a comic or picturesque, and minor, element of the social scene.[10] Even in the South, however, their situation was changing. Politically and legally, their status had actually regressed since the end of Reconstruction. But they had made economic progress and literacy was far more common than in 1865. It was in the early twentieth century that the chief organizations of the civil-rights movement, notably the NAACP, were founded. The objective of black Americans, then and for many years afterward, was to enjoy the same rights and status as white Americans. As W.E.B. DuBois put it, "We are fighting for the enforcement of the Constitution of the United States."[11] And the implicit belief was that if and when discrimination could be ended, blacks, given a fair chance, should catch up with white Americans.

As in the case of the Amerinds and the subjects of the colonial empires, the original coincidence of differences of color with other sorts of differences increasingly ceased to exist. The differences of language and religion had disappeared in the era of slavery. Cultural and class differences were gradually eroding, for it was no longer true that the freed slaves and their descendants were almost all illiterates of the lowest class.

PORTENTS OF CHANGE

World War I and its aftermath led to considerable change. Many blacks migrated to the North. There were changes in the South, too. After 1922, the worst feature of Southern life, lynching, sharply declined. (There was an average of about ten lynchings a year during the rest of the interwar era.) Gunnar Myrdal's research in the late 1930s and early 1940s concluded that much change had taken place for the better in the South. While the South was still very different from the North, it was, as he put it, becoming "Americanized." While many whites in the North considered blacks inferior, and there was much unofficial discrimination, there seemed, to Myrdal, to be little overt prejudice against middle- and upper-class blacks, whose numbers were growing. In parts of New England, discrimination seemed nonexistent. Most American whites, Myrdal thought, were willing to give blacks a better break, if they were aware of the facts, and this was true to a considerable extent in the South, as well as the North.[12]

But, as of 1941, as a later observer put it, the problems of blacks still "stood outside the mainstream of life in the United States."[13] Most blacks still lived in the South, and nearly half of those in the North were concentrated in just six big cities—New York, Chicago, Philadelphia, Pittsburgh, Cleveland, and Detroit. It is worth noting that, before World War II, and perhaps as late as the 1950s, it is likely that most white Americans—and almost certainly a majority of whites living outside the South—*had never seen a black person in the flesh*; an important, and nowadays often overlooked, factor in the situation. To many Northern whites—and especially those recently arrived from Eastern and Southern Europe—blacks were new and unfamiliar beings, if they encountered them. Their view of blacks was shaped by contemporary contacts, often unfortunate ones, in the slums of Northern cities, rather than by either traditional racial mythology or liberal sentiments, although it has been suggested that Eastern Europeans may have been influenced by a particular distaste for blacks' physical features. White Southerners, by contrast, were shaped by a long history of dealing with blacks, under very different circumstances; whatever else might be said about them, they at least were used to having them around.

The situation was pregnant with unpleasant consequences. For blacks, Northern whites were often maddeningly uncertain creatures. Whether the racial etiquette normal in the South was appropriate, or partly appropriate, or unnecessary, was often unclear. For lower-class whites, blacks were often just predatory slum dwellers; for blacks, hostility from Northern whites, especially recent immigrants, was even less tolerable than from Southerners. What seemed to them to be, and sometimes were, airs of superiority coming from bums just off the boat were even more outrageous than from white Southerners, who were merely repeating what they had been taught for many generations. What often started as basically class conflicts—after all, whites did not much care for *white* slum-dwellers—could easily become racial ones.

It is perhaps worth mentioning the existence of a less important, and opposite phenomenon. Some Northern whites had no contact with blacks at all, or encountered only middle-class or well-established Northern working-class blacks not too different from themselves. Such people often had trouble grasping the real social differences and conflicts produced by encounters between whites and very poor (and later underclass) blacks.

But the situation in the cities of the North was not much discussed between the World Wars, or even much later. There was a strong tendency, even for those whites who sympathized with blacks, to see race relations as a Southern regional issue. Perhaps still barely tenable before World War II, that view quickly became an anachronism, but it hung on, even among liberals, until the mid-1960s, before abruptly evaporating. Until then, there was a strong tendency among liberals to see the race problem as a product of a unique fiendishness of Southern whites (and perhaps a few aberrant Northerners who were mentally ill and better dealt with by psychiatrists than social reformers). Then, the liberal distaste for white Southerners, and the somewhat contradictory "psychiatric" approach to racial prejudice, would be turned full blast against the white population as a whole.

Despite the naive attitudes of the liberals of the era, in the 1930s racial issues reentered national politics for the first time since Reconstruction. The Roosevelt Administration clearly sympathized with blacks, and although generally sticking within the framework of "separate but equal," usually succeeded in ensuring that blacks got a fair share of federal assistance during the Great Depression. In 1940, the Ramspeck Act outlawed discrimination in the federal civil service. Readily bending to black pressure in 1941, the Roosevelt Administration created a Fair Employment Practices Commission to prevent discrimination in war-related industries. While the armed forces remained segregated during World War II, the position of blacks in the services improved. Especially in the Army, blacks broke out of the traditionally limited roles they had been allotted, and some reached high rank. The U.S. Army's two black infantry divisions were undistinguished in combat, but several black armored and artillery battalions fought well, as did black units in the Army Air Force. So did the men who volunteered for an experiment in semi-desegregation launched by General Eisenhower in 1945, in which black companies or individual platoons were inserted into white units. The fact that the smaller the black combat unit, the better its performance, showed intelligent observers that it was segregation, not any inherent inadequacy of the Negro soldier, that was the real problem; and this conclusion led to the decision to desegregate the armed forces in 1948.

A series of decisions by the Supreme Court and regulatory agencies began undermining the basis for discrimination. In 1935, in the *Scottsboro* case, the Supreme Court threw out a decision because blacks had been systematically excluded from jury duty. In 1950, in *Cassell v. Texas*, laws limiting black jury service were struck down. In *Gaines v. Missouri*, in 1938, the Court decided that blacks could demand entry into a regular, white state university if no "separate but equal" facility was being provided by the state. By 1950, a series of decisions in similar cases had turned aside attempts to evade this ruling. The Court, by then, had not explicitly repudiated the separate but equal doctrine, formulated in the 1890s, but segregationists were caught in a classic catch-22 situation. For the decision in the *McLaurin* case, in 1950, seemingly implied that *no* segregated institution would be equal and acceptable. In 1944, the Court struck down the "white primary," which had excluded blacks from an effective role in the Democratic Party in the South, by allowing only whites to vote in its primary elections. In 1948 the Court made discriminatory covenants in housing unenforceable. During the 1940s, the Interstate Commerce Commission slowly and painfully began demanding equality, then desegregation, in transportation.[14] Thus, contrary to a widespread myth, the decision in *Brown v. Board of Education* in 1954 was not a "nonviolent revolution" but a logical step in a course begun in the 1930s. But it is also necessary to note that a contrary myth—spread, oddly enough, by some of the same people— that holds that the Supreme Court was traditionally the trusty guardian of the nation's liberties, and a "progressive" institution, is also false. That now common belief would have evoked laughter, at least among educated people, up to the 1960s. Until the late 1930s, the Supreme Court never protected freedom of speech or the press against Congressional attack, and almost never intervened on behalf of unions, the lower classes, or minority groups, except in a few cases involving Indians. And, until then, it had gutted the protections that the Reconstruction lawmakers tried to give blacks.[15] Myths to the contrary, however, are important to the prestige of the Court, and to the American legal profession as a whole.

WHITE PUBLIC OPINION

Important as the trend of official and legal decisions, although it usually does not get as much attention, was the steady diminution of racial prejudice among whites, which was tracked by polls from the 1940s on. The change of views on a basic social issue was startling in its speed, and, again contrary to what is generally supposed, much of the change, especially in the views of Northern whites, took place in the 1940s and 1950s, rather than later. In 1942, only 42 percent of American whites thought that blacks were as intelligent as whites; by 1946, 53 percent did so, and by 1956, 77 percent agreed with that idea. Opinion on less abstract questions, such as accepting the integration of schools and blacks as neighbors, also changed. In 1942, less than a third of whites favored integrated schools, but by 1956 almost half did so; 56 percent favored them by 1959. Southern whites lagged behind Northerners but at a decreasing distance. The trends first visible in the 1940s continued, with but slight ups and downs.[16] It should be noted that if most white Southerners opposed equality and desegregation, they did not expect to win in the end. Polls as early as 1961 showed that 76 percent of white Southerners expected that there would soon be complete integration of public places.[17] Important changes and distinctions in the nature of their resistance should also be noted. The border states submitted to desegregation with little fuss; and while there was often bitter legal resistance to it in the Upper South, there was little violence against the civil-rights movement save in the Deep South. Things were notably different from the Reconstruction era. The original Ku Klux Klan had combined all classes under the traditional leaders of Southern society and ruthlessly murdered and burned as far north as Kentucky. In the 1950s and 1960s, "respectable" opponents of desegregation formed "White Citizen's Councils." The KKK was relegated to the dregs of Southern society, fanatics, hoodlums, and barroom bums of the sort who, as the old joke ran, "hated everybody but White Anglo-Saxon Protestants—and weren't too sure about them."

By 1948 the changes in white opinion, the legal situation, and the growth of black political power in the North had reached a point where a Democratic President sympathetic to civil rights could contemplate alienating much of the white South with equanimity. Although many Southern Democrats defected to the "Dixiecrats," Northern liberals and blacks were able to more than make up the difference and return President Truman to office. The South's position of strength—due to the normally solidly Democratic nature of its Congressional delegation and the seniority that gave it control of vital Congressional committees, and other effects of the then prevailing parliamentary rules, enabled Southerners to block Congressional civil-rights action for years. There seemed to be a near stalemate. But, in fact, their position was eroding. The desegregation of the military, begun in 1948, and the desegregation of Washington and of all Federal facilities in the South, decreed by President Eisenhower in 1953, left islands of integration even in the South. In the mid-1950s the Court's unanimous repudiation of the "separate but equal" doctrine and the Montgomery bus boycott inaugurated the well-chronicled heroic age of the civil-rights movement.

During the late 1940s and 1950s, an important shift in liberal and left-wing outlooks took place on matters related to race relations. In the 1930s, liberals and the left were sympathetic to blacks, but did *not* consider their predicament a central problem, and certainly not *the* central problem, of American society. They conceived of blacks as just the worst-off element of the lower class; and often viewed race prejudice as the result of a deliberate plot by the upper class in the South. Many persuaded themselves that poor whites would readily ally themselves with blacks against entrenched privilege; and most assumed that if the basic problems faced by workers and the poor were solved, whether by liberal reforms or some sort of socialism, black-white issues would shrink to unimportance. Observers like Gunnar Myrdal had to gently point out the unreality of such ideas and the fact that the upper classes were less bigoted toward blacks than poor whites.[18]

After World War II all this gradually seeped into the minds of liberals and leftists; and the prewar and wartime sentimentality toward the lower class—or, perhaps, just lower-class whites—faded. Liberals were increasingly concerned with things like civil liberties, race relations, and what were later called "quality-of-life" issues. They gradually realized that lower-class people did not necessarily share their views and interests; and that the middle and upper classes were often more "liberal" in their thinking about civil liberties and minorities than workers and the poor, a recognition greatly accentuated by the much-exaggerated threat of McCarthyism. They tacitly recognized, too, that in other countries Nazism and Communism had often appealed to lower-class people; the latter were not necessarily saints and democrats. This disillusionment was part of a general "conservative shift" in liberalism, typified by the rise of figures like Reinhold Niebuhr, Lionel Trilling, and Arthur Schlesinger, Jr. Curiously such ideas would later lend themselves to a resurgence of the extreme left, and to a virtual inversion of the attitudes of the 1930s.[19]

Another sort of "liberal" white, (utterly unlike the men mentioned above) of a kind that would hardly have been regarded as liberal in an earlier day, held a very different view of blacks. They did not regard Negroes as "as good as whites" (as most liberals would have put it), but saw them as degraded and inferior beings, every bit as much as any Southern segregationist. They simply did not think whites were any better. Indeed a variant of this type liked blacks precisely *because* they thought they were inferior. Although these diseased views only occasionally surfaced in the 1950s, they helped poison the situation later on.

THE CONCEPTUAL SHIFT OF THE 1960s

A drastic shift in attitudes took place within a few short years in the 1960s. It involved basic changes in the way Americans thought about their society (perhaps even their whole idea of civilization) and thought about the relations, past and present, between whites and other racial groups, and in how the interests of those groups, or their members, were defined. We have discussed some of these ideas earlier in this book, when dealing with specific historical myths. It is now time to try to analyze them more fully—at the risk of imposing more clarity on a set of often silly, sometimes monstrous, ideas than they really possess.

The concept of collective and hereditary guilt became popular. This was, as has been well said, a return to the "dark atavism of pre-Christian mythology."[20] Many believed that entire nations were responsible for crimes, real and alleged, committed in the past. This odd idea appeared, or revived, in connection with discussions of Nazi crimes, but quickly seeped into discussions of other matters. In thinking about race relations within the United States, it translated into the idea that present-day whites were responsible for earlier mistreatment of Amerinds and blacks. Such thinking is now so common that it is hard to realize that it played *no* role in liberal reformist arguments earlier. James Burnham, a bitter critic of liberalism, noted in 1964 that such ideas were not only novel but incompatible with traditional liberal principles.[21]

Liberalism aside, the idea of collective guilt was incoherent. It declared guilt without trial and annihilated individual responsibility. For a doctrine of the *general* inferiority of blacks, it substituted the *moral* inferiority of whites. Over and above the basic absurdity of holding people responsible for crimes, real or alleged, committed by their ancestors, it held people responsible for the crimes of *other people's* ancestors. It was senseless enough to blame descendants of Southern slave owners (singling out those slaveholders of all those who had existed) for slavery. It was still more absurd to argue that the many whites whose forebears had not been in North America before the Civil War and had never had anything to do with blacks were responsible for the situation of the latter—although perhaps no crazier than insisting that those whose ancestors had opposed slavery or fought for the Union were to blame.

A closely related phenomenon was the rise of "victimology." There was a growing tendency to divide the world, past and present, into "victims" and "victimizers," a tendency not solely apparent in racial matters, but of great impact on them. This point of view has grown steadily at the expense of both more pragmatic approaches and traditional views of rights. Oddly, this tendency often ended by inverting the true relation of victim and victimizer; in many instances, it was "discovered" that someone who committed a crime was *really* the victim. Criminals were really "victims of society" (the latter treated as a bland abstraction instead of an aggregate of predominantly decent individuals) instead of society being the victim of the criminals.[22]

The concepts of discrimination and racism were redefined. The standard for diagnosing these things shifted from hard, provable acts to anything seemingly having a disparate impact, and indeed to vague things such as thoughts. (It is arguable that the increased use of the term "racism" itself helped blur distinctions between conduct and ideas.) Further, it became widely believed that any difference between whites and blacks in the distribution of jobs, income, intelligence quotients, or test scores must be due to either discrimination against the less well off group or its actual, inherent inferiority. That ignored the fact that the distribution of such things as jobs and income between various groups of whites, and for that matter, other nonwhite groups such as Asians and West Indians, also differed considerably. In many cases where such differences could be found, no discrimination had existed, while in others, such measurements "favored" some minorities despite their suffering discrimination. It also ignored the likelihood that explanations existed for the poor performance of blacks other than the bare alternatives of *current* discrimination or innate inferiority. The difference between past and present discrimination was blurred, so what might well be the net effect of past discrimination was treated as if it were the result of current, continuing bias. Andrew Hacker's book, *Two Nations*, is an excellent example of this syndrome, indeed of the whole state of mind that made an undifferentiated and essentially unchanging white racism in both North and South the explanation of everything wrong in American society.

Definitions of racism became ever more elaborate, even baroque. A notable example is the concept of "institutional racism." This has been defined as "those established laws, customs, and practices which systematically reflect and produce racial inequalities in American society. If racist consequences accrue to institutional laws, customs, or practices, the institution is racist whether or not the individuals maintaining those practices have racist intentions."[23] Even more bizarre redefinitions of racism have been created to show that all of Western civilization has been permeated by racist ideas. Racism has been broadened, on the one hand, to prove that all whites are racist, and narrowed, on the other, to show that no blacks can be racist. Hunting for racism has turned to ever more abstruse, symbolic issues, and charges of racism have become ever vaguer and more irresponsible.[24]

The opinion forming elite of the mass media and academia and Federal courts discovered "group rights," and decided that they overrode both majority rule and the traditional rights of individuals. This was closely connected with the shift to hyperconsciousness of color and led to policies favoring blacks over whites. "Affirmative action," a slogan originally describing non-discriminatory efforts to advance blacks, became a global term to cover this change to reverse discrimination. It was argued that the heritage of slavery and discrimination left blacks unable to compete on even terms with whites, even with discrimination ended. This "shackled runner" argument was the most convincing argument for affirmative action. Those who used it, at first, often implied that preferential treatment for blacks was a special, regrettable, temporary measure.

It was argued that affirmative action put blacks in the positions they *would* have had had there been no slavery and discrimination. (Even few critics of affirmative action were so tactless as to point out that had slavery not existed there would be no blacks in the United States!)

Affirmative action was based on a false view of society. There was no way to know what percentage of positions blacks would occupy in such areas as schools or jobs in a "color-blind" situation. All other ethnic groups, after all, tended to "clump" in some social positions and to be "underrepresented" in others. The policy arbitrarily penalized individuals in the present to make up for suffering in the past; and favored people who might be, and often were, not particularly badly off. It favored middle-class blacks, but did little for the really badly off, and was a poisoned gift that threw a question mark over all successful blacks.

Strangely, few paid attention to a less divisive, simpler alternative to racial affirmative action—favoring all people from families with low incomes.

Affirmative action was soon extended to other minorities and women, including, absurdly, newly arrived immigrants. That produced endless quarrels between putative "victim" groups, and incidentally made nonsense of the "shackled runner" argument. That, however, mistaken its deductions, had at least rested on the incontestable truth that blacks *had* been treated worse than other Americans.[25]

The whole stress on group rights, historical victimization, and ethnicity triggered a "Balkanization" of American society, a tendency to split along racial, ethnic, and later sexual lines and argue about public policies as though those divisions were crucial. (It should be stressed here that most Americans, and almost certainly a majority of any subgroup, were not obsessed with such matters—indeed in the real world, intermarriage between various groups was growing. We are talking about the feelings of only a minority of any group—but often an influential and noisy minority.) The ugly term "white ethnic" was coined to describe whites descended from immigrants from southern and Eastern Europe, who often vied, unconvincingly, with blacks for "victim status." Many Jews, in particular, brooded endlessly about their history of victimization, although in some ways theirs was a special case. (The suffering had been all too real, but had taken place overseas and had little to do with life in America.)

Jews seem to have the most elaborate feelings of victimization of any American ethnic group other than blacks. Their attitudes even bear some similarities to those of blacks, despite the vast social gap between the situation of the two groups, and the neurotic state of mind of many American Jews may be worth discussion. Quite a few Jews suffer paranoid fears of the Christian majority and are obsessed with anti-Semitism, to a greater extent than the Jews of half a century ago, when, by all measurements, anti-Semitism was far more common. This seems closely connected to an obsession with the Nazi destruction of the European Jews. (An obsession far less common in the 1950s, when it was a much fresher memory.) Of course, even a paranoid would find it neither necessary nor possible to exaggerate Jewish suffering under the Nazis, but, nevertheless, distortions appear in some Jewish views of the Nazi experience. Notable examples are:

1. A frenetic insistence on distancing the Jews from other victims of the Nazis, especially Eastern European Christians.

2. Exaggerated tendencies to focus on the collaboration of other groups with the Nazis, and the real and alleged failures of the Allied governments to rescue Jews. Sometimes these quirks are carried to such an extreme that the Nazis themselves almost fade from view; the real villains become the Eastern European nationalities, or Roosevelt, Churchill, and their advisers! It should be noted that while Jews might have good reason to dislike many of their Eastern European neighbors, some of whom did collaborate with the Nazis or otherwise behaved badly, the latter were hardly prime movers in their destruction. And it is a further oddity that many Jews are particularly hostile to the Poles, who were strongly anti-Nazi and were rather less unfriendly than some other nationalities.

3. In a curious counterpoint to this, there is a tendency (manifested most clearly in some of the writings of Hannah Arendt) to blame the European Jews themselves for allegedly not resisting their fate and/or American Jews for supposedly not exerting their alleged influence on the U.S. government in trying to get the government to do more to save Jews. (These ideas are common enough—and so ill founded—that they suggest that, as in other expressions of ethnic grievances, self-hatred is mixed in with the self-pity and self-assertion.)

4. There is a bizarre tendency to harp on the theme that the Holocaust was a result of *Christian* anti-Semitism, a view accepted, oddly enough, by quite a few self-flagellating Christians. This is often carried to the extreme of practically ignoring the Nazis' actual ideas, particularly their racial concepts and their

hostility toward Christianity. In a way, by making the destruction of the European Jews merely an eruption of traditional Christian hatred, it trivializes it.[26]

Nathan Glazer, a careful observer of the "white ethnic" groups, judged that from the mid-1960s ethnic identity began gaining on the general American identity.[27] By the 1990s, no one even pointed out the incongruity of the fact that almost any parade in honor of this or that ethnic "homeland," which most of the marchers had never seen, and which their ancestors had been anxious to escape, drew more participants than commemorations of American national holidays. A curious tendency to "overidentification with one's ancestors" (often as one would have wished them to be or as it would be politically convenient for them to have been), of a kind that once had made the Daughters of the American Revolution figures of fun, became widespread. That "overidentification" was often revealed in a tendency to constantly employ the word "we," and use the present tense, when the sufferings of some *past* generation was actually being discussed.

Earlier, the treatment of blacks had been seen as an "exception" to the main thrust of American history, which was usually seen in optimistic terms. Now, there was so much concentration on the exception that it almost drove out the brighter aspects of the story (and other groups tried to pretend that they too were part of the exception.)[28]

This, perhaps, was just one example of a mental phenomenon that seems to have first appeared during the Vietnam War, and which has not been properly analyzed, or, perhaps, even noted, although by traditional ethical and intellectual standards, it was very odd indeed. Perhaps we can call it "extremist invert-projection." It consisted of this: once some event or phenomenon was widely condemned, pronounced a national disgrace, or generally denounced as a travesty of what the nation stood for—whether American involvement in Vietnam, or the Watergate scandal, or mistreatment of blacks—there was a strong tendency to see it as not just mistaken or wrong, but insist that it was *the very worst thing in history.* Then, once acceptance of that exaggeration—it was, usually, an exaggeration—became widespread, it then became fashionable to see, or project the evil, (or the fashionable image of that evil), onto the whole American, or Western past, and insist that it was an inextricable feature of the entire culture of the United States, or Western civilization as a whole, thus *inverting* the moral indignation on which the original reaction rested, and turning it against the whole of society instead of the real or alleged evil that had originally been denounced. (The original indignation, after all, had depended on the feeling that the evil being denounced was unusual or abnormal.) Thus, views originally quite appropriate, perhaps, in viewing the Ku Klux Klan, could be projected onto the entire white population of the United States, throughout its history. There is some resemblance in all this to what Lenin once called the "amalgam" technique of propaganda; but it appears to be an unconscious mimicking rather than a calculated copying.

For many blacks, their concept of their identity changed. Previously, the civil-rights movement had conceived of blacks as basically like everyone else "beneath the skin" wanting only integration and a fair share; or, in a more plausible variant, had assumed that blacks differed from white Americans no more than various white groups—for example Polish Americans or Swedish Americans—differed from each other. Now, there was a tendency to magnify, even harp, on real and supposed differences. The shift of names, from "Negro" to "black, " in 1966–1967 may have been psychologically significant. The two words might be precisely equivalent—on the page of a dictionary—but "white and Negro," in conventional English usage, merely conveys a degree of difference, while "white and black" perhaps unavoidably conveys overtones of *opposition*.

There was an increasing interest in and identification with Africa, and a tendency to wishfully magnify the persistence of Africanisms among the slaves and their descendants. Interest in Africa had naturally existed before, but there was a subtle difference. In the 1930s, and earlier, blacks had identified with Ethiopia and its struggle to stay independent. They had proudly noted that, in contradiction of hostile stereotypes, it was a civilized land and one of the oldest Christian countries in the world. Now, the focus was on newly independent ex-colonies, often pagan or Muslim. And there was a growing tendency (which seems to prey even on the minds of devout black Christians) to think of Christianity as a "white man's religion," associated with slavery, and a tropism toward the Islamic world—although Islam had also been founded by whites, and Moslems had enslaved blacks both before and after Westerners did so.

The older emphasis by reformers (which seems to have been well founded) that the suppression of blacks hurt not only them but whites, or most whites, and the nation as a whole, was abruptly replaced by a belief that not just a minority of slave-owners or exploiters, but whites in general, had profited from slavery and discrimination.[29] That view was closely related to, and supportive, of the concepts of collective guilt. It also promoted a view of relations between blacks and whites as an eternal "zero-sum game"—what whites gained blacks must lose, and vice versa, an idea that seems to lurk just under the surface of much public discussion, and to have at least partly replaced traditional ideas of justice in the minds of many blacks, and their professed sympathizers among whites. It should be noted that if the assumption of a complete dichotomy of interests were taken to its logical limits that would make whites who opposed slavery traitors, and those who fought in the Union armies fools. That would be a logical position to take—for the Ku Klux Klan.

The "disillusionment " of intellectuals and the opinion formers with the *white* lower class, observable since World War II, was carried to an extreme, perfectly inverting the left's dreams and stereotypes of the 1930s. (We might call this the Archie Bunker syndrome, after its most famous fictional incarnation.) It became fashionable for those claiming sympathy for minorities to believe that white workers were racists and reactionaries, and there was almost open disdain for the *white* poor.[30]

The historical difference between the treatment of blacks in the North and South was obliterated. American history as a whole was none too subtly "Southernized." In 1964, Charles Silberman neatly expressed the new view; the United States "all of it, North as well as South, West as well as East—is a racist society, in a sense and to a degree that we have refused, so far, to admit, much less face."[31] (This quote encompasses another shift in thinking; earlier, Americans would have said that the United States had a "race problem," or that "racism was a problem.") It was, of course, true enough that racism and discrimination existed in the North, too. And the old difference between North and South was in fact disappearing, and in fact had largely vanished by the 1980s, so to some degree this notion was merely a conventional error of projecting the present onto the past. Yet it was also a rather abrupt reversal within the context of the civil-rights movement, which had deftly exploited national revulsion against the peculiarities of the South.

There was another abrupt reversal in the attitude of the civil-rights movement and its supporters to law and order and violence. Earlier, they had argued that the law of the land supported black equality and had rightly emphasized that it was the segregationalists who were violent. After 1965, those who had bitterly condemned Southern resistance to court-ordered desegregation, much less rioting and violence, often palliated or even justified the urban riots of the 1960s. A slogan even suggested that "law and order" was a code-word for racism.

This was a doubly curious switch, for violence had always backfired when employed by the enemies of the civil-rights movement.

Indeed the shift in rhetoric, policies, and ideology by the movement and its supporters was so drastic, so bizarre, such a complete reversal of everything said earlier, that it is hard to avoid suspecting that for many involved the high-toned principles of freedom and equality had meant little, and that the civil-rights movement was just a cynical ethnic lobby grabbing as much as it could for its clients (who, to be sure, had been genuinely oppressed). That may well be true of some of its members; but, on the whole, this view should be resisted. The overt change in the movement coincided with so many other drastic changes in American society and attitudes that it is probable that the shift was a genuine change of opinion.

At further extremes, there were demands for self-determination and even out and out black separatism and nationalism. Although these last ideas had little popular appeal, actual resegregation began on some college campuses at the end of the 1960s, a trend which has since gone further; and more serious concessions were made to such views in public policy. The Voting Rights Acts were "interpreted" to demand gerrymandering so that blacks would be represented by their own race. Attempts were made to block or strongly discourage interracial adoptions. As Diane Ravitch has observed, there was a bizarre and unique alliance of the egalitarian and the particularistic—demands for equal treatment for all were combined with demands for special treatment for different groups.[32]

There was a general attack on conventional systems of merit and standards of excellence. If blacks did badly on standardized tests, it was because the tests were somehow culturally biased—although careful studies turned up no proof of this, and Asians outperformed whites on such tests. Soon it was argued that all existing standards were wrong; they had been invented by whites (or, as it was put a bit later, white males), as part of a conspiracy to hold others down. Objective or universal standards did not exist or could not be developed.[33]

In a way evocative of the extremes of early racism, the thesis of the immutability of group characteristics and contempt for any sort of standards spread through the intellectual world. A distorted form of cultural relativism served as a Trojan Horse for an all-out attack on Western culture. It was argued, or more exactly, asserted, that not only were all races equal in inherent capability but that all cultures were equal. In a drastic nonsequitur, cultures were increasingly identified with race, just as they had been a century ago. It was insinuated, then declared, that anyone who disagreed with this, or disparaged a particular culture—other than that of white Europeans and their descendants—must be a racist. (This involved a curious paradox; if no culture was any more advanced than any other, then a culture that was nonracist or antiracist, was no better than one that was fiercely racist.) The mainstream of American culture was increasingly identified by its critics with smaller subgroups—whites in general, or middle-class whites, or "WASPs" or "white males" or "white heterosexual males." It sufficed, for many, to identify an idea, institution, or standard with one of these categories to discredit it. There were ever more frantic attempts to argue that racism (that is, a belief in white superiority) was inextricably intertwined with Western cultural traditions as a whole in order to discredit the latter. To many, Western culture was not so much tainted with racism as identified with it, and particularly with the degradation of blacks. It would have been truer to say that it was Western culture that identified blacks as human beings; and the ideas described above would have been a counterproductive stance had racism still been a formidable threat, or really had broad social support. Liberals and leftists had hummed a rather different tune in the days when that had been true.

Cultural differences between white and black Americans, in particular, were wildly exaggerated, so that expressions like "white culture" and "black culture" no longer evoke skepticism. (The useful and seemingly more appropriate term "subculture" has dropped out of use.)

An interesting example of many of these muddled doctrines can be found in Paul Feyerabend's attacks on science: "When Blacks, Indians, and other suppressed races first emerged into the broad daylight of civic life, their leaders and their supporters among Whites demanded equality. But equality, racial equality included, then did not mean equality of traditions; it meant equality of access to one particular tradition—the tradition of the White Man. The Whites who supported the demand opened the Promised Land—but it was a Promised Land built to their own specifications and furnished with their own favorite playthings." Further, the ancestors of the nonwhites had "developed cultures of their own, colourful languages, harmonious views of the relation between man and man and man and nature whose remnants are a living criticism of the tendencies of separation, analysis, self-centeredness inherent in Western thought."[34] This is an interesting example of the incorporation of the myth of totally separate, immutable group identities with the myth that non-Western cultures are warm, ecologically sound and humane, and in all these respects superior to the West. The supposed historical "sin" of Western whites is transformed from excluding others from equal participation in their culture on grounds of color to assuming that they ought to participate. It should be noted that in practice, all this hostility to Western culture is rarely, if ever, associated with a real interest in the traditions of other civilizations. Instead, it is tied to admiration for recent "Third World" political creeds, which, on examination, turn out to be derived from originally Western ideas.

Parallel and in conjunction with all these other alterations in ideas and practices, a pair of very important changes took place in attitudes and policies toward social welfare and poverty. Early in the 1960s, liberals had kept, or revived, the old hope of doing away with the welfare system. They hoped to go further and permanently eradicate poverty in the United States. (Indeed, even some quite conservative elements shared that hope, although they were inclined to rely on sheer economic growth within the existing social and economic system to do the job.) But, as Charles Murray has shown, in an amazingly short period, between 1964 and 1967, American intellectuals and politicians in effect dropped the idea of eliminating welfare, while confusing the issue of poverty with that of racism—although most poor people were white. They concluded that there must be permanent income transfers, embracing bigger and bigger segments of the population. Ideas that the poor bore some responsibility for their situation (or at least for trying to get out of it) disappeared and many leaped to the opposite extreme of assuming that poverty was a *purely* social and structural problem in which encouraging the right sort of individual response was not a factor. Indeed, it was widely accepted that society did not have the right to force the poor to alter their behavior. The traditional distinction between "deserving" and "undeserving" poor was obliterated. Educational and legal policies also changed drastically in a short time, while vast sums were pumped into social programs.[35]

Unfortunately, the results were very different from what those responsible for these programs hoped and expected. The considerable progress made it eliminating poverty up to the mid-1960s—indeed since World War II—virtually came to an end. By later standards, some 30 percent of the American people had been poor in 1950; this had sunk to 18 percent by 1964 (before the "War on Poverty" began) and to 13 percent by 1968. The level of poverty changed little thereafter. Measurements of scholastic achievement began to drop. Crime rates, low and in some important respects falling in the 1950s, began to shoot upward.

These things—which disproportionately affected blacks—happened precisely as the walls of discrimination against blacks began collapsing. And, in fact, many blacks—probably most—were doing better; in terms of class and income, black Americans split into two groups, one improving its position, and rising out of the lower class, the other sinking far below it.[36] Blacks formed a disproportionate part of the underclass, which was rarely employed or perhaps indeed employable, where family life had disintegrated, crime and violence reached fantastic proportions, and drug addiction, AIDS, and other diseases were rife. Although underclass behavior was gradually seeping upward in the social scale, and the underclass was hardly racially exclusive, panic among blacks observing and experiencing it is a wholly understandable reaction. The fact that more and more whites were being sucked into the underclass, too, (a point whose importance cannot be overemphasized), curiously escaped many blacks and whites. The awful social crisis, which afflicted people of both races, and *not* racism, is almost certainly the central social problem of the United States, but it is often mistaken for, or misinterpreted as, a "racial" issue.

BLACK RACISM

Panicky reaction to this terrible social crisis, on top of the other phenomenona discussed in this chapter, has contributed to the rise of antiwhite racism among blacks—something not easy to distinguish, perhaps, from simple paranoia. Polls have indicated that a fourth of black Americans believe that the U.S. government deliberately feeds drugs into black neighborhoods; and 35 percent thought this at least possible. No less than 30 percent thought AIDS was, or could be, a government plot. A fanatical distrust of whites, and out and out expressions of hatred, have become common. This has generated extreme tension on many college campuses. There, and even more on lower levels of the educational system, successful blacks are berated for "acting white." "Hate crimes" by blacks against whites and Asians are common—more so, contrary to what is widely assumed, than hate crimes by whites against other groups. Racism appears in arguments that the educational system fails black children because the latter allegedly have a different "learning style" from whites. Races are inherently vastly different, and anyhow, all whites are racist. In a set of cultural stereotypes that can be found in many nationalist and racial theories as far back as the eighteenth century, it is argued that blacks are warm, emotionally expressive, and intuitive, unlike the cold and narrowly rational whites. The latter may not be all that smart anyway; some cranks—ensconced as tenured professors—have argued that melanin in the skin affects brain functioning (much as some Southern doctors did before the Civil War).

World history is radically recast, going far beyond any correction of past belittling of the cultural level and achievements of sub-Saharan Africa. "Afrocentrists," deriving some of their arguments from the African writer Cheikh Diop (but ignoring many more competent African historians) and building on the ideas of Grafton Smith, a cranky British writer of the 1920s, argue that Western civilization is an inferior offshoot of black African culture. Vastly exaggerating the cultural level of West Africa before the Europeans arrived, they proceed to "annex" ancient Egypt to black Africa by pretending that the ancient Egyptians were black. They further argue that all civilization in the Western world, and perhaps the world as a whole, derived from Egypt. The ancient Greeks created nothing, but "stole" and corrupted Egyptian culture, a fact European scholars concealed. In one variant, black Africans crossed the Atlantic and created the pre-Columbian civilizations of the Americas.

This of course is a tissue of nonsense. The ancient Egyptians were not blacks, but Mediterranean-type Caucasoids, who had surprisingly little to do with their neighbors to the south. Nor had the Greeks, or modern Europeans, ever concealed the real debt they owed to ancient Egypt. If anything, until the late nineteenth century, they exaggerated it, knowing nothing of the Sumerian civilization, much less the earlier proto-cities of Anatolia and Palestine which long predated Egypt or Sumeria.[37]

There is a peculiar obsession with "blackness," which is not at all the same thing as having a "black" skin. Black Americans can be damned, by other blacks, for not being really or sufficiently black, or for not "thinking black." This anxiety about being black is a bit peculiar when we consider that, at least until quite recently, black identity was very much a concept imposed by whites and was not a matter of choice or discussion. The newer mode of thought is incoherent in any case, but is doubly so if white racism is really still the overwhelming reality it is assumed to be. The quarrel over blackness, now an undefined and vague quality, and the common accusation of "acting white" seems to be a measure of how closely the identity of many blacks has become entangled with ideas of victimization. The very stigmata of oppression are identified with membership in one's race, escape from oppression identified with being white. There is, once again, a curious coincidence between the various sorts of racist; both identify the hapless slum-dweller as the "true" black.[38]

On the whole, however, black racism, and particularly its more fully articulated theories, does not really resemble the traditional white racist ideas about blacks too closely. Rather, with its elaborate self-glorifying delusions, annexations of other people's achievements, and diabolic conspiracies, it more closely resembles the ideas of the Nazis, although it is cruder and has even less of a factual underpinning. But it was even more futile. The emphasis on "blackness," identification with things African and distancing themselves from whites, was not unconnected with self-hatred. It was just as futile as any earlier neurotic attempts to pretend to be white. Genetically, black Americans would not cease being part-white just because they did not like the idea; nor could they cease being Americans, culturally. Indeed, by the spurious standards of blackness or Afrocentrism, they could never be more than second-rate blacks, or ersatz Africans.

The origins of these hatreds may be complex. It would be strange if some blacks did not react to oppression by hating all whites. As far back as the 1940s, even friendly observers like Eleanor Roosevelt and Gunnar Myrdal had been perturbed by the chauvinism and self-glorification of many black newspapers. Myrdal noted tendencies to see everything in terms of its "Negro" aspects, and to a cynical disregard of the rules when whites were in such a position that they could not hit back. He estimated that hatred of whites was a serious factor in black crimes against them. But he, and others, perhaps rightly, tended to discount this as part of an emotional reaction to a then overwhelming situation. They assumed that when blacks got fair treatment, such things would evaporate.[39]

That things got worse, instead, may be attributed to a number of factors. The desperate condition of the underclass inflamed traditional antiwhite prejudice and provided fuel for new sorts of paranoia. Racism and related conspiracy theories explained away the failure of blacks to be more successful as the real barriers in American society fell, and Asian immigrants operating in black neighborhoods prospered. Thanks to public policy and broad social attitudes, some middle- and upper-class blacks had a vested interest in separatism, or at least in harping on group identity. Some knew their positions might be due to affirmative action or other favoritism to minorities. And last, but not least, was the impact of a larger society that strangely distorted its own history to suggest that it, and only it, had victimized only blacks and a few other groups, and which often seemed to refuse to recognize that basic changes had taken place.

Notes

INTRODUCTION

1. Ralph Linton, *The Tree of Culture* (New York: Alfred Knopf, 1955), 28.

CHAPTER 1

1. Peter Tasker, *The Japanese* (New York: Dutton, 1987), 79–80; Ezra Vogel, *Japan as Number One* (Cambridge, Mass.: Harvard University Press, 1979), 160; Michael Banton, *Racial and Ethnic Competition* (Cambridge, England: Cambridge University Press, 1983), 272.
The above passage was written before the publication of Richard Herrnstein and Charles Murray's *The Bell Curve* (New York: Basic Books, 1994). It is noteworthy that even this book, despite its thesis that IQs and the difference between the average IQs of whites and blacks are largely genetically determined, concedes that the difference between whites and blacks has narrowed by three points in just a generation, and that studies of illegitimate German children fathered by Americans indicate that those who were fathered by blacks did not differ in intelligence from those whose fathers were white—data exceedingly hard to reconcile with the thesis that differences are primarily due to heredity. (Ibid., 269, 289–293, 310.) Indeed, the general thesis that intelligence is primarily hereditary is hard to reconcile with data showing considerable leaps in the intelligence

of adopted children over their natural mothers; some studies show jumps of as much as sixteen points.

The authors of *The Bell Curve* fail to note that the fifteen-point gap between average white and black IQs are paralleled in similar gaps in other societies with sharp ethnic/socioeconomic divisions. Chinese in Malaya have an average IQ fifteen points higher than the Malays, while European Jews in Israel average fifteen points higher than Jews from Arab countries. The genetic distance between Chinese and Malays is considerably smaller than that between whites and blacks in the United States, and is smaller still between the Jewish groups. (H. J. Eysenck and Leon Kamin, *The IQ Controversy*, New York: John Wiley, 1981), 84–85; Pierre Van den Berghe, *The Ethnic Phenomenon*, New York: Elsevier, 1981, 234.) The strikingly similar gaps are also incompatible with claims that the black-white IQ gap in the United States is the result of biases in the tests "favoring" the dominant group. No such bias has ever been shown; and it is hard to see how tests in three quite different societies could be rigged to produce such similar results. (And in Malaya the Malays, not the Chinese, are politically the controlling group.)

The Bell Curve is a classic example of the fallacy of trying to explain short-term social developments as the product of biological causes that are essentially unchanging. Much the same fallacy, incidentally, underlies the crudest sort of leftist environmentalism, which seeks to explain contemporary social disintegration and the rise in crime as simply the result of poverty or racism, factors that have either remained constant or waned as the underclass and crime rate have grown.

2. Such expressions in the public print—and the not too different figures of speech "white America" and "black America"—are of course common. For an example of the penetration of such expressions into scholarship, see Robert Berkhofer, *The White Man's Indian* (New York: Vintage, 1979), xv.

3. A book that perfectly epitomizes this notion is Ronald Segal, *The Race War* (New York: Bantam, 1967). Whatever else may be said of this book, it has the virtue of clearly expressing common but rarely coherently stated conceptions.

Notions that transform modern history into a story of Western aggressions, not necessarily seen in "racial" terms, have long been common; for an early influential example, see Arnold Toynbee, *The World and the West* (New York: Oxford University Press, 1953), 2–3.

4. Quoted in Arnold Beichman, *Nine Lies about America* (New York: Pocket Books, 1973), 42–43.

5. A term I have borrowed from Michael Banton, *Race Relations* (New York: Basic Books, 1967), 167. For an example, see UNESCO, *Race and*

Science (New York: Columbia University Press, 1961), 15, 62, 215 and Thomas Gossett, *Race* (Dallas: Southern Methodist University Press, 1963).

6. For example, Marvin Harris, *Culture, Man and Nature* (New York: Columbia University Press, 1977), 233.

7. See Segal, *The Race War*, especially 5–7, 17, 21, 31–32, 121, 182. For examples of this sort of view as applied to American history in a variety of forms, see Howard Zinn, *A People's History of the United States* (New York: Harper and Row, 1979); Robert Blauner, *Racial Oppression in America* (New York: Harper and Row, 1973), vii, 11–12, 73; Richard Drinnon, *Facing West* (Minneapolis: University of Minnesota Press, 1980); Joel Kovel, *White Racism* (New York: Pantheon, 1970). See also the articles by Robert Berkhofer, "The Native American and United States History" and John W. Blassingame, "The Afro-American from Mythology to Reality" in *The Reinterpretation of American History*, edited by William H. Cartwright and Richard L. Watson, Jr. (Washington, D.C: National Council for Social Studies, 1973).

8. Segal, *The Race War*, 7, comments, "Indeed, though the white supremacy doctrines and practices of the South African government are *gratuitously crude*, [my emphasis] they correspond closely enough to the radical realities of power and wealth in the world as a whole for the coloured poor everywhere to see in them a sort of magnifying mirror of their own domination by whites." Cf, the destruction of the European Jews, which some cultural critics portray as *both* the worst act in history and the logical, even typical, result of Western civilization.

9. Edmund Burke, *Reflections on the Revolution in France* (New York: Anchor, 1974), 156–157.

10. Philip Mason, *Patterns of Dominance* (New York: Oxford University Press, 1970), 137, 146.

11. Carleton Coon, *The Living Races of Man* (New York: Knopf, 1965, 115–117; George Murdock, *Africa* (New York: McGraw-Hill, 1959), 118, 402–403.

12. E. M. Bovill, *The Golden Trade of the Moors* (New York: Oxford University Press, 1966).

13. Nigel Heseltine, *Madagascar* (New York: Praeger, 1971), 9, 14.

14. Mason, *Patterns of Dominance*, 3–31; Winthrop Jordan, *White Over Black* (Chapel Hill, N.C.: University of North Carolina Press, 1968), ix–x, 2; David Brion Davis, *The Problem of Slavery in Western Culture* (Ithaca, N.Y.: Cornell University Press, 1966), 447; Leon Poliakov, *The Aryan Myth* (New York: Meridian, 1977), 135–136; Carl N. Degler, "Slavery and the Genesis of American Race Prejudice," *Comparative Studies in Society and Mobility* vol. 2, no. 1 (October, 1959), 49–66.

15. George Orwell, *Collected Essays, Journalism and Letters*, edited by Sonia Orwell and Ian Angus (New York: Harcourt, Brace and Jovanovich, 1968), vol. 2, 419.

16. For an excellent account, see Poliakov, *The Aryan Myth*, a work of far broader interest than its title might imply.

17. For a typical attempt to conflate and confuse all types of Western expansion, see Blauner, *Racial Oppression in America*, 11–12.

18. Mason, *Patterns of Dominance*, 4. I have derived many ideas from this work and the writings of Michael Banton. For a partly similar, partly contrasting, but extremely interesting interpretation, cf, Van den Berghe, *The Ethnic Phenomenon*.

19. Mason, *Patterns of Dominance*, 326–328.

CHAPTER 2

1. E. L. Jones, *The European Miracle* (Cambridge, England: Cambridge University Press, 1981), vii.

2. Karl A. Wittfogel, *Oriental Despotism* (New Haven, Conn.: Yale University Press, 1957); Jones, *The European Miracle*, especially 9, 89–90, 109–119, 160, 165, 206–208.

3. William H. McNeill, *Plagues and Peoples* (New York: Doubleday, 1976), 45.

4. Ibid., 20, 45; Pierre Gourou, *The Tropical World* (New York: John Wiley, 1968), 6–14; Jones, *The European Miracle*, 7, 22–23.

5. Jones, *The European Miracle*, 27–29.

6. Gourou, *The Tropical World*, 15–30, 63–66, 90–93; Jones, *The European Miracle*, 168.

7. Jones, *The European Miracle*, 175–178.

8. McNeill, *Plagues and Peoples* 64–67; Jones, *The European Miracle*, 192.

9. Jones, *The European Miracle*, 11–17; Carlo Cipolla, *Before the Industrial Revolution*, 2d ed. (New York: Norton, 1980), 5, 151.

10. Ralph Linton, *The Tree of Culture* (New York: Knopf, 1955), 445; Murdock, *Africa*, especially 36–39.

11. Roland Oliver and J. D. Fage, *A Short History of Africa*, revised edition (New York: Penguin, 1978), 43–53; Murdock, *Africa*, 33, 118, 397–398, 402–408, Jones, *The European Miracle*, 153–156.

12. Jones, *The European Miracle* 156; Alfred Crosby, *Ecological Imperialism* (Cambridge, England: Cambridge University Press, 1986), 17–18.

13. Jones, *The European Miracle*, 159.

14. Lynn White, *Medieval Religion and Technology* (Berkeley, Calif.: UCLA Press, 1978), 80, xix; cf, A. C. Crombie, *Medieval and Modern Science* (Cambridge, Mass.: Harvard University Press, 1963), vol. 1, 189.

15. White, *Medieval Religion and Technology*, especially 15–17, 24, 76; Lynn White, *Medieval Technology and Social Change* (New York: Oxford University Press, 1962); Crombie, *Medieval and Modern Science*, vol. 1, 133–193; William Carroll Bark, *Origins of the Medieval World* (Stanford, Calif.:

Stanford University Press, 1958), especially 27, 65–66, 69–70, 89–100; L. Sprague De Camp, *The Ancient Engineers* (New York: Ballantine, 1974), 322–383; Cipolla, *Before the Industrial Revolution*, 147–148, 167–184, 204–207, 221, 223; *Europe and the Rise of Capitalism*, edited by Jean Baechler, John A. Hall, and Michael Mann (Oxford, England: Blackwell, 1991).

16. Crombie, *Medieval and Modern Science* vol. 1, passim, vol. 2, 1, 3, 103–104; E. J. Dijksterhuis, *The Mechanization of the World Picture* (Oxford, England: Oxford University Press, 1961); Herbert Butterfield, *The Origins of Modern Science* (London, England: 1949); De Camp, *The Ancient Engineers*, 346–350.

17. De Camp, *The Ancient Engineers*, 302–310; Jones, *The European Miracle*, 175–191.

18. Archibald R. Lewis, *Naval Power and Trade in the Mediterranean AD 500–1100* (Princeton, N.J.: Princeton University Press, 1951), 250.

19. John H. Pryor, *Geography, Technology and War* (Cambridge, England: Cambridge University Press, 1988) 20–26, 44, 104–110; Lewis, *Naval Power and Trade in the Mediterranean*, 13, 71, 178, 220, 250–252; Archibald R. Lewis and Timothy Runyan, *European Naval and Maritime History 300–1500* (Bloomington, Ind.: Indiana University Press, 1985), 51–52, 56, 78; G. V. Scammell, *The World Encompassed* (Berkeley, Calif.: UCLA Press, 1981), 86–90; Frederic C. Lane, *Venice* (Baltimore: Johns Hopkins University Press, 1973), 7, 60; J. H. Parry, *The Age of Reconnaissance* (New York: New American Library, 1964), 52, 57–58.

20. Lane, *Venice*, 119–126, 129; Geoffrey Marcus, *The Conquest of the North Atlantic* (New York: Oxford University Press, 1980), 50, 54, 66, 78–79, 90–91, 100–101, 106–116, 119–121; Crosby, *Ecological Imperialism*, 46; Pryor, *Geography, Technology and War*, 39, 44, 87–88; Lewis and Runyan, *European Naval and Maritime History*, 74, 82–83, 158–159; Carlo M. Cipolla, *Guns, Sails and Empire* (New York: Pantheon, 1965), 74–78; Parry, *The Age of Reconnaissance*, 68–100, 105–115; Scammell, *The World Encompassed*, 1–19, 23–29, 38–56, 86–90, 126–127, 193, 206–208.

21. Cipolla, *Guns, Sails and Empire*, 21–90, 94–99; Parry, *The Age of Reconnaissance*, 137.

CHAPTER 3

1. Walter Prescott Webb, *The Great Frontier* (Austin, Texas: University of Texas, 1964).

2. Cf, W. H. McNeill, *Europe's Steppe Frontier* (Chicago: University of Chicago Press, 1964).

3. James Westfall Thompson, *Feudal Germany*, 2 vols. (New York: Frederick Ungar, 1962), vol. 2; Eric Christiansen, *The Northern Crusades* (Minneapolis: University of Minnesota Press, 1980); Herman Schreiber,

Teuton and Slav (New York: Knopf, 1965); George Vernadsky, *Kievan Russia* (New Haven, Conn.: Yale University Press, 1943).

4. Felipe Fernandez-Armesto, *Before Columbus* (Philadelphia: University of Pennsylvania Press, 1987), 43–70, 212–213.

5. Lewis and Runyan, *European Naval and Maritime History*, 167.

6. Davis, *The Problem of Slavery in Western Culture*, 42–44.

7. Charles Verlinden, *The Beginnings of Modern Colonization* (Ithaca, N.Y.: Cornell University Press, 1970), xii–xiv, xvii, 3, 5–6, 11–80; Fernandez-Armesto, *Before Columbus*, 88–219; Parry, *The Age of Reconnaissance*, 52, 57–58; Lane, *Venice*, especially 7, 42–43, 60, 69–70, 99, 132–133; W. H. McNeill, *Venice, the Hinge of Europe* (Chicago: University of Chicago Press, 1974); D. S. Chambers, *The Imperial Age of Venice* (New York: Praeger, 1970); David Jacoby, "From Byzantium to Latin Romania: Continuity and Change," 5, 8–10, in *Latins and Greeks in the Eastern Mediterranean*, edited by Benjamin Arbel, Bernard Hamilton, and David Jacoby (London: Frank Cass, 1989). It is noteworthy that despite the fame of Venice relatively little attention has been paid in the English-speaking world to medieval overseas expansion and related matters, except for the special and futile case of the Crusades, whose historical impact is exaggerated. Although much work on the subject has been done by Continental historians such as Verlinden, Fernandez-Armesto, and Pierre Chaunu, just one volume of Verlinden's vast scholarship on medieval colonization and slavery has been translated into English—testimony to the near-maniacal focus of English-speakers on post-Columbian issues.

8. Marcus, *The Conquest of the North Atlantic*, 164–178; Parry, *Age of Reconnaissance*, 31–34, 63–67, 146–148, 151, 162–164; Crosby, *Ecological Imperialism*, 71–79; Fernandez-Armesto, *Before Columbus*, 156–157, 166; Verlinden, *The Beginnings of Modern Colonization*, 13, 102–131.

9. Samuel Eliot Morison, *Admiral of the Ocean Sea* (Boston: Little, Brown, 1942), 161.

10. Fernandez-Armesto, *Before Columbus*, 7.

11. John Mercer, *The Canary Islanders: Their Prehistory, Conquest and Survival* (London, England: Rex Collings, 1980); Crosby, *Ecological Imperialism*, 79–103; Fernandez-Armesto, *Before Columbus*, 7, 169–214, 224; Parry, *Age of Reconnaissance*, 162–164, 189; Verlinden, *The Beginnings of Modern Colonization*, 132–157.

12. Mercer, *The Canary Islanders*, 213.

CHAPTER 4

1. Hottentots, however, had domesticated cattle. The vast differences within the broad pattern labeled "Neolithic" should not be underestimated; for American Indians alone, see Alvin Josephy, Jr., *The Indian*

Heritage of America (New York: Bantam, 1969), and for Polynesians, Robert C. Suggs, *The Island Civilizations of Polynesia* (New York: New American Library, 1960). Cf, Gary Nash, *Red, White and Black* (Englewood Cliffs: Prentice Hall, 1974), especially xiv, 3, 20–21, 238, 317–319, for a typical homogenized and idealized version of Indian cultures. The books by Zinn and Drinnon cited in Chapter 1, Note 7, represent more extreme, but still common, views as does David Stannard's *American Holocaust* (New York: Oxford University Press, 1992), perhaps the most coherent exposition of such ideas. It portrays white-Amerind relations as a dress rehearsal—indeed a bigger version—of the destruction of the European Jews, which shrinks to a minor episode. Noteworthy features of the book are its portrayal of medieval and early modern Europeans as subhuman brutes and the pre-Columbian Americas as a near Eden; its failure to distinguish between the unintentional harm done Amerinds by disease and the deliberate actions of white settlers; its attempts to assimilate all other Europeans to the "Black Legend" version (unfortunately accurate) of Spanish conduct; and its identification of all Western civilization, and especially the USA, with Nazi Germany. It is rather difficult to convey the tone of hatred for Western civilization—ultimately perhaps, all civilization—that oozes from the works of Zinn, Drinnon, and Stannard. Kirkpatrick Sale's *The Conquest of Paradise* is in some respects an attempt to popularize a slightly watered-down version of their ideas.

2. Crosby's *Ecological Imperialism*, despite its silly title, is a superb and important interpretation of this problem. See especially 17–18, 28, 197–212. See also Josephy, *The Indian Heritage of America*, especially 283, 301, 326; Wilcomb Washburn, *The Indian in America* (New York: Harper and Row, 1975), especially 104–107; A. Grenfell Price, *White Settlers and Native Peoples* (Westport, Conn.: Greenwood Press, 1970—originally published in 1950), 190; McNeill, *Plagues and Peoples*, 61–64, 124–127; Stuart Fiedel, *The Prehistory of the Americas* (Cambridge, England: Cambridge University Press, 1987), 355–356. Just how steep the drop in population was is still unclear. The unreliability of estimates of the pre-Columbian population of the Americas is indicated by the fact that scholars using the same raw data have estimated the population of Hispaniola, the first large island contacted by Europeans, as ranging from 120,000 to 8 million! (The latter figure is almost as high as Alfred Kroeber's traditional estimate—almost certainly too low—of the population of the whole Western Hemisphere.) Irving Rouse, the leading contemporary expert on the pre-Columbian Caribbean, estimates the population of Hispaniola in 1492 at 500,000. Rouse, *The Tainos* (New Haven, Conn.: Yale University Press, 1992), 7; Cf, Carl O. Sauer, *The Early Spanish Main* (Berkeley, Calif.: UCLA Press, 1966), 51–58, 64–68, 203–204. Recent estimates of the hemispheric population have tended to draw back from the very high figures common in the 1960s

and 1970s, which rose as high as 113 million, with 12.25 million in North America north of the Rio Grande. A widely accepted recent estimate is a pre-Columbian population of 54 million, with some 3.8 million north of Mexico. Whatever the original Amerind population of the United States was, it was reduced to about 500,000 by 1900. Virtually all modern figures are higher than James Mooney's well-known traditional estimate, modified by Kroeber, of 1.1 million people in the United States and Canada, which itself was based on a misunderstanding—Mooney's aim was to secure a baseline or minimal figure, not estimate the actual population. His work may have been quite accurate—not for 1492, but for the early seventeenth century, when European colonists arrived and estimated Indian numbers, long after the latter may have been hit by epidemics. Physical archaeological evidence suggests that, at least in the Southeast, the most advanced area of North America, the pre-Columbian population may have been four times as large as he supposed. Cf, J. Leitch Wright, *The Only Land They Knew* (New York: Free Press, 1981), 22–32, 79, 296 n.53. There are many uncertainties and controversies involved; for example, whether epidemics actually spread beyond the Southeast and Southwest during the sixteenth century, or only reached the north after the English and French began settling. Estimates for Latin America, especially, may be influenced by factors—migration and absorption by mixture with whites and blacks—that make the decline appear steeper than it really was. The physical basis for the populations involved is not always clear—cf, for example, the remarks in Wright, *The Only Land They Knew*, 7–11 on agriculture with those of Charles Hudson, *The Southeastern Indians* (Knoxville, Tenn.: University of Tennessee Press, 1976), 273–295. For discussions of the pre-Columbian population see *The Native Population of the Americas*, edited by William Denevan, 2d. ed. (Madison, Wisc.: University of Wisconsin Press, 1992); David Henige, "Primary Source by Primary Source: On the Role of Epidemics in New World Depopulation," *Ethnohistory* (Summer, 1986), 293–312; "Exchange Between Henry Dobyns, Dean R. Snow, Kim Lanphier and David Henige," *Ethnohistory* (Summer, 1989), 285–307.

3. Washburn, *The Indian in America*, 107; Hudson, *The Southeastern Indians*, vi; Daniel Richter, *The Ordeal of the Longhouse* (Chapel Hill, N.C: University of North Carolina Press, 1992), 265–266.

4. Price, *White Settlers and Native Peoples*, especially 19, 120.

5. Alden T. Vaughan, *New England Frontier* (New York: Norton, 1979), especially xiv, 20–21, 43; Karen O. Kupperman, *Settling with the Indians* (Totowa, N.J.: Rowman and Littlefield, 1980), 2, 35–36, 40–42, 107–110; Berkhofer, *The White Man's Indian*, 6, 42; Poliakov, *The Aryan Myth*, 135–137; Francis Bremer, *The Puritan Experiment* (New York: St. Martin's, 1976), 199–202; Jordan, *White Over Black*, xv, 89, 162–167; Davis, *The Problem of Slavery*, 10, 169–182; Ronald Sanders, *Lost Tribes and Promised Lands* (Bos-

ton: Little, Brown, 1978), 364–374; Robert Wauchope, *Lost Tribes and Sunken Continents* (Chicago: University of Chicago Press, 1962); Grace Woodward, *The Cherokees* (Norman, Okla.: University of Oklahoma Press, 1963), 36; Rouse, *The Tainos*, 14.

6. Kenneth R. Andrews, *Trade, Plunder and Settlement* (Cambridge, England: Cambridge University Press, 1984), 37–38; Karen O. Kupperman, *Roanoke* (Totowa, N.J.: Rowman and Allanheld, 1984), 57–59, 67–68; Kupperman, *Settling with the Indians*, vii, 2–4, 27–28, 46–71, 106, 111–117, 122, 143, 186–188; Bremer, *The Puritan Experiment*, 199–202; Alden Vaughan, "From White Man to Red Skin," *American Historical Review* (October, 1982), 917–953, is an important article.

7. J. C. Beaglehole, *The Exploration of the Pacific*, 3rd. ed. (Stanford, Calif.: Stanford University Press, 1968), 43, 49, 64; William L. Schurz, *The Manila Galleon* (New York: Dutton, 1939), 291.

8. Sanders, *Lost Tribes and Promised Lands*, 102, 202; Kupperman, *Settling with the Indians*, 111–112.

9. Kupperman, *Roanoke*; Kupperman, *Settling with the Indians*; Vaughan, *The New England Frontier*; Alden Vaughan, *American Genesis* (Boston: Little, Brown, 1975), 32–36.

10. Richter, *Ordeal of the Longhouse*, 83; George T. Hunt, *The Wars of the Iroquois* (Madison, Wisc.: University of Wisconsin Press, 1940), especially 5, 41.

11. Washburn, *The Indian in America*, 135–136; W. J. Eccles, *France in America* (New York: Harper and Row, 1972), 37, 45, 66, 90, 95–100; Francis Parkman, *Count Frontenac and New France Under Louis XIV* (New York: Literary Classics of America, 1983). Cf, Francis Jennings, *The Ambiguous Iroquois Empire* (New York: Norton, 1984) especially xviii, 10, 195–196, for a different view of the Iroquois.

12. Edward H. Spicer, *Cycles of Conquest* (Tucson, Ariz.: University of Arizona Press, 1968), 210–212; Ruth Underhill, *The Navahos* (Tulsa: University of Oklahoma Press, 1970).

13. Cf, the tone of Theda Perdue, *The Cherokees* (New York: Chelsea House, 1987), 39–47; Hudson, *The Southeastern Indians*, 449.

14. Spicer, *Cycles of Conquest*, 1, 46, 133–134, 137–151; Woodward, *The Cherokees*, 84–86, 119–120, 123–127; Mason, *Patterns of Dominance*, 118–124, 326–328; Hudson, *The Southeastern Indians*, 295, 436, 449; Crosby, *Ecological Imperialism*, 224–267.

15. Sauer, *The Early Spanish Main*, 203–204; Jacob Burckhardt, *The Civilization of the Renaissance in Italy* (New York: Harper, 1975) vol. 1, 119; Morison, *Admiral of the Ocean Sea*, 291, 481–495, 562–572; Rouse, *The Tainos*, 150–154.

16. Eccles, *France in America*, 8, 35, 38.

17. Vaughan, *The New England Frontier*, passim; Bremer, *The Puritan Experiment*, 199–203; Eccles, *France in America*, 158–159; Francis Parkman, *A Half Century of Conflict* (New York: Literary Classics of America, 1983), 540–548.

18. For New England's relations with the Indians, and the origins of King Philip's War, Vaughan, *New England Frontier* (New York: Norton, 1979); Washburn, *The Indian in America*, 82–84, 112–113.

19. Spicer, *Cycles of Conquest*, 160–162, 210–226, 239–243; Underhill, *The Navahos*, 112–113; Frank McNitt, *Navajo Wars* (Albuquerque, N.Mex.: University of New Mexico Press, 1972), especially vii–viii, 12–13; Robert M. Utley, *Frontiersmen in Blue* (New York: Macmillan, 1967), 80–84; Odie B. Faulk, *Crimson Desert* (New York: Oxford University Press, 1974) 42–87; Lynn Bailey, *The Long Walk* (Los Angeles: Westernlore Press, 1964).

20. Wright, *The Only Land They Knew*, 79–83, 126–150; Hudson, *The Southeastern Indians*, 434–438, 465–467.

21. Leach, *Flintlock and Tomahawk*, 23; Parkman, *A Half Century of Conflict*, 554–555, 558.

22. Robert Utley, *Frontier Regulars* (New York: Macmillan, 1973), 239–247, 357–358; Faulk, *Crimsoned Desert*, 67–68.

23. Faulk, *Crimson Desert*, 36.

24. Paul Andrew Hutton, *Phil Sheridan and His Army* (Lincoln, Neb.: University of Nebraska Press, 1985), 145.

25. Ibid., 144–145, 181–186, 195–198, 363; Tom Gibson, *The Maori Wars* (London, England: Leo Cooper, 1972); Utley, *Frontiersmen in Blue*, especially 45, 51–52, 191; and Francis Prucha, *Sword of the Republic* (Bloomington, Ind.: Indiana University Press, 1969) provide numerous examples.

26. Dan Thrapp, *The Conquest of Apacheria* (Norman, Okla.: University of Oklahoma, 1967), 88–94; Faulk, *Crimsoned Desert*, 166.

27. Don Russell, "How Many Indians Were Killed," *The American West*, vol. 10, no. 4 (July, 1973), 42–47, 61–63; Washburn, *The Indian in America*, 207. A full-scale examination of the myths about the Indian Wars spread by writers like Dee Brown (*Bury My Heart at Wounded Knee*) would be tediously long. The most famous massacre of Indians, that of Wounded Knee, was not a massacre at all, cf, Utley, *Frontier Regulars*, 407 and S.L.A. Marshall, *Crimsoned Prairie* (New York: Scribner's, 1972), 238–260. An overall view of the United States wars with the Indians may be obtained in the aforementioned works of Utley and Prucha. Regional studies of interest include Marshall, *Crimsoned Prairie*, for the Plains wars, Faulk, *Crimsoned Desert*, for the Southwest, and William Leckie, *The Conquest of the Southern Plains* (Norman, Okla.: University of Oklahoma Press, 1963).

28. Faulk, *Crimson Desert*, 3–24; Vaughan, *New England Frontier*, 342; Utley, *Frontier Regulars*, 4–5.

29. Vaughan, *New England Frontier*, 312, 319, 324–325; Leach, *Flintlock and Tomahawk*, 152–154, 242–243; Utley, *Frontier Regulars*, 376–387; Thrapp, *The Conquest of Apacheria*, especially 126.

30. Kupperman, *Roanoke*, 114–117; Thrapp, *The Conquest of Apacheria*, 6–9.

31. Wright, *The Only Land They Knew*, 88–90; Francis Parkman, *The Conspiracy of Pontiac* (New York: Literary Classics of America, 1991), 703, 709, 713, 718; Washburn, *The Indian in America*, 144–145.

32. Thrapp, *The Conquest of Apacheria*, vii; Spicer, *Cycles of Conquest*, 134, 216; Utley, *Frontier Regulars*, 188, 194, 297–298; Underhill, *The Navahos*, 107–108, 115.

33. Thrapp, *The Conquest of Apacheria*, 176; Spicer, *Cycles of Conquest*, 217–221; Faulk, *Crimson Desert*, 80–81, 87–89, 187; Bailey, *The Long Walk*, 165–227.

CHAPTER 5

1. Introduction to *Race Prejudice and the Origin of Slavery in America*, edited by Raymond Starr and Robert Detweiler (Rochester, Vt.: Schenkman, 1990), iv; Eugene Genovese, *Roll, Jordan Roll* (New York: Vintage, 1974), 2–3; Rush Limbaugh, *The Way Things Ought to Be* (New York: Pocket Books, 1992), 200.

2. Andrew Hacker, *Two Nations* (New York: Ballantine, 1993), 3, 13–14, 17.

3. Jared Taylor, *Paved with Good Intentions* (New York: Carroll and Graf, 1993), 9.

4. For example, the famous debate in the 1950s between Oscar and Mary F. Handlin and Carl Degler, reprinted in *Race Prejudice and the Origin of Slavery in America*, edited by Raymond Starr and Robert Detweiler (Rochester, Vt.: Schenkman, 1990). Oscar and Mary F. Handlin, "Origins of the Southern Labor System," 25–40 and Carl Degler, "Slavery and the Genesis of American Race Prejudice," 41–55. Somewhat more coherently, Winthrop Jordan, the greatest historian of racial concepts in America, has suggested, "Rather than slavery causing prejudice or vice versa, they seem to have generated each other." *White Over Black*, 80.

5. P. Kirby, *The Making of Early England* (New York: Schocken, 1965), 238; Ruth Mazo Karas, *Slavery and Society in Medieval Scandinavia* (New Haven, Conn.: Yale University Press, 1988), 30; William Philips, Jr., *Slavery from Early Roman Times to the Early Transatlantic Trade* (Minneapolis: University of Minnesota Press, 1988), 3, 59–63.

6. Philips, *Slavery from Early Roman Times to the Early Transatlantic Trade*, 36–168; Lane, *Venice*, 7, 128–133, 349–350; Scammell, *The World Encompassed*, 106, 174–175, 215; Verlinden, *The Beginning of Modern Coloniza-*

tion, 11, 18–20, 27–92; Fernandez-Armesto, *Before Columbus*, 19–24, 36; Davis, *The Problem of Slavery in Western Culture*, 31, 42–44; Marcus, *The Conquest of the North Atlantic*, 139, 168–169.

7. John Thornton, *Africa and Africans in the Making of the Atlantic World* (Cambridge, England: Cambridge University Press, 1992), 28, 74–75, 80–86; Parry, *Age of Reconnaissance*, 146–148, 151; Scammell, *The World Encompassed*, 252–254; Philips, *Slavery from Early Roman Times to the Early Transatlantic Trade*, 131, 155.

8. Philips, *Slavery from Early Roman Times to the Early Transatlantic Trade*, 3–4; C. Duncan Rice, *The Rise and Fall of Black Slavery* (New York: Harper and Row, 1975), 4, 6–9; Verlinden, *The Beginning of Modern Colonization*, 30.

9. Rice, *The Rise and Fall of Black Slavery*, 2, 21; Robert McColley, "Slavery in Virginia 1619–1660: A Reexamination" in *New Perspectives on Race and Slavery in America*, edited by Robert H. Abzug and Stephen F. Maizlish (Lexington, Ky.: University Press of Kentucky, 1986), 22.

10. Rice, *The Rise and Fall of Black Slavery*, 2.

11. Wright, *The Only Land They Knew*, 126–150, 168; Hudson, *The Southeastern Indians*, 435–438, 447; Spicer, *Cycles of Conquest*, 160–161; Underhill, *The Navahos*, 55, 79–82, 192–193; Lynn R. Bailey, *Indian Slave Trade in the Southwest* (Los Angeles: Westernlore Press, 1966), especially 20–29, 109–137, 177–192; Jordan, *White Over Black*, xiv, 89; Davis, *The Problem of Slavery in Western Culture*, 169–186; Frank McNitt, *Navajo Wars*, 12–13, 69.

12. Marvin Harris, *Patterns of Race in the Americas* (New York: Walker, 1964), 16–17, 68–70; Hacker, *Two Nations*, 84; Peter I. Rose, *The Subject Is Race* (New York: Oxford University Press, 1968), 53.

13. Murdock, *Africa*, 403; Jordan, *White Over Black*, xiv, 5.

14. Jordan, *White Over Black*, ix–x; 5ff; Mason, *Patterns of Dominance*, 30 31; Carl N. Degler, *Neither Black Nor White* (New York: Macmillan, 1971), 210–212; Degler, "Slavery and the Genesis of American Race Prejudice," 49–66; Davis, *The Problem of Slavery in the History of Western Culture*, 447; G. P. Dunston and R. F. Hobson, "A Note on an Early Ingredient of Racial Prejudice in Western Europe" in *Race*, vol. 6, no. 4 (April, 1965), 334–339.

15. Hiroshi Wagatsuma, "The Social Perception of Skin Color in Japan" in *Color and Race*, edited by John Hope Franklin (Boston: Houghton Mifflin, 1968), 129–165. Anecdotal evidence suggests that Chinese and Korean attitudes were similar to those of the Japanese. It is worth noting, incidentally, that the Japanese describe the lighter shades of their own skin as "white." They never, save under Western influence, call themselves "yellow," and their main pejorative for Caucasians, "keto," means "hairy barbarian." It does not refer to skin color.

16. Burckhardt, *The Civilization of the Renaissance in Italy*, vol. 2, 292 n1.

17. Philips, *Slavery from Early Roman Times to the Early Transatlantic Trade*, 192 ff.; Scammell, *The World Encompassed*, 252–254; Parry, *Age of Reconnaissance*, 282–283.

18. Rice, *The Rise and Fall of Black Slavery*, 52–53, 64–65; Vaughan, *American Genesis*, 146–149; McColley, "Slavery in Virginia 1619–1660: A Reexamination," 11–24; J. H. Parry, *Trade and Dominion* (New York: Praeger, 1971), 18, 50.

19. Davis, *The Problem of Slavery in the History of Western Culture*, 12; Kenneth Stampp, *The Peculiar Institution* (New York: Vintage, 1965), 95.

20. Cf, Stampp, *The Peculiar Institution* for the pre–Civil War South, and Rice, *The Rise and Fall of Black Slavery* for slavery in the Americas in general. Degler, *Neither Black Nor White*, supplies a valuable comparison of slavery in the American South and Brazil.

21. Bremer, *The Puritan Experiment*, 204–207; Rice, *The Rise and Fall of Black Slavery*, 91; Jordan, *White Over Black*, 200–201.

22. Stampp, *The Peculiar Institution*, 194–196, 350ff; Gunnar Myrdal, *An American Dilemma* (New York: Harper, 1962), 97–100, 107–108, 582, 701; Ashley Montagu, *Man's Most Dangerous Myth* (Cleveland: World, 1964), 100–101, 293–316; The sexual mythology surrounding blacks has proven particularly persistent and has often been inverted in the twentieth century. It was noted by George Orwell in his 1945 article, "Notes on Nationalism." Norman Mailer's well-known 1957 essay, "The White Negro," is a classic case.

23. Peter G. Foote and David M. Wilson, *The Viking Achievement* (New York: Praeger, 1970), 76; Karas, *Slavery and Society in Medieval Scandinavia*, 63–64; John W. Blassingame, *The Slave Community* (New York: Oxford University Press, 1979), 50–63, 228.

24. Cf, Degler, *Neither Black Nor White*, especially 102–104, 196, 237 ff; Banton, *Racial and Ethnic Competition*, 28; Mason, *Patterns of Dominance*, 276, 285, 312; Davis, *The Problem of Slavery in the History of Western Culture*, 274–275, 280.

25. Wendell Stephenson, *Isaac Franklin* (Gloucester, Mass.: Peter Smith, 1968), 80; Frederic Bancroft, *Slave Trading in the Old South* (Baltimore: J. H. Furst, 1931), 328–329; Jordan, *White Over Black*, 168.

26. Robert Stuckert, "Race Mixture: The African Ancestry of White Americans" in *Physical Anthropology*, edited by Peter B. Hammond (New York: Macmillan, 1964), 192–197.

27. Rice, *The Rise and Fall of Black Slavery*, 390.

28. Davis, *The Problem of Slavery in the History of Western Culture*, 332–333, 392–393; Rice, *The Rise and Fall of Black Slavery*, 153–223, 335; Jordan, *White Over Black*, 271–578.

29. Ulrich B. Phillips, *American Negro Slavery* (New York: D. Appleton, 1918), 84, 123–124.

30. Jordan, *White Over Black*, 282–283, 293, 311–368.

31. E. Merton Coulter, *The Confederate States of America* (Baton Rouge, La.: Louisiana State University Press, 1950), 8–10.

32. Stampp, *The Peculiar Institution*, 28, 57–85, 98–105, 125–126, 164–166, 168, 336–338; Blassingame, *The Slave Community*, 107–108, 249, 250, 272, 280; Genovese, *Roll, Jordan Roll* 7–8, 152; George Rawick, *The American Slave: A Composite Autobiography*, vol. 1 (Westport, Conn.: Greenwood, 1972); Joseph Glathaar, *The March to the Sea and Beyond* (New York: New York University Press, 1985), 106–107.

33. Blassingame, *The Slave Community*, 47, 313; Stampp, *The Peculiar Institution*, 87–88, 148.

34. Coulter, *The Confederate States of America*, 254.

35. Stampp, *The Peculiar Institution*, 118, 134–135, 164–168, 172, 179–182, 188–190, 208, 214, 426; Blassingame, *The Slave Community*, 81–83, 261–268; Genovese, *Roll, Jordan Roll*, 14, 17–18, 22–24, 71, 123.

36. Stampp, *The Peculiar Institution*, 282–284; Genovese, *Roll, Jordan Roll*, 63–64. Blassingame, *The Slave Community*, 252–254, is unusual in arguing that lack of enough food was common.

37. Blassingame, *The Slave Community*, 149–177, 180–181, 252–254; Stampp, *The Peculiar Institution*, 111, 148, 245–249, 252, 293, 296, 305, 341–350; Genovese, *Roll, Jordan Roll*, 58–59, 450–459; Bancroft, *Slave-Trading in the Old South*, 197, 208.

38. Stampp, *The Peculiar Institution*, 415; Bancroft, *Slave-Trading in the Old South*, especially 354; Stephenson, *Isaac Franklin*, 80, 84, 171.

39. Stampp, *The Peculiar Institution*, 380–381, 416; Kenneth Stampp, *The Era of Reconstruction* (New York: Knopf, 1965), 168; John Hope Franklin, *Reconstruction* (Chicago: University of Chicago Press, 1961), 87–90; Benjamin Quarles, *The Negro in the Civil War* (Boston: Little Brown, 1953), xii–xiii; Bruce Catton, *A Stillness at Appomattox* (New York: Pocket Books, 1958), 261–262; Henry Hitchcock, *Marching with Sherman*, edited by M. A. DeWolfe Howe (New Haven, Conn.: Yale University Press, 1927), 71.

40. *The Autobiography of Oliver Otis Howard* (New York: Baker and Taylor, 1907), 274–275, 292, 335, 374; Stampp, *The Era of Reconstruction*, 165.

41. Douglas Southall Freeman, *Robert E. Lee* (New York: Scribner's, 1935), vol. 4, 254; Stampp, *The Era of Reconstruction* 14, 138–139; Franklin, *Reconstruction*, 91–98.

42. *The Autobiography of Oliver Otis Howard*, 310, 374, 317; Stampp, *The Era of Reconstruction*, 79–81.

43. Stampp, *The Era of Reconstruction*, 15, 20, 23, 30–32, 36–38, 41, 46, 81–85, 87–89, 91; Franklin, *Reconstruction*, 48–52, 60–63, 66–67.

44. Myrdal, *An American Dilemma*, 69–70, 73–75, 85, 224–228, 438, 447, 582–583, 667–671.

45. Stampp, *The Era of Reconstruction*, 215; Myrdal, *An American Dilemma*, 440.

46. Samuel Eliot Morison, *The Oxford History of the American People* (New York: New American Library, 1972), vol. 1, 213–215.

47. For example, see the letter by Richard Pipes, *Commentary* (January, 1994), 19.

48. Rice, *The Rise and Fall of Black Slavery*, 3; Nash, *Red, White and Black*, especially 156–167.

49. Davis, *The Problem of Slavery in the History of Western Culture*, 47ff; Karas, *Slavery and Society in Medieval Scandinavia*, 15.

50. Segal, *The Race War*, 17–19.

51. Rice, *The Rise and Fall of Black Slavery*, 17–19.

52. For example, Segal, *The Race War*; and Nash, *Red, White and Black*, 157–159.

53. Rice, *The Rise and Fall of Black Slavery*, 108–112; L. H. Gann and Peter Duignan, *Burden of Empire* (Stanford, Calif.: Hoover Institution Press, 1967), 154–162.

54. Nathan Glazer's introduction to Stanley Elkins, *Slavery* (New York: Grosset and Dunlap, 1963); Segal, *The Race War*, 31–34, 121, 182; Frank Tannenbaum, *Slave and Citizen in the Americas* (New York: Knopf, 1947); Arnold Toynbee, *A Study of History* (Oxford, England: Oxford University Press, 1947) vol. 1, 211–219, 223–225, 464–465.

55. Davis, *The Problem of Slavery in the History of Western Culture*, 21, 29–31, 59–61.

56. Stampp, *The Peculiar Institution*, 217–221; Degler, *Neither Black Nor White*, 20, 25–34; Rice, *The Rise and Fall of Black Slavery*, 39, 64–65; Davis, *The Problem of Slavery in the History of Western Culture*, 234–242, 269.

57. Degler, *Neither Black Nor White*, 61–68, 75; Davis, *The Problem of Slavery in the History of Western Culture*, 223–242, 269, 282–283; Rice, *The Rise and Fall of Black Slavery*, 91, 100–101, 265–275, 283, 292.

58. Eric Williams, *Capitalism and Slavery*, is the classic exposition of this view; cf, also Segal, *The Race War*, 33; Nash, *Red, White and Black*, 156.

59. Rice, *The Rise and Fall of Black Slavery*, 103–105; Davis, *The Problem of Slavery in the History of Western Culture*, 153–156; Parry, *Trade and Dominion*, 48, 96–97, 102, 107, 278, 365 n. 20.

60. Nash, *Red, White and Black*, 238; Edmund Morgan, "Slavery and Freedom," *Journal of American History*, vol. 59 (1972–1973), 25; One variation on the Hobson-Lenin theme, however, manages to exceed even this in silliness; the anthropologist Marvin Harris once suggested that the prosperity of America and Australia is due to the exploitation of . . . New Guinea! This is an example of the sort of late Marxism that smacks more of Groucho than Karl. Cf, Harris's *Cows, Pigs, Wars, and Witches* (New York: Vintage, 1978), 131–132.

61. Stampp, *The Peculiar Institution*, 426–428.

CHAPTER SIX

1. Geoffrey Fairbairn, *Revolutionary Guerrilla Warfare* (Baltimore: Penguin, 1974), 288–289. Cf, Hans Kohn, *Is the Liberal West in Decline?* (London, England: Pall Mall Press, 1957). For a much harsher view of colonial rule, however, see Van den Berghe, *The Ethnic Phenomenon*, 85–119.

2. Holden Furber, *Rival Empires of Trade* (Minneapolis: University of Minnesota Press, 1976), 77–79, 230–234, 244, 257, 260, 268; O.H.K. Spate, *Monopolists and Freebooters* (Minneapolis: University of Minnesota Press, 1983), 91–92, 112–113; Parry, *Age of Reconnaissance*, 207, 212, 215–216; Parry, *Trade and Dominion*, 8, 65–66, 77, 91, 278–280.

3. Schurz, *The Manila Galleon*, 22–25, 37–38, 54, 91–92; O.H.K. Spate, *The Spanish Lake* (Minneapolis: University of Minnesota Press, 1979), 157–161.

4. Parry, *Age of Reconnaissance*, 216–219, 266–270; Parry, *Trade and Dominion*, 76–79, 159, 166–170, 198; George M. Kahin, *Nationalism and Revolution in Indonesia* (Ithaca, N.Y.: Cornell University Press, 1952), 1–15; D. K. Fieldhouse, *The Colonial Empires* (New York: Delacorte, 1965), 271–272, 279, 283, 332–337, 381–384. Cf, John Strachey, *The End of Empire* (New York: Praeger, 1959), for a sober argument that the plunder of Bengal was important for British industrialization and Harris, *Culture, Man and Nature*, 233, 456, 467–472, for claims that colonial rule aborted development.

5. Cipolla, *Guns, Sails and Empire*, 36; Kupperman, *Roanoke*, 169–170; Schurz, *The Manila Galleon*, 396; Fieldhouse, *The Colonial Empires*, 26, 93–96; Allen Sievers, *The Mystical World of Indonesia* (Baltimore: Johns Hopkins University Press, 1974), 87–122; *The Cambridge History of Southeast Asia*, vol. 1, edited by Nicholas Tarling (Cambridge, England: Cambridge University Press, 1992), 503–506, 597.

6. Parry, *Trade and Dominion*, 91, 278; Spate, *Monopolists and Freebooters*, 91.

7. Quoted in D. K. Fieldhouse, *Economics and Empire* (Ithaca, N.Y.: Cornell University Press, 1973), 30.

8. William L. Langer, *The Diplomacy of Imperialism* (Cambridge, Mass.: Harvard University Press, 1935); Fieldhouse, *Economics and Empire*, 62–369; Fieldhouse, *The Colonial Empires*, especially 178–241, 380–381; Gann and Duignan, *Burden of Empire*, especially 4–71, 163–208; Ronald E. Robinson, John Gallagher, and Alice Denny, *Africa and the Victorians* (New York: St. Martin's Press, 1961).

9. Walt W. Rostow, *Stages of Economic Growth* (Cambridge, Mass.: Cambridge University Press, 1960), 110.

Monty Penkower, *The Jews Were Expendable* (Urbana, Ill.: University of Illinois Press, 1983), especially vii; Edward Norden, "For and Against the Holocaust Museums," *Commentary* (August, 1993), 23–32; Jonathan D. Sarna, "Anti-Semitism and American History," *Commentary* (March, 1981), 42–47. Cf, Gary Tobin and Sharon Sassler, *Jewish Perceptions of Anti-Semitism* (New York: Plenum Press, 1988), 7, 19, 44–45, 90–92, 118–119, for a rather different interpretation from that given above, which concedes that American Jews are more "sensitive" about anti-Semitism and that at least 10 percent suffer from exaggerated fears.

27. Glazer, *Affirmative Discrimination*, 17; Sykes, *A Nation of Victims*, passim, Van Den Berghe, *The Ethnic Phenomenon*, 190, 214, 228.

28. Cf, Myrdal, *An American Dilemma*, lxxxiii.

29. Nash, *Red, White and Black*, 238; Stanley Masters, "Affirmative Action Should Be Strengthened" in *Racism in America: Opposing Viewpoints* edited by William Dudley and Charles Cozle (San Diego: Greenhaven Press, 1991), 139–146; Joel Kovel, *White Racism* (New York: Pantheon, 1970). The older view is implicit in virtually everything published before the 1960s, notably Myrdal's *An American Dilemma* and Stampp's *Peculiar Institution*; for another example, see Dorothy Baruch, *The Glass House of Prejudice* (New York: Morrow, 1946), especially 10–12, 33.

30. Beichman, *Nine Lies About America*, 81–97; Glazer, *Affirmative Discrimination* 177; Magnet, *The Dream and the Nightmare*, 143; Hacker, *Two Nations*, 100–101.

31. Charles Silberman, *Crisis in Black and White* (New York: Random House, 1964), 9–10.

32. Ravitch, *The Troubled Crusade*, 213–214, 268–270; D'Souza, *Illiberal Education*, 11–12, 47–48; Taylor, *Paved with Good Intentions*, 191–193, 248–249, 252–253.

33. Roger Freeman, *The Wayward Welfare State* (Stanford, Calif.: Stanford University Press, 1981), 21–22, 195; D'Souza, *Illiberal Education*, 10, 44, 48–50, 151, 246; Taylor, *Paved with Good Intentions*, 130–135, 158–159, 170–172, 180–181, 283; Capaldi, *Out of Order*, 86, 96, 111–112, 130–132; Terkel, *Race*, 182; Hacker, *Two Nations*, 23, 141–146.

34. Paul Feyerabend, *Science in a Free Society* (London, England: NLB, 1978), 76, 118.

35. Murray, *Losing Ground*, especially 9, 23–25, 42–47, 56–64, 172; Magnet, *The Dream and the Nightmare*, 16–19, 31, 36, 118–122, 127.

36. Murray, *Losing Ground*, passim; Magnet, *The Dream and the Nightmare*, passim.; Patterson, *America's Struggle Against Poverty*, 13, 79–80, 86–102, 164–182; Taylor, *Paved with Good Intentions*, 10–14, 24–27, 287–332; Freeman, *The Wayward Welfare State*, 209–213.

37. Paul R. Gross and Norman Levitt, *Higher Superstition* (Baltimore: Johns Hopkins University Press, 1994), 203–214, 246–247; Gann and Duig-

nan, *Burden of Empire* 127–132; David O'Connor, "Ancient Egypt and Black Africa," in *The Rise and Fall of Civilizations* (Menlo Park, N.J.: Cummings, 1974), 403–409; *The Cambridge History of Africa* vol. 1 (Cambridge, England: Cambridge University Press, 1978), 899–902; Colin Renfrew, *Before Civilization* (New York: Knopf, 1973), 31–33; Glyn Daniel, *The First Civilizations* (New York: Crowell, 1968), 185–187, 200, n.16. It is typical of actual European attitudes that Sir Arthur Evans, the discoverer of the Minoan culture, the first civilization in Europe, believed that it had been sparked by predynastic Egyptian refugees fleeing the unification of Egypt. Unfortunately, this proved to be a romantic idea of the sort that ought to be true but isn't; later scholars could not substantiate it. Arthur Evans, *The Palace of Minos* (New York: Biblo and Tannen, 1964), vol. 1, 13, 16–19, 66, vol. 2, 24–26, vol. 4, 172–173, 986–987.

38. Taylor, *Paved with Good Intentions*, 43–55, 64–65, 69–75, 93–106, 113–115, 200, 227–228, 248–249, 252–258, 271–275; D'Souza, *Illiberal Education*, 11, 47–48, 50, 66, 235, 248; Magnet, *The Dream and the Nightmare*, 145–146, 217–218.

39. Myrdal, *An American Dilemma*, 751–753, 760 763, 783, 975–976; Joseph Lash, *Eleanor and Franklin* (New York: New American Library, 1971), 868–869.

Selected Bibliography

Abzug, Robert H., and Maizlish, Stephen F., eds. *New Perspectives on Race and Slavery in America*. Lexington, Ky.: University Press of Kentucky, 1986.

Allen, Frederick Lewis. *The Big Change*. New York: Perennial, 1986.

Andreski, Stanislav. *The African Predicament*. New York: Atherton, 1969.

Andrews, Kenneth R. *Trade, Plunder and Settlement*. Cambridge, England: Cambridge University Press, 1984.

Bailey, Lynn R. *Indian Slave Trade in the Southwest*. Los Angeles: Westernlore Press, 1966.

Bailey, Lynn R. *The Long Walk*. Los Angeles: Westernlore Press, 1964.

Bancroft, Frederic. *Slave Trading in the Old South*. Baltimore: J. H. Furst, 1931.

Banton, Michael. *Race Relations*. New York: Basic Books, 1967.

―――. *Racial and Ethnic Competition*. Cambridge, England: Cambridge University Press, 1983.

Bark, William Carroll. *Origins of the Medieval World*. Stanford, Calif.: Stanford University Press, 1958.

Barnett, Correlli. *The Collapse of British Power*. New York: Morrow, 1972.

Baruch, Dorothy. *The Glass House of Prejudice*. New York: Morrow, 1946.

Barzun, Jacques. *Race*. New York: Harper and Row, 1965.

Beaglehole, J. C. *The Exploration of the Pacific*. 3rd ed., Stanford, Calif.: Stanford University Press, 1968.

Beichman, Arnold. *Nine Lies about America*. New York: Pocket Books, 1973.

Berkhofer, Robert. *The White Man's Indian*. New York: Vintage, 1979.

Blackburn, Gilmer. *Education in the Third Reich*. Albany, N.Y.: State University of New York Press, 1985.

Blassingame, John W. *The Slave Community*. New York: Oxford University Press, 1979.

Blauner, Robert. *Racial Oppression in America*. New York: Harper and Row, 1973.

Bolick, Clint. *Changing Course*. New Brunswick, N.J.: Transaction, 1988.

Bovill, E. M. *The Golden Trade of the Moors*. New York: Oxford University Press, 1966.

Bremer, Francis. *The Puritan Experiment*. New York: St. Martin's Press, 1976.

Burckhardt, Jacob. *The Civilization of the Renaissance in Italy*. New York: Harper, 1975.

Burke, Edmund. *Reflections on the Revolution in France*. New York: Doubleday, 1961.

Burnham, James. *Suicide of the West*. New York: John Day, 1964.

Butterfield, Herbert. *The Origins of Modern Science*. New York: Macmillan, 1957.

Capaldi, Nicolas, *Out of Order*. Buffalo, N.Y.: Prometheus Books, 1985.

Carrington, C. E. *The British Overseas*. Cambridge, England: Cambridge University Press, 1968.

Catton, Bruce. *A Stillness at Appomattox*. New York: Pocket Books, 1958.

Chafets, Ze'ev. *Devil's Night*. New York: Random House, 1990.

Chambers, D. S. *The Imperial Age of Venice*. New York: Praeger, 1970.

Christiansen, Eric. *The Northern Crusades*. Minneapolis, Minn.: University of Minnesota Press, 1980.

Cipolla, Carlo M. *Guns, Sails and Empire*. New York: Pantheon, 1965.

Cohn, Norman. *Warrant for Genocide*. Chico, Calif.: Scholars Press, 1981.

Coon, Carleton. *The Living Races of Man*. New York: Knopf, 1965.

Coulter, E. Merton. *The Confederate States of America*. Baton Rouge, La.: Louisiana State University Press, 1950.

Crombie, A. C. *Medieval and Modern Science*. 2 vols. Cambridge, Mass.: Harvard University Press, 1963.

Crosby, Alfred. *Ecological Imperialism*. Cambridge, England: Cambridge University Press, 1986.

Dallin, David. *German Rule in Russia*. New York: Macmillan, 1957.

Daniel, Glyn. *The First Civilizations*. New York: Crowell, 1968.

Davis, David Brion. *The Problem of Slavery in Western Culture*. Ithaca, N.Y.: Cornell University Press, 1966.

Dawidowicz, Lucy. *The War Against the Jews*. New York: Bantam, 1976.

De Camp, L. Sprague. *The Ancient Engineers*. New York: Ballantine, 1974.

Degler, Carl N. *Neither Black Nor White*. New York: Macmillan, 1971.

Denvan, William, ed. *The Native Population of the Americas*. second edition. Madison, Wisc.: University of Wisconsin Press, 1992.

D'Souza, Dinesh. *Illiberal Education*. New York: Free Press, 1991.

Dijksterhuis, E. J. *The Mechanization of the World Picture*. Oxford, England: Oxford University Press, 1961.

Drinnon, Richard. *Facing West*. Minneapolis, Minn.: University of Minnesota Press, 1980.

Dudley, William and Cozle, Charles, eds. *Racism in America: Opposing Viewpoints*. San Diego, Calif.: Greenhaven Press, 1991.

Eccles, W. J. *France in America*. New York: Harper and Row, 1972.

Elkins, Stanley. *Slavery*. New York: Grosset and Dunlap, 1963.

Eysenck, H. J., and Kamin, Leon. *The IQ Controversy*. New York: John Wiley, 1981.

Fairbairn, Geoffrey. *Revolutionary Guerrilla Warfare*. Baltimore, Md.: Penguin, 1974.

Faulk, Odie B. *Crimson Desert*. New York: Oxford University Press, 1974.

Fernandez-Armesto, Felipe. *Before Columbus*. Philadelphia, Pa.: University of Pennsylvania Press, 1987.

Feyerabend, Paul. *Science in a Free Society*. London, England: NLB, 1978.

Fiedel, Stuart. *The Prehistory of the Americas*. Cambridge, England: Cambridge University Press, 1987.

Fieldhouse, D. K. *The Colonial Empires*. New York: Delacorte, 1965.

Fieldhouse, D. K. *Economics and Empire*. Ithaca, N.Y.: Cornell University Press, 1973,.

Foote, Peter G., and Wilson, David M. *The Viking Achievement*. New York: Praeger, 1970.

Franklin, John Hope, ed. *Color and Race*. Boston, Mass.: Houghton Mifflin, 1968.

Franklin, John Hope. *Reconstruction*. Chicago, Ill.: University of Chicago Press, 1961.

Freeman, Douglas Southall. *Robert E. Lee*. 4 vols. New York: Scribner's, 1935.

Freeman, Roger. *The Wayward Welfare State*. Stanford, Calif.: Stanford University Press, 1981.

Furber, Holden, *Rival Empires of Trade*. Minneapolis, Minn.: University of Minnesota Press, 1976.

Gann, L. H., and Duignan, Peter. *Burden of Empire*. Stanford, Calif.: Hoover Institution Press, 1967.

Genovese, Eugene. *Roll, Jordan Roll*. New York: Vintage, 1974.

Gibson, Tom. *The Maori Wars*. London, England: Leo Cooper, 1972.

Glathaar, Joseph. *The March to the Sea and Beyond*. New York: New York University Press, 1985.

Glazer, Nathan. *Affirmative Discrimination*. Cambridge, Mass.: Harvard University Press, 1987.

Gourou, Pierre. *The Tropical World*. New York: John Wiley, 1968.

Gregory, Ross. *America 1941*. New York: Free Press, 1989.

Gross, Paul, and Levitt, Norman. *Higher Superstition*. Baltimore, Md.: Johns Hopkins University Press, 1994.

Hacker, Andrew. *Two Nations*. New York: Ballantine, 1993.

Hammond, Peter B., ed. *Physical Anthropology*. New York: Macmillan, 1964.

Harris, Marvin. *Culture, Man and Nature*. New York: Columbia University Press, 1977.

Harris, Marvin. *Patterns of Race in the Americas*. New York: Walker, 1964.

Herrstein, Richard, and Murray, Charles. *The Bell Curve*. New York: Basic Books, 1994.

Heseltine, Nigel, *Madagascar*. New York: Praeger, 1971.

Hibbert, Christopher. *The Great Mutiny*. New York: Penguin, 1980.

Hilberg, Raul. *The Destruction of the European Jews*. Chicago, Ill.: Quadrangle, 1961.

Hitchcock, Henry. *Marching with Sherman*. ed. M. A. DeWolfe Howe. New Haven, Conn.: Yale University Press, 1927.

Hohne, Heinz. *Order of the Death's Head*. New York: Ballantine, 1971.

The Autobiography of Oliver Otis Howard. New York: Baker and Taylor, 1907.

Hudson, Charles. *The Southeastern Indians*. Knoxville, Tenn.: University of Tennessee Press, 1976.

Hunt, George T. *The Wars of the Iroquois*. Madison, Wisc.: University of Wisconsin Press, 1940.

Hutton, Paul Andrew. *Phil Sheridan and His Army*. Lincoln, Neb.: University of Nebraska Press, 1985.

Jones, E. L. *The European Miracle*. Cambridge, England: Cambridge University Press, 1981.

Jordan, Winthrop. *White Over Black*. Chapel Hill, N.C.: University of North Carolina Press, 1968.

Josephy, Alvin Jr., *The Indian Heritage of America*. New York: Bantam, 1969.

Kahlin, George M. *Nationalism and Revolution in Indonesia*. Ithaca, N.Y.: Cornell University Press, 1952.

Karas, Ruth Mazo. *Slavery and Society in Medieval Scandinavia*. New Haven, Conn.: Yale University Press, 1988.

Kirby, P. *The Making of Early England*. New York: Schocken, 1965.

Kohn, Hans. *Is the Liberal West in Decline?* London, England: Pall Mall Press, 1957.

Kolarz, Walter. *Russia and Her Colonies*. New York: Praeger, 1953.

Kovel, Joel. *White Racism*. New York: Pantheon, 1970.

Kupperman, Karen O. *Roanoke*. Totowa, N.J.: Rowman and Allanheld, 1984.

_____. *Settling with the Indians.* Totowa, N.J.: Rowman and Littlefield, 1980.

Lane, Frederic C. *Venice.* Baltimore, Md.: Johns Hopkins University Press, 1973.

Langer, William L. *The Diplomacy of Imperialism.* Cambridge, Mass.: Harvard University Press, 1935.

Laqueur, Walter. *Russia and Germany.* Boston, Mass.: Little Brown, 1965.

Lash, Joseph. *Eleanor and Franklin.* New York: New American Library, 1971.

Leach, Barry. *German Strategy Against Russia.* New York: Oxford University Press, 1972.

Leckie, William. *The Conquest of the Southern Plains.* Tulsa, Okla.: University of Oklahoma Press, 1963.

Lewis, Archibald R. *Naval Power and Trade in the Mediterranean, A.D. 500–1100.* Princeton, N.J.: Princeton University Press, 1951.

Lewis, Archibald R., and Runyan, Timothy. *European and Maritime History, A.D. 300–1500.* Bloomington, Ind.: Indian University Press, 1985.

Limbaugh, Rush. *The Way Things Ought to Be.* New York: Pocket Books, 1992.

Linton, Ralph. *The Tree of Culture.* New York: Knopf, 1955.

Lorimer, Douglas A. *Colour, Class and the Victorians.* Leicester, England: Leicester University Press, 1978.

Lukas, Richard C. *The Forgotten Holocaust.* Lexington, Ky.: University Press of Kentucky, 1986.

McNeill, William H. *Europe's Steppe Frontier.* Chicago, Ill.: University of Chicago Press, 1964.

_____. *Plagues and Peoples.* New York: Doubleday, 1976.

_____. *Venice, the Hinge of Europe.* Chicago, Ill.: University of Chicago Press, 1974.

McNitt, Frank. *Navajo Wars.* Albuquerque, N. Mex.: University of New Mexico Press, 1972.

Magnet, Myron. *The Dream and the Nightmare.* New York: Morrow, 1993.

Mallory, J. P. *In Search of the Indo-Europeans.* London, England: Thames and Hudson, 1989.

Marcus, Geoffrey. *The Conquest of the North Atlantic.* New York: Oxford University Press, 1980.

Marshall, S.L.A. *Crimsoned Prairie.* New York: Scribner's, 1972.

Mason, Philip. *Patterns of Dominance.* New York: Oxford University Press, 1970.

Mellaart, James. *The Neolithic in the Near East.* New York: Scribner's, 1975.

Mercer, John. *The Canary Islanders: Their Prehistory, Conquest and Survival.* London, England: Rex Collings, 1980.

Montagu, Ashley. *Man's Most Dangerous Myth*. Cleveland, Ohio: World, 1964.

Morison, Samuel Eliot. *Admiral of the Ocean Sea*. Boston, Mass.: Little, Brown, 1942.

Morison, Samuel Eliot. *The Oxford History of the American People*. 3 vols. New York: New American Library, 1972.

Murdock. George. *Africa*. New York: McGraw-Hill, 1959.

Murray, Charles. *Losing Ground*. New York: Basic Books, 1984.

Myers, Henry A., ed. *Western Views of China and the Far East*. 2 vols. Hong Kong: Asian Research Service, 1982–1984.

Myrdal, Gunnar. *An American Dilemma*. New York: Harper, 1962.

Nash, Gary. *Red, White and Black*. Englewood Cliffs, N.J.: Prentice Hall, 1974.

Newby, I. *Jim Crow's Defense*. Baton Rouge, La.: Louisiana University Press, 1965.

Nolte, Ernest. *Three Faces of Fascism*. New York: Holt, Rinehart and Winston, 1966.

Nordau, Max. *Degeneration*. 2d ed. New York: D. Appleton and Co., 1895.

Oliver, Roland, and Fage, J. D. *A Short History of Africa*. Rev. ed. New York: Penguin, 1978.

Orwell, George. *Collected Essays, Journalism and Letters*. eds. Sonia Orwell and Ian Angus. New York: Harcourt, Brace and Jovanovich, 1968.

Owen, Francis. *The Germanic People*. New York: Dorset Press, 1990.

Parkman, Francis. *The Conspiracy of Pontiac*. New York: Literary Classics of America, 1991.

——— . *Count Frontenac and New France Under Louis XIV*. New York: Literary Classics of America, 1983.

——— . *A Half Century of Conflict*. New York: Literary Classics of America, 1983.

Parry. J. H. *The Age of Reconnaissance*. New York: New American Library, 1964.

——— . *Trade and Dominion*. New York: Praeger, 1971.

Patai, Raphael, and Wing, Jennifer. *The Myth of the Jewish Race*. New York: Scribner's, 1975.

Perdue, Theda. *The Cherokees*. New York: Chelsea House, 1987.

Phillips, Ulrich. B. *American Negro Slavery*. New York: D. Appleton, 1918.

Philips, William Jr. *Slavery from Early Roman Times to the Early Transatlantic Trade*. Minneapolis, Minn.: University of Minnesota Press, 1988.

Poliakov, Leon. *The Aryan Myth*. New York: Meridian, 1977.

——— . *The History of Antisemitism*. Vol. 4. New York: Vanguard Press, 1985.

Price, A. Grenfell. *White Settlers and Native Peoples*. Westport, Conn.: Greenwood Press, 1970. (Originally published 1950.)

Prucha, Francis. *Sword of the Republic*. Bloomington, Ind.: Indiana University Press, 1969.

Pryor, John H. *Geography, Technology and War*. Cambridge, England: Cambridge University Press, 1988.

Quarles, Benjamin. *The Negro in the Civil War*. Boston: Little Brown, 1953.

Rawick, George. *The American Slave: A Composite Autobiography. Vol. 1.* Westport, Conn.: Greenwood Press, 1972.

Renfrew, Colin. *Archaeology and Language*. New York: Cambridge University Press, 1988.

Rice, C. Duncan. *The Rise and Fall of Black Slavery*. New York: Harper and Row, 1975.

Rich, Norman. *Hitler's War Aims*. New York: Norton, 1977.

Richter, Daniel. *The Ordeal of the Longhouse*. Chapel Hill, N.C.: University of North Carolina Press, 1992.

Robinson, Ronald E., Gallagher, John, and Denny, Alice. *Africa and the Victorians*. New York: St. Martin's Press, 1961.

Rose, Peter I. *The Subject Is Race*. New York: Oxford University Press, 1968.

Rostow, Walt W. *Stages of Economic Growth*. Cambridge, England: Cambridge University Press, 1960.

Rouse, Irving. *The Tainos*. New Haven, Conn.: Yale University Press, 1992.

Sanders, Ronald. *Lost Tribes and Promised Lands*. Boston, Mass.: Little, Brown, 1978.

Sauer, Carl O. *The Early Spanish Main*. Berkeley, Calif.: UCLA Press, 1966.

Scammell, G. V. *The World Encompassed*. Berkeley, Calif.: UCLA Press, 1981.

Schreiber, Herman. *Teuton and Slav*. New York: Knopf, 1965.

Schurz, William L. *The Manila Galleon*. New York: Dutton, 1939.

Seaton, Albert. *The Russo-German War*. New York: Praeger, 1971.

Segal, Ronald. *The Race War*. New York: Bantam, 1967.

Shirer, William. *The Rise and Fall of the Third Reich*. New York: Crest Books, 1973.

Silberman, Charles. *Crisis in Black and White*. New York: Macmillan, 1964.

Southern, David. *Gunnar Myrdal and Black-White Relations*. Baton Rouge, La.: Louisiana State University Press, 1987.

Spate, O.H.K. *Monopolists and Freebooters*. Minneapolis, Minn.: University of Minnesota Press, 1983.

——— . *The Spanish Lake*. Minneapolis: University of Minnesota Press, 1979.

Spicer, Edward H. *Cycles of Conquest*. Tucson, Ariz.: University of Arizona Press, 1968.

Stampp, Kenneth. *The Era of Reconstruction*. New York: Knopf, 1965.

——— . *The Peculiar Institution*. New York: Vintage, 1965.

Stannard, David. *American Holocaust*. New York: Oxford University Press, 1992.

Starr, Raymond, and Detweiler, Robert. *Race Prejudice and the Origin of Slavery in America*. Rochester, Vt.: Schenkman, 1990.

Stephenson, Wendell. *Isaac Franklin*. Gloucester, Mass.: Peter Smith, 1968.

Strachey, John. *The End of Empire*. New York: Praeger, 1959.

Suggs, Robert C. *The Island Civilizations of Polynesia*. New York: New American Library, 1960.

Sykes, Charles. *A Nation of Victims*. New York: St. Martin's Press, 1992.

Tannenbaum, Frank. *Slave and Citizen in the Americas*. New York: Knopf, 1947.

Tasker, Peter. *The Japanese*. New York: Dutton, 1987.

Taylor, Jared. *Paved with Good Intentions*. New York: Carroll and Graf, 1993.

Terkel, Studs. *Race*. New York: New Press, 1992.

Thompson, James Westfall. *Feudal Germany*. 2 vols. New York: Frederick Ungar, 1962.

Thornton, John. *Africa and Africans in the Making of the Atlantic World*. Cambridge, England: Cambridge University Press, 1992.

Thrapp, Dan. *The Conquest of Apacheria*. Norman, Okla.: University of Oklahoma, 1967.

Toynbee, Arnold. *A Study of History*. Oxford, England: Oxford University Press, 1947.

———. *The World and the West*. New York: Oxford University Press, 1953.

Underhill, Ruth. *The Navahos*. Tulsa, Okla.: University of Oklahoma Press, 1970.

UNESCO. *Race and Science*. New York: Columbia University Press, 1961.

Utley, Robert. *Frontier Regulars*. New York: Macmillan, 1973.

———. *Frontiersmen in Blue*. New York: Macmillan, 1967.

Van den Berghe, Pierre. *The Ethnic Phenomenon*. New York: Elsevier, 1981.

Vaughan, Alden. *American Genesis*. Boston, Mass.: Little, Brown, 1975.

———. *New England Frontier*. New York: Norton, 1979.

Verlinden, Charles. *The Beginnings of Modern Colonization*. Ithaca, N.Y.: Cornell University Press, 1970.

Vernadsky, George. *Kievan Russia*. New Haven, Conn.: Yale University Press, 1943.

Vogel, Ezra. *Japan as Number One*. Cambridge, Mass.: Harvard University Press, 1979.

Waite, Robert. *The Psychopathic God*. New York: Basic Books, 1977.

Washburn, Wilcomb. *The Indian in America*. New York: Harper and Row, 1975.

Wauchope, Robert. *Lost Tribes and Sunken Continents*. Chicago, Ill.: University of Chicago Press, 1962.

Webb, Walter Prescott. *The Great Frontier*. Austin, Texas: University of Texas Press, 1964.

West, Cornel. *Race Matters*. Boston: Beacon Press, 1993.

White, Lynn. *Medieval Religion and Technology*. Berkeley, Calif.: UCLA Press, 1978.

———. *Medieval Technology and Social Change*. New York: Oxford University Press, 1962.

Wilson, William Julius. *The Truly Disadvantaged*. Chicago: University of Chicago Press, 1987.

Wittfogel, Karl A. *Oriental Despotism*. New Haven, Conn.: Yale University Press, 1957.

Woodward, Grace. *The Cherokees*. Norman, Okla.: University of Oklahoma Press, 1963.

Wright, J. Leitch. *The Only Land They Knew*. New York: Free Press, 1981.

Zinn, Howard. *A People's History of the United States*. New York: Harper and Row, 1979.

Index

About the Author

ALAN J. LEVINE, an historian specializing in Russian history, international relations, and World War II, has published many articles about World War II and the Cold War. He is the author of *The Soviet Union, the Communist Movement and the World: Prelude to the Cold War* (Praeger, 1990), *The Strategic Bombing of Germany, 1940–1945* (Praeger, 1992), *The Missile and Space Race* (Praeger, 1994), and *The Pacific War* (Praeger, 1995).

CHAPTER 7

1. Poliakov, *The Aryan Myth*, especially 7, 38–42, 61–62.

2. Ibid., 176.

3. Ibid., 21–30, 155–181, 217–224; Jacques Barzun, *Race* (New York: Harper and Row, 1965), 18–31, 35–49; Banton, *Race Relations*, 16–50.

4. Fieldhouse, *The Colonial Empires*, 328.

5. J. P. Mallory, *In Search of the Indo-Europeans* (London, England: Thames and Hudson, 1989), Colin Renfrew, *Archaeology and Language* (Cambridge, England: Cambridge University Press, 1988); Thomas V. Gamkrelidze and V. V. Ivanov, "The Early History of the Indo-European Languages," *Scientific American* (March, 1990), 110–116.

6. Orwell, *Collected Essays, Journalism and Letters*, vol. 4, 252–253.

7. Ernest Nolte, *Three Faces of Fascism* (New York: Holt, Rinehart and Winston, 1966), 278–286; Barzun, *Race*, 48–134; Poliakov, *The Aryan Myth*, 183–283; James Mellaart, *The Neolithic in the Near East* (New York: Scribners, 1975), 99; Francis Owen, *The Germanic People* (New York: Dorset Press, 1990), 48–50.

8. Max Nordau, *Degeneration*, 2d ed. (New York: D. Appleton and Co., 1895), 209–210.

9. Raphael Patai and Jennifer Wing, *The Myth of the Jewish Race* (New York: Scribner's, 1975), 11–14; Lucy Dawidowicz, *The War Against the Jews* (New York: Bantam, 1976), 25, 221–222.

10. Nolte, *Three Faces of Fascism*, 303, 406–407, 411, 412, 418ff; Norman Rich, *Hitler's War Aims* (New York: Norton, 1977), 3–10; William Shirer, *The Rise and Fall of the Third Reich* (New York: Crest Books, 1973), 47–50, 124–126; Gilmer Blackburn, *Education in the Third Reich* (Albany, N.Y.: State University of New York Press, 1985); Robert Waite, *The Psychopathic God* (New York: Basic Books, 1977), 83–85, 117; Dawidowicz, *The War Against the Jews*, 38–44; Norman Cohn, *Warrant for Genocide* (Chico, Calif.: Scholars Press, 1981); Walter Laqueur, *Russia and Germany* (Boston: Little Brown, 1965), 51–104; Leon Poliakov, *The History of Antisemitism*, vol. 4 (New York: Vanguard Press, 1985), especially 103, 142–153, 170–172.

11. Dawidowicz, *The War Against the Jews*; Raul Hilberg, *The Destruction of the European Jews* (Chicago: Quadrangle, 1961); Heinz Hohne, *Order of the Death's Head* (New York: Ballantine, 1971), 367–453.

12. Hohne, *Order of the Death's Head*, 332–346; Richard C. Lukas, *The Forgotten Holocaust* (Lexington, Ky.: University Press of Kentucky 1986).

13. Shirer, *The Rise and Fall of the Third Reich*, 1225–1229, 1234, 1241–1242, 1288–1289; Hohne, *Order of the Death's Head*, 347–366; Albert Seaton, *The Russo-German War* (New York: Praeger, 1971), 115; Barry Leach, *German Strategy Against Russia* (New York: Oxford University Press, 1972), 197; David Dallin, *German Rule in Russia* (New York: Macmillan, 1957).

10. Fieldhouse, *The Colonial Empires*, 239–241, 332–333, 362–363, 364–371, 380–392; Fieldhouse, *Economics and Empire*, 35–36, 50–61, 342, 355, 369; Gann and Duignan, *Burden of Empire*, 39–70; Robinson, Gallagher, and Denny, *Africa and the Victorians*, 7–13, 79–83, 409, 419–422, 428–432, 458. Cf, Correlli Barnett, *The Collapse of British Power* (New York: Morrow, 1972), 10–11, 74–82, 132–135, 165–232 for a cold-blooded analysis of what colonies contributed, or didn't contribute, to British strength.

11. Stanislav Andreski, *The African Predicament* (New York: Atherton, 1969), 22, 106, 111. Cf, also Gann and Duignan, *Burden of Empire*, passim; Fieldhouse, *Economics and Empire*, 342; Fieldhouse, *The Colonial Empires*, 357–364.

12. Murdock, *Africa*, 229, 412.

13. Spate, *The Spanish Lake*, 107; Henry A. Myers, "Introduction" in *Western Views of China and the Far East*, edited by Henry A. Myers (Hong Kong: Asian Research Service, 1982), vol. 1, 35.

14. Myers, "Introduction," 35–37; Chong-kun Yoon, "Sinophilism During the Age of Enlightenment: Jesuits, Philosophes and Physiocrats Discover Confucius" in *Western Views of China and the Far East*, edited by Henry A. Myers (Hong Kong: Asian Research Service, 1982), vol. 1, 149–178; Victoria M. Siu, "Nineteenth Century China and the Far East in the Eyes of British and American Diplomats" in *Western Views of China and the Far East*, edited by Henry A. Myers (Hong Kong: Asian Research Service, 1984), vol. 2, 29–35.

15. Parry, *Age of Reconnaissance*, 263–265; Mason, *Patterns of Dominance*, 99–100.

16. John Strachey, *The End of Empire* (New York: Praeger, 1959), 54–55; Christopher Hibbert, *The Great Mutiny* (New York: Penguin, 1980), 37–39.

17. Parry, *Trade and Dominion*, 310–316; C. E. Carrington, *The British Overseas* Part 1 (Cambridge, England: Cambridge University Press, 1968), 193; Furber, *Rival Empires of Trade*, 322.

18. Andreski, *The African Predicament*, 224–225.

19. Walter Kolarz, *Russia and Her Colonies* (New York: Praeger, 1953), 5–6.

20. Harold R. Isaacs, "Group Identity and Political Change" in *Color and Race*, 75–76; Michel Leiris, "Race and Culture" in *Race and Science* 215.

21. Langer, *The Diplomacy of Imperialism*, 91–92.

22. Douglas A. Lorimer, *Colour, Class and the Victorians* (Leicester, England: Leicester University Press, 1978), especially 11–13, 15, 64–67, 107, 131–160, 172; Robinson, Gallagher, and Denny, *Africa and the Victorians*, 8–10, 467–471.

sudden reversal of course. Indeed, even more extreme views are occasionally expressed, in attempts to obliterate even the memory of the progress achieved before the 1960s. As the head of the ACLU has said, "During the 1950s, racial segregation was the *law of the land*, enforced by state sanctioned terror." Ira Glasser, "The Myth of the Much More Moral 1950s," *Long Island Newsday*, August 7, 1995 (emphasis mine). Note also the fantastic pretense that the prevailing interpretation of the Constitution not only allowed segregation but actually mandated it—a claim even the Ku Klux Klan might not have dared to make!

16. D. Garth Taylor, Paul B. Sheatsley, and Andrew Greeley, "Attitudes Toward Racial Integration," *Scientific American* (June, 1978), 42–49; Bruno Bettelheim and Morris Janowitz, *Social Change and Prejudice* (Glencoe, Ill.: Free Press, 1964), 11–14; Ben Wattenberg, *The Real America* (New York: Doubleday, 1979), 243–251; Taylor, *Paved with Good Intentions*, 31.

17. Myrdal, *An American Dilemma*, xliii.

18. Ibid., 69–70, 73, 75.

19. Allen Matusow, *The Unraveling of America* (New York: Harper, 1984), 3–8; David Southern, *Gunnar Myrdal and Black-White Relations* (Baton Rouge, La.: Louisiana State University Press, 1987), 106–107; Van den Berghe, *The Ethnic Phenomenon*, 2–4.

20. Beichman, *Nine Lies About America*, 166.

21. James Burnham, *Suicide of the West* (New York: John Day, 1964), 194; Beichman, *Nine Lies About America*, 155–166; Taylor, *Paved with Good Intentions*, 125–128.

22. Sykes, *A Nation of Victims*, is a book-length analysis of this; Magnet, *The Dream and the Nightmare*, especially 155; Taylor, *Paved with Good Intentions*, especially 287; D'Souza, *Illiberal Education*, 10, 242–243.

23. Quoted in *Racism in America*, 71.

24. D'Souza, *Illiberal Education*, 244; Magnet, *The Dream and the Nightmare*, 205; Nicolas Capaldi, *Out of Order* (Buffalo, N.Y.: Prometheus Books, 1985), 122, 133–134; Sykes, *A Nation of Victims*, 82, 167, 200–202; Taylor, *Paved with Good Intentions*, 14–16, 23–61, 64–107. Cf. Hacker, *Two Nations*, especially 93–94.

25. Capaldi, *Out of Order*, especially 16–18, 23–33, 36–39, 122, 130, 134; Lewis M. Killian, "Black Power and White Reactions: The Revitalization of Race-Thinking in the United States," 48–49, 51–53; Clint Bolick, *Changing Course* (New Brunswick, N.J.: Transaction, 1988), especially 53–69; Taylor, *Paved With Good Intentions*, 123–212, 239–243; Diane Ravitch, *The Troubled Crusade* (New York: Basic Books, 1983), 287–292; D'Souza, *Illiberal Education*, 37, 48–50; Nathan Glazer, *Affirmative Discrimination* (Cambridge, Mass.: Harvard University Press, 1987). Cf. Hacker, *Two Nations*, 131, 134–141.

26. Richard Rubenstein, *Approaches to Auschwitz* (Atlanta: John Knox Press, 1982); Alan Dershowitz, *Chutzpah* (Boston: Little, Brown, 1991),

CHAPTER 8

1. Lewis M. Killian, "Black Power and White Reactions: The Revitalization of Race-Thinking in the United States, *Annals of the American Acad-
emy of Political and Social Science* (March, 1981), 43. Cf. the interesting
remarks of Van den Berghe, *The Ethnic Phenomenon*, 217, 236–237, 281,
292–297.

2. Charles Sykes, *A Nation of Victims* (New York: St. Martin's Press,
1992), 97.

3. Dinesh D'Souza, *Illiberal Education* (New York: Free Press, 1991), 7,
147, 151. See also 59, 63–64, 66, 244.

4. Beichman, *Nine Lies About America*, 87; Hacker, *Two Nations*, 4.

5. Jim Wallis, "White Racist Attitudes Are a Serious Problem" in
Racism in America: Opposing Viewpoints, edited by William Dudley and
Charles Cozle (San Diego: Greenhaven Press, 1991), 26.

6. Ze'ev Chafets, *Devil's Night* (New York: Random House, 1990), 178.

7. Cornel West, *Race Matters* (Boston: Beacon Press, 1993), 18, 73. West
is black; but cf. many similar remarks by the white author Andrew Hacker
in *Two Nations*, especially 4, 13–14, 22, 167–169. For a review of Hacker, cf.
Arch Puddington, "Is White Racism the Problem?" *Commentary* (July,
1992), 31–36.

8. Studs Terkel, *Race* (New York: New Press, 1992), 206.

9. Charles Murray, *Losing Ground* (New York: Basic Books, 1984);
Myron Magnet, *The Dream and the Nightmare* (New York: Morrow, 1993);
William Julius Wilson, *The Truly Disadvantaged* (Chicago: University of
Chicago Press, 1987).

10. Frederick Lewis Allen, *The Big Change* (New York: Perennial, 1986),
178–179. Cf. Myrdal, *An American Dilemma*, 601.

11. Myrdal, *An American Dilemma*, 758, 828.

12. Banton, *Racial and Ethnic Competition*, 252–283; Myrdal, *An American
Dilemma*, 46–49, 219, 383, 438, 462–466, 526, 565, 601–603, 630, 1010–1014;
Dixon Wecter, *The Age of the Great Depression 1929–1941* (New York:
Macmillan, 1948), 164–166; Ross Gregory, *America 1941* (New York: Free
Press, 1989), 192–222; I. Newby, *Jim Crow's Defense* (Baton Rouge, La.:
Louisiana State University Press, 1965).

13. Gregory, *America 1941*, 195.

14. Myrdal, *An American Dilemma*, xxiii, 549, 629–633; Diane Ravitch,
The Troubled Crusade (New York: Basic Books, 1983), 122; Clint Bolick,
Changing Course (New Brunswick, N.J.: Transaction, 1988), 43; Fred Powl-
edge, *Free at Last?* (Boston: Little Brown, 1991), 14–16, 29.

15. Raoul Berger, *Government by Judiciary* (Cambridge, Mass.: Harvard
University Press, 1978), 222, 306, 331–332. Cf. *The New York Times*, May 18,
1994, 24–25. Hardly a single news account, on the fortieth anniversary of
Brown v. Board of Education, failed to repeat the myth that it represented a

ISBN 0-275-95037-9

HARDCOVER BAR CODE